SOURCE MY GARMENT

The Insider's Guide To Responsible
Offshore Manufacturing

Adila Cokar

ISBN: 978-1-9995579-2-8 (sc)
ISBN: 978-1-9995579-0-4 (hc)
ISBN: 978-1-9995579-1-1 (e)

Lulu Publishing Services rev. date: 06/17/2019

LOVE AND GRATITUDE

My rock

MY DAD.

MY MOM. SAMI COKAR brother from another mother.
BRAINS AKA Rubina Cokar. **MADIHA & ZAINAB MOLANI.**
**MANI AND THE ASTRO APPARELS FAMILY. DINESH &
THE WOODROSE GARMENTS FAMILY. ANNE PRINGLE
& ALEX GILL** Social Innovation Zone. **ANDREA ROMERO**
Fashion Zone. **KEVIN & MARIE** MARSDD. **JENNIFER
MACINNIS** Ryerson Legal Counsel. **JOEL GREGORIO**
Sovereign State. **OLEG AMURJUEV** YEDI Institute.
KATRINA MCKAY Uplevel Solutions. **EMILY FOUCAULT**
Think Hatch. **LISA ZAMPARO** The Wealth Company.
ALEEM ARIF BanoEmee. **AKHIL SIVANANDAN** Green
Story. **VERA BELAZELKOSKA** Ulula. **REBECCA PICKARD**
Source Studio. **MAUREEN BRADSHAW** Lovbird Design.
JAZMIN WELCH Fleck Creative Studio. **JODY ABERDEEN.**
ANDREW La Daveed. **SHARON GREENO** Kwantlen
University College. **NATASHA WALJI. SONAL SUDRA.**
**ALISHA DAMANI. TANIA D'SOUZA. KRISTEN FUNG.
SAROO SHARDA. NOOR KIDWAI. NABEELA COKAR.**
JANNI DEPP & DAVIE BECKHAM - my fur babies.

CONTENTS

*make
every
day
count*

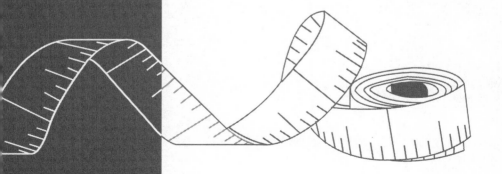

AN INTRODUCTION

Dear apparel makers, fashion innovators & designer entrepreneurs,

Sew, you've had these designs in your head for a long time, and now you've finally decided to take the leap to push them into production. It's a big step. If you're a beginner to all of this, it can be intimidating, but that's okay. If you're reading this, you're in good hands! Throughout my career, as both a designer and a product development consultant, I've managed hundreds of designs, from initial concept through to bulk production. In that time, I've learned almost every lesson and hit every roadblock you can imagine - and trust me, it wasn't easy. However, they all helped me learn many strategies to ensure that the development process runs as smoothly as possible, every garment gets manufactured to your specifications, and every shipment is delivered on schedule.

Good planning is the key to success, and that's what this book is all about. Straight up: You can't succeed in offshore garment manufacturing without proper planning. I'll help you understand just how long a product's life-cycle can be, from concept to completion. Planning what needs to get done prior to production, and allocating time for all of the steps, will speed up your production process, lower your costs (always good!), and prevent other mistakes that can cost you a lot of money, time, and even customers. Your goal is simple: manage your delivery expectations and know your process - the whole thing, from start to finish. And then, wash, rinse, and repeat for new deliveries.

Most newbie designers walk into offshore manufacturing hoping to go into production within a month. If this sounds suspiciously like you, then my friend, know that this is unrealistic, especially considering the number of people who are working on each product. The time between the initial design to the start of production, known as "product development," is a lengthy and complicated process. Product development typically takes anywhere from two months to a year to work through. That's right. We are not even talking about manufacturing and shipping here (yikes!). It seems unreasonable, but if you want a successful outcome, you've got to allow yourself the time to work through the process correctly. It requires thoughtful and strategic planning to ensure goals are met.

Do you want that win-win-win in your business? Of course you do! So read on, and learn how to accomplish your goals.

To be successful in manufacturing a product, a designer entrepreneur has a responsibility to understand and communicate how a product is "engineered." If you have a creative personality, as I do, this might go against your grain at first. After all, clothing design is an art form, isn't it? Actually, it's an art AND a science, and it's on you to work through product development, conveying the specifics and other information in a document called a "tech pack." You and your design will evolve and go through many iterations as you move through the process. The time and patience you invest early on will only help you improve quality, control costs, and save you time.

In short, the product development process helps to ensure that you and the factory are on the same page prior to production so that issues are minimized during manufacturing. The time spent prior to production ensures that everything is made correctly, and your customers get what they've ordered.

Production is one of the most challenging aspects of launching a fashion line. Any new entrepreneur in this field knows this in a very real way. You have to learn how to properly communicate your design requirements with your manufacturer- especially if they are overseas. Bad communication, sometimes even a complete lack of communication, can cause failures in the manufacturing process. Confusion at the factory level results in increased costs, delays, poorer quality products, and many more headaches. The two things you can have the greatest control over are a thorough understanding of your design and the product development process. In that way, you'll be able to ensure success throughout the manufacturing process and in the final product.

In the final analysis, the truth is very simple: if you want to make it in the apparel business, you need to learn every facet of it. Any monkey can design a cute dress or two, but real fashion entrepreneurs can crank out products that consumers need, prepare for production, plan effectively, manage budgets, avoid potential manufacturing problems, manage a team, design sustainably - and do it season after season.

As you move forward with your idea, be prepared to dance with dreaming and doing. As you embark on this exciting and transformative journey, I want you to know:

YOU ARE NOT ALONE. WE ARE IN THIS TOGETHER.

SO, THROUGH ALL THE LONG HOURS,

LATE NIGHTS, ACHES AND PAINS.

BRING IT. THIS IS YOUR YEAR.

LET THE JOURNEY BEGIN.

HOW TO USE THIS BOOK (AND WHAT TO EXPECT)

Before we go any further on this journey, you'll need to know that this won't be a straight road. It gets pretty curvy in places.

This book is meant to give you an overview of what to expect and how to plan your business. Just as every person is unique in their personality and how they do things, so is every apparel business. Although there is a beginning and an end to the book, and a step-by-step process, there will be times that we bounce from topic to topic. We might also cover the same topics from different perspectives within different chapters.

You will find that you will likely be referring to a multitude of different chapters or steps at any given time, just as your business might need to go from one step to another. If you're planning on ordering products more than once a year, it's pretty much guaranteed that steps will overlap. It's up to you to figure out what is your best plan of action and how you want to do things.

Expect curves and twists and turns along the way. If you find yourself thinking "Hey, I've read this before," look at it with a critical eye. Why is this coming up again now? What's different this time? Have a full read-through,and then set out a strategy that will produce the best results and optimize profits for your business.

All set? Then let's begin!

"A JOURNEY OF A THOUSAND MILES BEGINS WITH A SINGLE STEP"

- LAO TZU

TIME MANAGEMENT AND DELIVERIES

OVERVIEW

"WITHOUT PATIENCE, WE WILL LEARN LESS IN LIFE. WE
WILL SEE LESS. WE WILL FEEL LESS. WE WILL HEAR LESS.
IRONICALLY, RUSH AND MORE USUALLY MEAN LESS."

- MOTHER TERESA

I've got news! The role of a fashion designer has drastically changed. Long gone are the days of haute couture, working on the art of hand sketches, and draping. When fashion design was more of an art that took quality time. Thanks to technology and *a lot* more global competition, the creative process of the fashion designer has been turned upside down. Clothing is now designed to be mass produced. Manufacturing multiple products means that garments need to be designed, developed and delivered much quicker. The calendar is our new best friend.

Today, fashion designers of all stripes - corporate, small business, and freelance alike - find themselves with greater power over the entire product development process, providing more collaboration and even technical insights into how it's all done. Specializing in one particular role in the fashion industry doesn't get you too far these days, as fashion designers (now considered "designer entrepreneurs") are expected to fill far more roles than ever before.

Designer entrepreneurs are a new breed of innovators, wearing several hats, including that of the product developer and a project manager. This means ensuring things get done in a timely fashion and managing deadlines. Additionally, they take on a slew of new responsibilities, including research, updating data, keeping consistent communication and collaboration, and getting into the nitty-gritty of technical details and costs. It's not enough to just say how you want your shirts to look and feel: you have to be able to talk the talk (meaning technical descriptions) and walk the walk.

You might be saying to yourself: "This isn't why I got into this business. I just want to make amazing clothes. Why should I care about all this stuff?" I get it, this may not be your favorite part of the process, but if you can't strategically work through and understand the product development so you can manage timelines and deliveries; it will be hard to bring in the moola.

Sew... what's involved in the product development process?

> Research, research and more research! Product and consumer research, testing, shopping the market, and trend research are all necessary. If you thought your research days were over when you graduated from school, think again!
> Managing and organizing the entire process: workflows and time management, adhering to deadlines.
> Maintaining and updating information as constant design revisions are made. Updating and storing most revised files for patterns, artwork or technical drawings, and much more.
> Finding, collaborating with and seeking expertise from your tribe. Conducting meetings with the pattern maker, sample sewer, graphic designer, technical designers, and more.
> Creating artwork for care labels, main labels, prints, embroideries, and more.
> Evaluating and approving samples; preparing fit comments.
> Controlling and understanding costs while balancing your design requirements.
> Hand-sketching and CAD illustrations.
> Creating the blueprint (known by the pros in this industry as the "tech pack"). Understanding and conveying specifications and technical information. Effectively communicating sewing requirements, both seams and stitches.
> Selecting fabrics and materials for prototypes and production.
> Understanding the business of fashion - product labeling, product rules and regulations that affect the design, and much more.
> Sourcing fabric, trims, and, of course, a manufacturer.

Whew! Seems like an awful lot of work, doesn't it? Just remember, as Steve Jobs would say: "The only way to do great work is to love what you do." As you master your craft, the feeling of "work" goes away, and it transforms into a passion. It becomes second nature.

If you want to grow your brand, keep costs down, and speed up delivery times, understanding product development is the key. It is what will get your designs successfully manufactured. Not only will you feel more in control, but you will also move ahead with much more confidence. Partner with a garment manufacturer and you'll do it all while ensuring that your customers get the highest quality merchandise faster and at a better price.

What qualities and skills do successful designer entrepreneurs possess?

> We have a thirst to learn.
> We have the drive to see our vision come to life.
> We propel society forward with big leaps of creative disruption.
> We exhibit strong communication and interpersonal skills.
> We can prioritize projects and handle multiple tasks while managing time effectively to meet deadlines.
> We are able to develop and maintain productive relationships and communicate effectively with internal and external partners.
> We exhibit strong attention to detail.
> We are able to seek out and take guidance from experts and collaborate within a team.
> We are proactive, resourceful, and have strong problem-solving skills.
> We are fearless. We have the insatiable need for more, more, more!

Sew... what are your #designgoals? Simply put: Responsibly design a product that maximizes profits and minimize expenses, while achieving your aesthetic objectives.

Time-Tested and True: **Breaking Down The Complexities Of The Manufacturing Process:**

Fact is, things are going to get a little crazy... There are many complexities involved in manufacturing, which is why beginners must fully understand the process before starting. Even with little training or education, beginners can learn the ins and outs of offshore garment manufacturing. Moving into production is not a simple endeavour, but being organized and efficient will save you time, headaches, and money. Being organized will ensure the best possible outcomes in design, which will generate higher sales. (And who doesn't want higher sales?)

It all starts with research and design. Once you have worked through finalizing the designs and creating prototypes, you're ready to begin the second phase of product development with the factory.

The factory starts by creating a counter sample, based on your prototype, which can be manufactured in bulk production. Counter sampling not only prepares styles for bulk production, but it also provides a firm cost. During counter sampling, the factory provides samples for approval so you can make comments for improvement or give the green-light for production. The factory submits several options for every component for you to provide feedback. In many cases, you'll have to adapt your design to reduce costs while meeting quality standards and working with factory capabilities. The more complex the design, the more time it takes.

Generally, the manufacturing process never flows from one step to another. For example, while working through product development with the factory, you may realize that it is taking you much longer than you planned. To save time, you might revisit the color selection process and decide to take out a color, so everything goes a bit faster.

The diagram below illustrates the complexities involved in creating and manufacturing a new style. Although the steps involved appear to be in sequence, product development is fluid: it can go back and forth from any point in the process. Every case is unique.

PRODUCT DEVELOPMENT
& ORDER PROCESS

SHOP THE MARKET	RESEARCH & ANALYZE THE MARKET	FIND YOUR NICHE

FABRIC RESEARCH & SELECTION	COLOUR SELECTION	PRODUCT SELECTION & MIX

VISION & MOOD BOARD	SKETCH & LINE DRAWINGS	ESTIMATE TARGET COSTS & CREATE MOCK P.O	EDIT THE LINE

TECHNICAL SKETCHES	RESEARCH LEGAL COMPLIANCE & TESTING REQUIREMENTS	COLLABORATE WITH TECH PACK DESIGNER	COLLABORATE WITH GRAPHIC ARTIST

PROTOTYPE: COLLABORATE WITH PATTERN MAKER	PROTOTYPE: COLLABORATE WITH SAMPLE SEWER	PROTOTYPE FIT SESSION: REVISION OR APPROVAL

ASSEMBLE PRE PRODUCTION PACKAGE	REQUEST FOR QUOTE	FABRIC APPROVAL	ROUGH COSTS/ ESTIMATES	FACTORY SUBMITS COUNTER SAMPLE

COUNTER SAMPLE APPROVALS & COMMENTS FIT SESSION	FINAL SAMPLE APPROVALS	COSTS PROVIDED FOR PURCHASE ORDER	GRADING	PRE PRODUCTION SAMPLE

PRODUCTION	LOGISTICS	CUSTOMS	DELIVERY ☺

Planning and Time Management: **Good Things Take Time**

> "IF YOU REALLY LOOK CLOSELY, MOST OVERNIGHT
> SUCCESSES TOOK A LONG TIME."
>
> **- STEVE JOBS**

Sew... as I mentioned just now, product development typically takes anywhere from two months to a year to work through. A lot of thought, care, and attention must go into every detail of the design.

To determine how long the manufacturing process will take, you've got to consider everything. Always allow a buffer of time for unforeseen delays, such as bad weather, delayed sample shipments, or power outages at the factory. Even just one hour lost can delay deliveries.

The time it takes to design, manufacture, and ship your product is dependent on many variables: your total order quantity and the number of units per style; the complexity of design; type of fabric being manufactured; and the delivery method. Simpler orders with higher volumes are much easier for a factory to handle and therefore also make the process much quicker. Working with the factory minimums always takes more time.

Allowing more time to work through product development may not seem ideal: heck, we all want results yesterday, am I right? However, allocating enough time will allow you to fully understand every aspect of each design. Your well-developed knowledge will help clearly communicate every product detail and specification to the factory, reducing error and confusion. As a result, it will lead to realistic expectations from the people you are working with and enable you to better communicate what is expected to the factory.

A work-back schedule and a time-and-action calendar can help you organize, prepare, and plan the product development and the manufacturing process. Most importantly, it will help you manage customer expectations for delivery dates. The key to success is referring to both of them on a daily basis to ensure that you're on track and meeting target dates. (More on these awesome organizational tools ahead.)

After working through the plan, most designers realize that numerous steps have taken a lot more time than expected. Over the years, I've found that the brands that allowed more time to work through these steps always yielded better results with the finished product.

Without careful planning, designers risk receiving poor quality products, late deliveries, and uncontrollable delays that, in turn, affect sales. The more time you spend on product development, the more likely it will be that you avoid costly mistakes.

Order Lead-Times

Sew... when will I get my goods?

In the apparel industry, lead-time - commonly referred to as turnaround time - is the total amount of time required to complete a product from receiving an order to the shipment of goods to the distributor.

Estimated lead-times from the initial order to final delivery vary based on a variety of factors, including the type of fabric structure, design complexity, and delivery method.

There are two components that make up lead-time: production and logistics.

Production order lead time is the length of time necessary to process an order. This includes procuring raw materials, cutting and sewing, finishing, and packing. The factory determines a ship date and an estimated lead-time needed for production. The factory coordinates with the suppliers and the production floor to give a more accurate lead time once the order is placed.

Logistics (transit/delivery) lead time is the time it takes to move the finished products from the factory to the buyer (the person that placed the purchase order: namely, you and/or your customers). The transit time includes trucking the products from the factory to the closest port or airport, shipping via sea or air, as well as the time it takes to move the products via truck from the destination to the warehouse.

Estimating Production Lead Time

Estimating production lead-times typically involves the time it takes to produce the fabric. Processing and ordering fabrics takes the longest time in the manufacturing process. Better factories will work with mills to procure and develop fabric. Cut-and-sew factories never stock fabric, only small quantities for sampling purposes. Of course, you have the option of delivering the material to the factory, if the factory allows it. However, that requires a lot more work on your end: you'll need to run around, source fabrics, approve them for quality, manage shrinkage, store the material, and deliver it to the factory. If you can place an order without having to send the fabric to the factory, it'll save you a lot of time and effort.

What's your best practice, then? Work with a factory that works with mills. Your fabric will be customized to your needs. This way, you will also be able to control product quality. The yarn is bought, weaved or knitted, dyed and washed as per your specifications. The fabric finishes, washes, fiber quality weight, shrinkage, dye colors, and so on, can all be controlled. The bonus in having your fabric manufactured from scratch is your ability to reproduce it for future orders.

Unlike most fabric wholesalers, mills never go out of stock. Being able to know the process right from the yarn, where the fabric is made, gives you greater control over the supply chain. You are able to trace your supply chain. How cool is that? Most brands have no idea where each part of their products comes from, how they were made, or, in many cases, if anyone was hurt along the way. You want to make sure you're in the loop at every step. Washes and finishes are impossible for third parties to test, so when the fabric is manufactured from scratch, you know the exact recipe.

Consumers and brands all strive for quality, but quality does take time. Big brands are notorious for asking for unreasonable turnaround times to get the product into stores. When you pressure factories to speed up the process, they might start engaging in unethical practices - scheduling long hours, compromising safety rules, etc., all of which will harm workers, which nobody wants to do. Furthermore, you risk selling a cheaper product that doesn't meet industry standards, which can hurt your reputation and possibly lead to lawsuits.

❊ GOLDEN NUGGET

You can request unofficial test reports from the factory. The mills always provide the factory with final fabric information and internal test results to ensure standards are met. Knowing the exact count or weight is useful information for the tech pack. Official test reports can also be conducted by a third party at a cost. Just ask the factory to provide you with them.

Let's talk about fabric structure for a moment. Lead time is determined by the fabric structure.

- **Knit fabrics** take approximately 75 to 90 days for the mills to develop and manufacture.
- **Woven fabrics** take approximately 120 to 150 days for the mills to develop and manufacture.

Garment factories are typically set up based on the structure of the fabric they can sew. Knit and woven fabrics require different machinery. Stitching the garments in either structure requires specific manufacturing processes. Also, knit and woven fabrics require different sewing capabilities and skill sets. Sewing operators are generally experienced in one or the other, not both. This means that if both fabrics are on one purchase order, you may need to work with two separate factories. As explained above, knit fabrics are faster to stich and produce.

Estimating Delivery Times

Delivery method timelines vary. The faster you want your product in the hands of the consumer, the higher the cost. Working further in advance and planning more efficiently will help you save money.

Approximate Delivery Times (within North America)

> By sea: approximately 30 to 45 days
> By air courier: approximately 4 to 5 days
> By air freight: approximately 7 to 10 days
*Consult a customs broker to better estimate transit time

Your delivery method is dependent on the budget and urgency of delivery. Also, consider how much margin per-piece each product can allow for delivery. The more significant the product margin, the more the profit, which will enable you to ship via air if necessary. If you know that customers will pay for a product at a higher cost, then you should have the margin to ship by air. If you order larger volumes or have a shipment with heavier weight products, planning ahead and shipping by sea can save you money.

Pre-Production Lead Times

In the beginning, it'll take time to fully understand the entire manufacturing process. If you have more than one delivery, it can get tricky, because you'll be working on different steps at any given point.

Average lead-time from prototyping and pre-production to delivery varies according to each order. Work through each timeline and estimate how long you would spend on each step. The work back schedule acts as a guide to help plan the amount of time needed to efficiently organize and manage tasks. (More ahead on the workback schedule.)

Photo | *Custom Design Manufacturing Process*

What's Your (Proto)type?

Sew... now let's talk about prototypes and counter samples.

Before an order is placed, you have to allocate time for designing prototypes. You can only work through design changes and direction at the prototyping stage. Designer entrepreneurs collaborate with other apparel industry professionals to create tech packs, patterns, graphics, and samples to build the perfect prototype, which the factory uses to develop a counter sample. The time spent on creating your prototype will help you perfect your design for functionality, fit, and aesthetic. Moving slowly through prototyping gives everyone involved a chance to provide you with valuable feedback before moving ahead with the factory.

Here are the steps to success:

Prototype: The first sample that is created from a pattern is your prototype. Usually, it's the designer who steers the ship, with the help of many other people, including tech pack designers, graphic designers, sample sewers, fit models, and pattern makers.

Counter Sample: Using the prototype as a guide, the factory creates a counter sample to get sewing efficiencies, understand what machinery is necessary, and estimate cost. The counter sample is also made to prepare each style for bulk production.

✻ GOLDEN NUGGET

Prototype development should always be done locally. You will have to collaborate with a team to create the design. There will be many design iterations, so the only way to control what you want is to work closely with people to perfect the design. Product development done locally will save you time, money, and makes the process much easier to manage.

Prototype Time Frame

The time frame for creating prototypes is determined by the size of your product line, the complexity of the designs, and the pace of workflow. The pattern maker, sample sewer, graphic designer, and the tech-pack designer all contribute to the workflow. Typically, the prototype process can take anywhere from 8 weeks to 18 months to complete, depending on the intricacies of your product, and your tribe's (the product development team's) schedule.

Counter Sample Time Frame

From what I've experienced with factories, counter sampling two to six styles can take anywhere from 8 to 12 weeks on average. This includes working through comments and approvals and courier transit time. The clearer and more thorough the information you send, the quicker the process. If you can, take a trip out there to work through counter sampling to speed up this step.

Counter Sampling & Approvals

After you create the prototype, which should be made as close to the "perfect" sample as possible, you and your team will assemble a detailed pre-production package for the factory. This package includes a fabric swatch, tech pack, prototype, reference samples, and a pattern, which the factory uses as a guide to develop a counter sample. Along with the counter samples, all components, including trims, embellishments, and so on, will be sent back for comments and approvals before production begins. (More on this in Part 3)

Counter Sampling With The Factory

When the factory receives the pre-production package, the first thing they'll do is analyze, weigh, and possibly test the fabric standard you've provided them with. They then work with their network of suppliers and mills to source options based on the fabric standard. Sourcing can take two weeks or more. Once the fabric options are couriered back to you, select the best option so the factory can provide you with an estimate. If the estimate is agreeable, move on to the next step.

Next, the factory develops a counter sample based on the provided prototype(s) for each design, reference samples, and tech packs. The counter sample is made using available fabric in a similar construction and weight of the approved material, to ensure proper fit. The designer gives approvals and comments for quality, fit, and stitching. The sample may be recreated two or three times until it is perfected for production. Every time you give the factory feedback seeking necessary changes, the factory will send you another package with those changes for sign-off. The counter sample helps the factory determine the set-up of machinery required and evaluate stitching efficiencies, which help provide a more accurate cost.

Along with the counter sample(s), the factory develops other approvals and provides mock-ups or options for all components and materials. The designer approves or rejects all of these, giving feedback on necessary changes. Everything from trims, embroideries, prints, packaging, tags, lab dips (swatches of fabric test dyed to hit a color standard you provide), and all other components are sourced by the factory. For example, the factory may provide a few options for buttons based on your reference sample, leaving it up to you to decide which ones to use for production.

The factory must source the materials from numerous fabric suppliers, dyeing mills, washers, printers, trims suppliers, and label makers to give you new and revised samples. They will need time to coordinate with their suppliers to create these samples. Often, delays can occur due to wait times to get service, because, well, the factory is working with a LOT of different companies. And, you know very well what it's like to depend on other people to get your job done.

Typically, the factory needs two to three weeks to send a package for approval. Keep in mind that every time you request a re-submission of a sample, it will cost more and push the delivery date out further. In some cases, if the issues or error will not affect a sale, it may be better to make an approval, rather than delay the shipment. You may consider the factory's mistake as an error, however, it can be deemed acceptable if it does not affect the overall goal of your design. Remember: it's not about if they did it "correctly," it's about determining whether the garment is sellable or not. Doing so will save both time and money, as well as help the factory.

❇ GOLDEN NUGGET

Avoid requesting that the factory revise a sample more than three times. Sampling is a costly process for the factory, and what's more, the factory may not have workers with the appropriate skill set or the necessary machinery to complete the sample to your standard. As much as it might be inconvenient, if you're not the least bit happy with what they've given you, consider a plan B. If it takes more than three revised samples, it's time to drop that style or maybe look for a new factory that better understands your requirements.

Work-Back Schedule

SEW...

Now that you've got a general understanding of estimating both production and delivery lead times, you can make a plan. While it may feel easier, even exciting, to start planning a project with a kick-off date, manufacturing offshore requires us to work backwards from an end date or goal. Otherwise, how can you ensure everything gets done to meet the delivery date? The work-back schedule is a guide to help plan what needs to be done on a weekly basis to keep you on track to achieve your deadlines.

The work back schedule starts with establishing all the tasks that you need to get done from initial design to product delivery. This includes allocating time needed to complete steps such as design, prototyping, counter sample and so on. The tasks are entered into the calendar starting with the the date you want to receive your goods. Finally you add the rest of the tasks required to meet that date.

It's important to factor in additional cushion time for unforeseen and often uncontrollable setbacks that can happen during the manufacturing process. Managing timelines, delays, and changes requires careful planning. Remember: delays can come from your end, from the factory, suppliers, or couriers, and even from uncontrollable setbacks such as severe weather. If you place two orders in a year, you must include a schedule with each order.

Do you want to be profitable? Of course, you do! Just remember that planning is crucial to profitability. As you begin this iterative process, you will learn to design and plan for at least two seasons ahead. Doing so will give you greater control of your business (as well as no shortage of $$$).

» BEST PRACTICE

Once you start the whole manufacturing cycle, it's hard to keep up. Give yourself a head start. Before you begin working with factories, design, sample, and plan products for at least three orders ahead.

General Guidelines & Instructions For Creating A Work Back Schedule:

Using Excel is the best way to create a roadmap, mapping out columns for departments (eg. design, marketing, product development & production) at the top, and dates (months by week) on the left.

1 *Delivery Date*: What date do you expect to see your product? Enter the date.

2 *Estimate Production Lead Times*: Based on the following fabric structure, back out the following production lead times (these dates are based on minimum orders when factories are working with fabric mills, reduce time if you are purchasing stock fabric):

   – Knit fabrics take approximately 75 (11 weeks) to 90 days (13 weeks) to develop the fabric with a mill and produce it.

   – Woven fabrics take approximately 120 (17 weeks) to 150 (22 weeks) days to develop fabric with a mill and produce it.

3 *Estimate Transit Lead/Delivery Lead Times*: How will the product move from the factory to you? Select a suitable delivery mode from below. Next, back out approximate time frame required. Add a few extra days to give yourself a buffer. You can also speak to a customs broker to get a better idea of transit times.

   *Don't forget to factor in the time it takes to move the goods from the factory to the port/airport and when it reaches your country, to your door.

   Remember:Approximate Delivery Times (within North America):

   – By sea, approximately 30 to 45 days
   – By air courier, approximately 4 to 5 days
   – By air freight, approximately 7 to 10 days

4 *Counter Sampling*: Allow roughly 4 to 6 weeks for the factory to source materials and supplies, as well as work with you on counter sampling. This is a critical time for preparing for production. If possible, the factory may be able to provide

you with an estimated time frame. Just know that this time it takes to counter sample is also dependent on the number of times you may ask for a revised sample.

5 *Design/Research/Prototyping/Sales & Marketing*: This can vary from product to product and company to company. This will be a long process, so break down the steps for better accuracy.

Are you planning more than one shipment in a year? Add the 2nd delivery date and follow Steps 1-5 again to map out a plan.

Photo | *Workback Schedule*

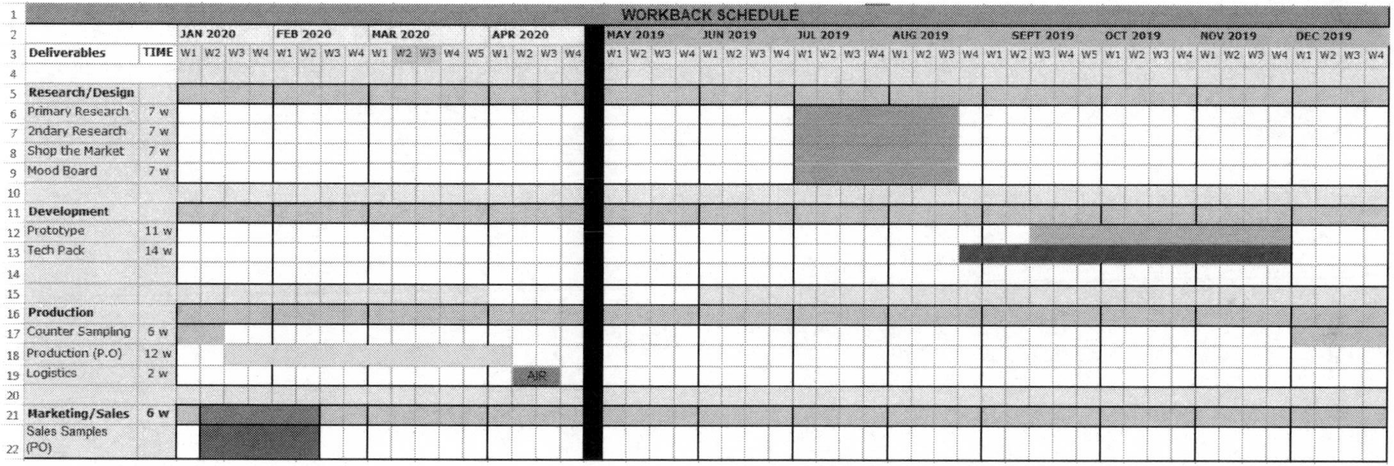
WORKBACK SCHEDULE
JAN 2020
FEB 2020
MAR 2020
APR 2020
MAY 2019
JUN 2019
JUL 2019
AUG 2019
SEPT 2019
OCT 2019
NOV 2019
DEC 2019
Deliverables
TIME
Research/Design
Primary Research 7 w
2ndary Research 7 w
Shop the Market 7 w
Mood Board 7 w
Development
Prototype 11 w
Tech Pack 14 w
Production
Counter Sampling 6 w
Production (P.O) 12 w
Logistics 2 w
AIR
Marketing/Sales 6 w
Sales Samples (PO)

Example: If you want to receive your goods the 3rd week of April 2020, for example, project kick off date would be the 1st week of July 2019 (the entire process taking you 10 months)

What To Expect When You're Expecting (Design)

Here are some factors to consider when managing your time efficiently.

1   Expect to spend at least *two months* working through design. The fine details of the product development process such as selecting fabrics, shopping the marketplace, gathering samples, researching quality standards for prints, trims, labels and other items, partnering with sample makers and pattern makers, developing logos and marketing materials: all of these take time. Researching your target market and competitors to creating mood boards also take time.

2   Expect to spend at least four months reviewing and commenting on samples, working with partners locally and the factory offshore.

3   Expect to spend a lot of time working on the details of each tech pack. On a regular basis, you'll need to update the tech pack as changes are made to the product, or new information is received from partners. Updates will be done from prototyping, possibly right up until the end of production. Accurate, up-to-date packages are crucial for the successful production of current and future orders.

4   Expect to learn the art of clearly and simply communicating every detail of each design with the product development team and the factory.

5   Expect to undergo a long process of working through product development to perfect each design and to get it production ready.

6 Expect to spend several hours approving, and commenting on each counter sample sent from the factory. Thorough and detailed notes, image comments, and fit sessions are required for every design.

Learn From The Big Guys (and Gals)

The manufacturing process is time-intensive. Manufacturing offshore requires preparation for a lengthy time commitment. Even fast fashion brands such as The Gap, Ralph Lauren, and Zara plan a year or more ahead. They understand the complexities of the production process. Numerous factories, suppliers, and industry players are involved in the manufacturing process, making it virtually impossible to quickly turn around mass produced items. Truly, manufacturing is an art, centered around people, and deserves the time necessary to produce a quality product.

Fast fashion brands such as H&M understand that creating new styles is a costly and lengthy process. These retailers rarely create new patterns. Take a closer look: you'll see that season after season, they repeat the majority of their styles, making only slight variations in fabrics, styles, embellishments, and colors. Garments previously sold are proven to be successful. *Sew,* why reinvent the wheel? Products previously manufactured are generally resold, but tweaked to speed up delivery.

Established brands work off of basic blocks. A block is a pattern silhouette that is used season after season with minor changes. An example would be a T-shirt or skirt that remains the same but changes its color, trim, length, or maybe even gets a pocket added to it. A brand creates a collection of blocks and then manipulates the blocks to create new styles.

By working off basic blocks and only making minor revisions, these brands are able to turn the finished product around in just a few months, and scarily enough, some are even quicker (though their ethical standards are debatable).

Working with basic blocks helps mitigate risk and is both a money and time saver. As exciting as designing might be, reinventing the wheel each season will dramatically increase the total cost of production. You save money in pattern making and product development. You also assume less risk in production sewing or fit issues.

The factory has experience manufacturing your product, so assumes less risk in sewing and production. You also assume less risk in producing a garment that does not fit, if consumers have indicated they are happy. If you have a product that has generated a lot of sales, maximize your return by using the existing blocks and make slight modifications to them to create new styles.

» BEST PRACTICE

Do you have staple pieces, such as a top, pant or skirt you will regularly want to produce? Ask the pattern maker to create and work off of basic blocks. Not only will you save time and money, you will minimize your chances of product issues. Trust me: your future self will thank you.

Love Takes Time, Love Makes Time

No matter how much you're making, products designed from scratch and manufactured overseas take a considerable amount of time to process. All established brands work through initial design, product development, and pre-production.

Although it may take up to a year to turn around a new design development, progress can be made over time. Building long-term relationships with partners helps you both to improve the manufacturing process. Better communication and understanding grows over time. You'll improve and deepen your relationships with all of your partners, including and especially the factory and the product development team. Less confusion ensues because the prototyping team and the factory's staff understand the brand standards, expectations, and the production process, helping to complete orders much, much faster. Factories especially have a steep learning curve, with many more communication challenges compared to working with the local product development team.

Likewise, you must also learn how your partners work. Every partner has procedures that make it faster and easier for them to do their work. Additionally, their capabilities may help you design better products. For example, you may learn over time that the factory may have a strong skill set in embroideries, something which can be integrated into the products going forward. You will master the factory-buyer procedures such as ordering products and better understanding the delivery timelines for your specific products. Nurturing long-lasting relationships enables growth and speeds up all processes.

When you learn, it enables you to tweak things, which saves you time and money in the long run. Once we develop mutual expectations and understanding of processes and procedures of the factory production, orders become quicker to process. You will both develop a shared understanding with each new order that is placed. You will also get better at planning ahead and the long turnaround times will not be so much of an issue.

> "COMING TOGETHER IS A BEGINNING. KEEPING TOGETHER
> IS PROGRESS. WORKING TOGETHER IS SUCCESS."
> **- HENRY FORD**

Purchase Orders

Purchase orders have a start and an "estimated" end date. However, most brands will usually fill out another order to replenish stock so inventory is not fully depleted. You and the factory should mutually agree upon the delivery date before you place your order, along with an estimated delivery date set on the order itself. Purchase orders should be placed once a factory has made a counter sample and the fabric has been approved. You may also need to revise the purchase order with updated prices if major changes occur from the time they provided an initial estimate to the approved counter sample.

Meeting Delivery Dates

Let's talk a little bit about pressure. Although it is essential to meet delivery expectations, really try to avoid putting excessive pressure on the factory. Mutual agreements must be made before placing the official order. Always leave a buffer for late deliveries. Just like any other company, factories want to receive payment for services rendered, which means they will work diligently to complete and ship your order to the supplier before the set deadline. Although factories are working with many clients and most likely higher volumes, they have no reason to not complete your order on time. Everyone is trying their best.

Pressuring factories to deliver your orders faster will likely produce a lower quality standard. More importantly, pressure and threats negatively impact the factory's work environment, which often leads to unethical practices. After all, factories and suppliers can only output a certain number of units each day.

❇ GOLDEN NUGGET

To avoid delays, many brands shipping within the same year will send the factory a new production package as soon as the first PO is placed. Repeat Steps 1 to 3 during this timeframe.

Paperwork: Ordering Process

The ordering process is the same for both sampling and bulk orders; however, there are cost differences. (See Part 2 for more information).

The ordering process involves the six following steps.

Photo | *Purchase Order Process*

1 Program Overview

The designer submits a number of items, called a pre-production package or program, to the factory. The factory then reviews the entire program. A pre-production package typically includes the prototype(s), reference samples, tech pack(s), artwork file(s), a mock purchase order, a line sheet, and a fabric swatch. The mock purchase order gives the factory a target price per unit and budget that you are looking to work with. The product prototype(s) and other physical materials can be sent at a later time once the designer green-lights the estimate. In this case, the tech pack(s), artwork file(s), mock purchase order and a line sheet suffice for a quick estimate. (See Part 5 for a detailed pre-production package checklist).

2 Estimates

The factory reviews the pre-production package and sources similar fabrics based on the quality standard provided. In return, the factory provides fabric options, and the designer selects one so the factory can produce an estimate. If the price is agreeable to both the designer and the factory, the remaining components - prototype, color standard, reference materials, and pattern - are sent to the factory.

3 *Counter Sample*

The factory makes a counter sample using a similar, available fabric to achieve sewing efficiencies, establish machinery requirements, and to source all other materials in the product. The designer makes comments or gives approvals on product trims, quality standard selection, and other items that impact price. Once all items and details —materials, fit and stitching, embellishments, trims, tags, and more— are approved, the factory can calculate a final cost for each product. Because there are numerous suppliers in the manufacturing process, calculating prices is a very timely and exhaustive process for the factories. At this point, you can get an estimate for a turnaround time should you place an order.

4 *Purchase Order*

Commitments between both buyer and seller are typically discussed in person, over the telephone, by fax, or via email. After this, the designer or buyer places an official purchase order (PO) noting:

> Colors and style numbers
> Description of the product (fiber/weight etc.)
> Product price (typically FOB, discussed in Part 2)
> Total order quantity and size break-down
> Packing instructions
> Testing requirements
> Delivery terms and address
> Whatever else has been agreed upon

» BEST PRACTICE

If colors, style numbers, delivery address, or other details change during production or counter sampling, be sure to update the PO to avoid potential issues. Additional charges may apply to any changes made once the PO is placed.

5 *Proforma Invoice*

In return to the PO, the factory or seller will send a proforma invoice to confirm the agreement. A proforma invoice is an estimated invoice submitted by the factory to a buyer in advance of a shipment or delivery of goods. It states complete details for the agreement of sale. It should also state the factory name, confirm delivery date and banking information to wire the deposit.

Normally, a letter of credit is opened on the basis of this proforma invoice sent by the seller. It's best to open a letter of credit, a letter issued by a bank to another bank (typically in a different country) to serve as a guarantee for payments made to a specified person under specified conditions. When you open a letter of credit with the bank or provide the factory with fifty percent deposit of the purchase order, they can procure fabric and pay suppliers and workers. The factory works with several partners, suppliers, and the production department, and must coordinate with everyone to establish a firm turn-around time or estimated delivery date.

At this point, they should also be able to send you a time and action (TNA) calendar for the manufacturing and production process. (More on the TNA ahead)

6 *Manufacturing/Production*

Once the order is placed, and the fabric is procured, the factory manufactures a sample of each style using the exact production fabric and sends it to the designer for approval. This is called the pre-production sample. Upon approval, they will start cutting.

7 *Final Invoice*

Once all the garments are packed and ready to ship, the factory generates a packing slip and a commercial invoice. The final invoice for products is paid before delivery and may include the shipping fees if requested. A packing slip of all styles, sizes and colors comes with each carton. You can also ask for a top of production (TOP) sample from the finished production, before sending final payment.

Costs generally don't include shipping expenses, since it's difficult to estimate until products are packed. Duty rates, importation and shipping fees are usually handled by your customs broker, which allows you more control.

Please Note: To avoid shortages from damage during manufacturing, the factory cuts a small percentage of extra pieces of each style. Expect anywhere around 5-8% of pieces in the final invoice. Again, the more you order, generally the lower the shortage or surplus.

Purchasing Sales Samples & Lead Times

After placing a PO for bulk production and all the materials are in-house, the factory will provide you with a pre-production (PP) sample. When you place an order, you can request a specific size and color for the pre-production sample to use as sales samples. If you require more than one sample of a style, you should fill out a samples purchase order. Remember you should also receive a top-of-production (TOP) sample of each style after production.

Since every order is unique, the factory will only provide you with a sampling cost after reviewing the entire sample order. The most cost-effective way to order samples is by purchasing and requesting samples to be delivered when all the materials are in-house. There are no added costs for the factory to manufacture or order fabrics separately and therefore the main cost will be in stitching. Depending on your timelines and needs, first, see if PP samples or TOP sample will suffice for sales samples. The time allocated to logistics and delivery can be used to work with the sales samples. Typically, startup brands order one or two units of each color and style to use for photo shoots and sales samples.

Lengthy turnaround time is mainly due to fabric and the dyeing process. Unfortunately, the turnaround times for sampling styles in the exact fabric are not much faster than manufacturing fabric in a small batch production order. For this reason, sampling PO's and bulk production orders are placed together, so delivery dates don't get pushed out further.

If you require any other color or fabric other than what is on order, costs are at a premium since materials need to be made in smaller quantities.

Time And Action (TNA) Plan

SEW, let's take a quick breath. How are we doing so far?

If this seems like a lot to take in, remember your outcome: beautifully-designed products, excellently-made, delivered on time, at efficient prices. This is the result of mastery of the product development process, and I've got a few more tips and tricks for you yet!

Let's talk about TNA: The time and action plan.

Managing a production order is no different than managing a project. Every order brings in a list of tasks that are needed to be done, from issuing the purchase order to shipping the product. You might need to carry out some tasks one after the other while carrying out others simultaneously, all depending on the order needs. There are a lot of complexities in managing each order. You'll need to have a definite plan, clearly-defined responsibilities, and the time and resource requirements for each task.

The time and action (TNA) calendar is one of the most essential tools for managing the manufacturing process. A TNA calendar helps to establish a lead time for the order: that is, the time an order takes to complete, from the moment the factory receives the order to the final shipment to the buyer. Merchandisers at the factory prepare a plan in a spreadsheet, listing key processes in one column and planned dates of action for each process in another. They'll list every product with expected delivery dates for sample approvals, fabrics, trims, cut dates, quality control, packing dates, delivery dates and more, according to style. The merchandisers will then follow the TNA calendar on a daily basis to keep orders on track. Before or immediately after you place an order, request a TNA calendar from the factory so you can follow up and ensure orders are meeting targets.

As I said earlier, some tasks come one after the other and others move at the same time. Just as there can be a lot of processes, there can be a lot of people involved in fulfilling an order. Secondly, each order is unique regarding process and time demand. A detailed plan with clear responsibilities is a must for each purchase order to stay on track.

Photo | *The Time & Action Plan*

TIME AND ACTION PLAN

S/no	Style	Colour	Fabric Name	QTY	Knitting		Dyeing		Compacting		Fabric inhouse	Cutting		Sewing		Checking		Packing	
					Start	End	Start	End	Start	End	Date	Start	End	Start	End	Start	End	Start	End
1	W5F17-S/S tee	Grey	Single Jersey-160 GSM	150	We will recieved the final approval on 30-06-2019							7/5/2019	7/5/2019	7/7/2019	7/14/2019	7/17/2019	7/19/2019	7/20/2019	7/24/2019
2	WLSCT17-L/S Tee	Grey	Single Jersey-160 GSM	100	will be start the production							7/6/2019	7/7/2019	7/10/2019	7/17/2019	7/18/2019	7/21/2019	7/24/2019	7/26/2019
3	LSTD17-L/S tunic dress	Grey	Single Jersey-160 GSM	175								7/10/2019	7/12/2019	7/13/2019	7/20/2019	7/24/2019	26-207-2019	7/27/2019	7/31/2019
4	RGD17(Raglan Tee)	Grey	100% French Terry Fleece-Organic Cotton-320 GSM	210	6/26/2019	7/10/2019	7/11/2019	7/31/2019	8/1/2019	8/5/2019	8/7/2019	8/9/2019	8/11/2019	8/14/2019	8/18/2019	8/21/2019	8/24/2019	8/25/2019	8/29/2019
5	SWH (HOODIE)	Grey	100% French Terry Fleece-Organic Cotton-320 GSM	50	6/27/2019	8/11/2019	8/13/2019	03/008/2019	8/4/2019	8/8/2019	8/10/2019	8/11/2019	8/15/2019	8/16/2019	8/22/2019	8/23/2019	8/28/2019	8/29/2019	8/31/2019
6	JLST-JACKET	Grey	100% French Terry Fleece-Organic Cotton-320 GSM	175	6/30/2019	7/5/2019	7/6/2019	8/3/2019	8/4/2019	8/8/2019	8/10/2019	8/16/2019	8/18/2019	8/21/2019	8/31/2019	9/1/2019	9/5/2019	9/6/2019	9/10/2019
				860															

Minimum Order Quantities (MOQ's)
From The Factory's Point Of View

Now, let's take a minute and put ourselves in the factory's shoes (or, more accurately steel-toed safety boots).

There are a lot of reasons why a lot of the big players in fashion, order in bulk quantities. The unfortunate truth is that the factory considers minimum order quantities (MOQ) to be lower priorities compared to their other orders. However, it's important to understand that the factory accepts your order as an investment to help you grow, and thus expects that future orders will be much larger. Factories that take minimum orders have a 30 percent efficiency rate, which means they are not making as much as they should. Minimum orders also affect lead-times: the higher the order volume, the faster it will move through the manufacturing process.

Table-1 | Line efficiency at different order quantity

Order Qty.	Average Style Efficiency
100-500	30%
501-1000	35%
1001-3000	40%
3001-8000	50%
8001-10000	55%
10000 plus	60%

Photo: *Line Efficiency At Different Order Quantity,* *Source: Online Clothing Study*

Suppliers and factories are set up for large orders, thus making production move faster. Materials purchased at larger volumes often use machinery that is set up for easy management. Buying in higher quantities translates to higher profits for the factory. Higher profits pushes the order as a top priority. As a result, designers with smaller volume orders will be deprioritized, because the orders are more difficult to manage and may experience longer lead-times.

It's critical, then, for you to discuss these scenarios openly with the factory and have a single point of contact you can liaise with to keep production moving at a steady pace. Requesting time and action calendars helps manage expectations of delivery dates.

In reality, the factory's work environment is incredibly fast-paced, since staff are working on several orders at once. Therefore, some patience and empathy are required on your part. Remember: you're cultivating a long-term relationship with the factory, which will, over time, make your entire process smoother, cheaper, and more meaningful. Think of the factory as a best friend or sibling who's completely different than you, who maybe never grew out of the partying phase or who has a deep interest in politics, but who has loaned you her favorite dress when you really needed it and drives you to work at the last-minute when your car breaks down. You may not completely understand what it's like in their world, but you can always count on them to have your back (and you'll still have theirs).

How Sample Approval Delay Affects PO Delivery Dates

Delays in sampling approvals, manufacturing and delivery dates are a well-known part of offshore garment manufacturing. The nature of the business can be very unpredictable. Most often, delays from overseas are out of any individual's control.

For example, manufacturers in some countries can face numerous setbacks during the monsoon season: power outages, inability to print, dangerous travel conditions coming and going from villages to factories or delivery to the port of exit, and so on. A designer should be thoroughly aware of the reality that festivals, weather, unreliable electricity, fabric dyeing accessibility, and more can all affect lead times in this regard. Every country is unique. What works in the West may be impossible in a developing country, or in a culture influenced by different traditions, business practices, or even weather conditions.

Factories have no time to explain the details of what causes delays. Only as your relationship and communication grows, over time, will you fully understand their pain points. Trusting relationships are built on a willingness to learn how the factory and partners work most effectively and what obstacles they face. Investing in human relationships will result in increased value added to your product. The factory has numerous approvals and clients that they are working with at any given moment. Deadlines are not just the factories' issues or faults. Remember, they are working with several suppliers.

» BEST PRACTICE

It is your responsibility, then, to provide comments on the packages on time or it will adversely impact deadlines for delivery. When the package arrives, it should be treated with urgency. Allow at least a few hours to work through, understand, and give comments on all approvals that they're requesting. Take no more than 48 hours to reply with your comments and issues, or it will push your lead time and delivery date even further out. Delays on your end can also drastically impact your production turnaround times.

You Want It When?

Delays can occur for some of the following reasons:

1 *Back-and-Forth Communication* (a.k.a. phone and email tag) The back-and-forth nature of communicating with the factory can cause delays. Time differences and response times come into play. The factory is working with multiple buyers, and the sampling department may need some time to address your sampling approvals and comments. The faster you send your approvals or comments, the faster the process moves along. If you get held up with an approval, it will cause even more delays in the process. Every time you ask the factory to re-submit an approval sample, it sets production back by another two weeks. You may not be able to control how quickly the factory responds to you, but you can control how fast you reply to the factory. Respond to any written correspondence within the same business day and any sample approvals within no more than 48 hours.

2 *Holidays*

Religious observance, cultural events, and holidays are extremely important for some countries. Holi, for example, one of India's biggest festivals that celebrates color, can cause a significant setback in production. Garment workers may travel to their native villages for the festival and then allow their visits to stretch to a week or more. What's more, a wedding in the family is not merely a weekend affair.

Every country has its own unique holidays. While you may be on a regular workday, the factory may be on holiday. Similarly, when the factory is in production, you may be on holiday. Holidays also affect lead times. Always ask for these dates at the onset of the project, so you understand if you are not receiving prompt replies.

3 *Courier Delays*

Misconnected flights, customs delays, incorrect addresses, no one to receive the package, lost packages: all of these can cause delays in delivery. Also, not all carriers are built the same concerning service. In my opinion, FedEx generally has the best service. Prices may be slightly higher, but the chances of your package being lost are much lower. In case of emergency and for your records, always have a second set for whatever you send to the factory.

4 *Weather*

Weather you like it or not (pardon my pun), delays can arise due to a multitude of weather conditions. Weather disruptions may happen during sampling approvals and production order delivery.

Take, for example, monsoons. Unless you've lived through monsoons in a city in which electricity is sporadic, or roads are unpaved, you may not fully understand how production schedules can be affected by what you might consider a simple rainstorm. Monsoon season in India lasts from June to September. Monsoons make screen printing almost impossible. This may seem silly, but the high humidity levels make the ink bleed and make drying next to impossible. Excessive heat can also start the gelling process and make inks thick and hard to print.

Sew... that was Part 1. I know, it was A LOT, but don't worry!

In Part 2, we'll get to the fun stuff: we're going to talk design! To ensure that you're designing products that will sell, not only do you need to consider styles, aesthetic, quality, and materials, you also need to ensure that the design is thoughtfully researched to fill a demand. Designing uses not only creativity but a crucial understanding of what your market demands. Let's keep going!

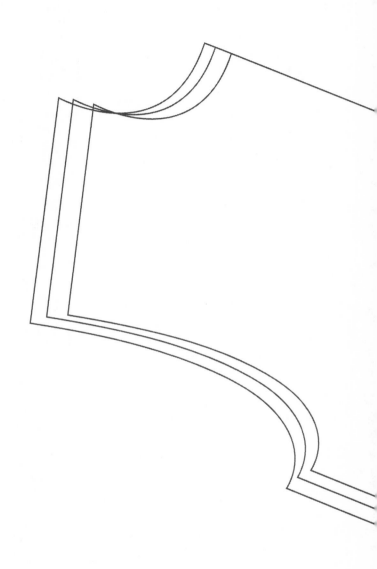

DESIGNING FOR PRODUCTION

OVERVIEW

Sew, let's talk design. After all, isn't that why you got into this business?

Apparel design and product development are two processes that go hand in hand. As Albert Einstein said, "creativity is intelligence having fun." They both require time, thought, patience, love, and energy. You've got to balance your left brain and your right brain, yin and yang working in harmony to create something new and beautiful. Apparel design is the first step in the product development process.

At the design stage, you are taking your idea, conceptualizing it, and establishing the direction for both function, quality, and aesthetic. Design typically requires you to create a mood board; research the market (which also entails competition analysis); shop the market; and select fabrics, trims, colorways and creating sketches, and styles. It's a lot, but do it all right, and the end result will be a beautiful new creation that generates profits and takes the world by storm.

Translating one design into a scalable, well-built product is an art. As a designer entrepreneur, you must consider material selection, cost, target market, and production requirements when working through every design detail. Remember: it's not enough to just have a fantastic idea in your head, you must ensure that you've got a proven method to bring it into reality.

Product development, as a broad term, may be defined as taking a design idea and working through the process of getting it ready for production; ultimately coming out with samples. One thing to always keep in mind is that when you're working through product development, your design will also evolve. The product development process will involve many iterations, and you may need to consider deviations from the original design. The more thought that you put into the entire process, the more successful the outcome. Rushing and not taking the much needed time to develop the product always leads to costly mistakes.

Successful brands start the process by doing a significant amount of research before adopting a product into their offerings. Ultimately, the goal is to find a niche, prove it can sell, and fill the demand. startups selling fewer items will minimize risk, improve manufacturing efficiencies, and help manage reasonable budgets. Starting with one to six designs will help maintain control while streamlining the process of growth. I recommend not offering more than two colors for any given style or product. This may seem small, but there is a lot to manage and juggle, especially if the product comes in multiple sizes.

One of the most critical aspects of manufacturing any successful product is choosing and understanding the right fabric(s) for the product. Think about it: material is the most costly part of any product, so you need to understand it in great detail if you want to avoid wasting money. By details I mean everything from structure, properties, washes, and count, to composition, weight, how it's constructed, washing instructions, and much, much more. You need the recipe.

Now, if you're something of a fabric nerd and have extensive knowledge about the materials, you can convey exact fabric requirements to the factory manager. If you don't specify in detail what you want, how can you expect a factory to deliver? It's a little like going to Starbucks and ordering a "coffee." Well, what kind? Dark roast? Latte? Venti, double shot, non-fat, no whip, extra-foam, caramel macchiato? You've got to be specific about what you want.

The fashion designer's relationship with fabric is at the heart of the creative process. The right choice of material is fundamental to good design and is instrumental to its manufacturing success.

Let's talk about our old friend, the factory. There are significant advantages in allowing the factory to source the fabrics and work directly with a mill. The cut-and-sew factories have more substantial buying power than a small brand. The factory can directly work with mills and negotiate the best price. Mills manufacture, dye, and finish the fabrics. In the long run, since the material was created to spec, you know the exact recipe and can easily reproduce it. There is no guarantee when working with a fabric supplier that it can be replicated. Let the factory deal with procurement, delivery, storage, coordination, and quality control.

Higher-end brands don't skimp out on quality. Let's compare, for example, Old Navy to Banana Republic, two clothing retailers owned by American multinational corporation Gap Inc. Starting with the fabric, quality standards differ between the companies. Old Navy uses a lower quality fiber and avoids preshrinking fabric to cut costs. Banana Republic, on the other hand, manufactures pre-shrunk quality fabrics that have the best hand feel and use only premium quality yarns. The better the quality, the happier the customer.

A great way to materialize ideas is by creating well-thought out vision and mood boards. In this chapter, I'll show you how these boards help you to plan and provide an intuitive way to brainstorm, organize, and play with your research. Much like a business plan, combining the right images, colors, and text to tell one cohesive story is much harder than it seems (although, if you're anything like me, you'll agree that making a vision and mood board is waaaay more fun than writing a business plan). While a vision board visually showcases a business plan, and the mood board visually showcases the product direction, I'm a firm believer that using both will help you solidify your goals and bring them to life.

Warning: **Failing To Conduct Market Research Can Result In A Death Sentence For Your Business**

Never underestimate the importance of market research. Not bothering with market research is an easy way to condemn your business vision to an early grave. No matter what size or type of enterprise you run, performing market research is critical to your overall success, as it serves as the foundation of the entire business strategy, determining everything from sales and marketing to product development. Research is essential to the creative process. The insights you get from your research data direct you to actual product design, as well as pricing and marketing strategies.

Typically, when entrepreneurs hear the phrase "market research," their thoughts immediately go to *competitive research*, since it helps to see how they measure up to others within the marketplace. While researching competitors is an important aspect of market research, it's not the only aspect.

Target market research, or the collection of data regarding customers' preferences and behaviours, is also essential. Understanding the target consumer will ultimately help you to address their problems so you can design better products that "speak" to consumers.

As long as consumers have problems, they will always shop for solutions. People will always look for better, faster, and smarter ways to accomplish everyday tasks. And fortunately for many entrepreneurs, there is still much room for improvement in many existing products. The biggest challenge for most startups is finding these painful problems and coming up with solutions for them.

Using a combination of research methods can help you create a targeted business strategy that's based on cold hard facts rather than on feelings. Ultimately, research enables you to confidently make business decisions,that will, in turn, generate growth.

Market Research; **It's Not Just For The Big Boys (Or Gals)**

For good reason, big brands pay big bucks for private research companies to gather and interpret data. These corporations rely on these research companies for comprehensive information and analysis of consumer spending and shopping behavior, so that they can design customized solutions and drive better business decisions. Careful examination of quality research ultimately reduces risk. In addition to businesses that provide customized solutions, many of the more prominent brands use third party market research companies, such as WGSN (World Global Style Network), who are paid upwards of $10,000 yearly for memberships. The same information is accessible to all their members.

NOW... I'm not suggesting paying for all this, especially when you can do it at a fraction of the cost. In fact, the research should be both collected and analyzed by the designer. Getting your hands dirty is the best way to drive better business decisions. (Whatever you do, just don't get any of it on the garments).

Forbes magazine famously notes that 90% of startups fail. Nine out of ten! What?! Now that is a hard stat to swallow. Cold statistics like these, however, are not intended to discourage you, but to encourage you to work smarter.

Forbes reported the top reason that startups fail is: "They make products no one wants."[1] A careful survey of failed startups determined that 42% of them identified the "lack of a market need for their product" as the single biggest reason for their failure. If you're going to spend your time making a product, then spend your time making sure it's the right product for the right market."

If you have an idea, great! Research it! Wouldn't you feel a lot better being able to validate an idea before you invest the big bucks? The research will confirm your key startup assumptions and give you actionable insights into how to price, design, and select every component that goes into each product.

When To Research

Research is not a "set it and forget it" activity. Researching the target audience and analyzing the competition are activities that you need to do before you start a business, and then on a daily basis once you've got everything humming along.

By conducting research on a regular basis, you can keep up with the dynamics of the economy. You can also adjust to new regulations and technological breakthroughs.

Part of being prepared with market research is avoiding unpleasant surprises. Intuition and experience can be helpful at times, but research and facts often paint a more accurate picture of what is happening in the market.

Pre-launch: The data collected before launch helps you analyze who the target market is and if it is big enough to support your fashion business. You want to learn what consumers need. Most importantly, are you solving a problem? Scope out the competition. What makes you different and how can you have a competitive edge over them?

Post-launch: Ongoing target audience and competitive research will help you find more customers. The data collected will help you implement insights that attract repeat business. Existing businesses must still gather and analyze research for insights into successful marketing campaigns to offer new products. Are the various ways they promote something you can do?

❊ GOLDEN NUGGET

Subscribe to competitor newsletters or online magazines that cater to your target market for up-to-date information that keeps you on top of what's going on. It may also spark inspiration or new ideas.

Market Mix: **What To Zone In On**

The marketing mix is a crucial tool to help understand what the product or service can offer and how to plan for a successful product offering. To know where you need to focus, it's important to understand some instrumental "P" words:

Product — Improve your product or service based on findings of what your customers really want and need. Focus on things like function, appearance, and return policies, all of which help you to design and finalize which products will go into production.

It's vital for you to understand consumer pain points. Consumer feedback at any given point leads you to what is missing and the challenges they face. Their feedback helps you design better products suited to your brand. You can gather information about anything from fit and color preferences to quality and function. It enables you to make selections for each component of the product when working through product development. Your target customer will be able to direct you with quality standards for something as small as a simple zipper. They can help to you know when to choose the reputable and world's largest zipper manufacturer, YKK, over a no-name brand.

Beyond prospective clients, current clients and sales orders also indicate what is and isn't working with regards to your product.

Price — How a product is priced will directly affect how it sells. There are many techniques for establishing what you want to sell a product for. Firstly, it's important to see what the market bears. You can directly ask your target market what they think of the prices you set, but remember that branding also affects pricing. The perceived value is what a customer believes the product is worth, rather than an actual cost of the product on offer. If a product is priced higher or lower than its perceived value, then it will not sell.

Placement — Decide where and how to distribute the products. Compare the characteristics of different locations and the value of points of sale (retail, wholesale, online, pop-up shops, trade shows, etc.).

Promotion — Promotion is just the communication aspect of the entire marketing function. Figure out how to best reach particular market segments (teens, parents, students, professionals, etc.) in areas of advertising and publicity, social media, and branding.

Types Of Research

Ready to become a research nerd? When conducting market research, you should gather two types of data: primary and secondary analysis. There are various methods of collecting each one.

Primary Research
Primary research is original information gathered through your own efforts to respond to a specific question or set of questions aimed at your target customer. Sure, you can hire a market research

company, but, if you truly want to gain an understanding and strategize, better to get your hands dirty. You can gather your data via surveys, focus groups, and a multitude of other methods from past, prospective, and current customers.

Secondary Research
Secondary research is data that's already compiled and organized for you. It involves gathering statistics, reports, studies and other data from organizations such as government agencies, trade associations, and your local chamber of commerce. It also exploits existing resources like company records, surveys, research studies, and books, and applies the information to answer the question(s) you are asking.

Before You Begin

1. First, it is essential to establish clear goals for the market research activity you're about to undertake. Make sure you have defined what you need to know and why. Establish clear objectives for gaining insight into shopping behaviors, product attributes, demographics and more.

Let's say you want to develop innovative products that make it easier for working moms to contribute to a healthy planet. Your research goal, then, is to understand how they live their lives, so that you can respond more effectively to their needs with informed and inspired design solutions. For example, Apple Cheeks Diapers, featured on Dragons Den, created a reusable diaper for the modern parent. *Sew,* what sets them apart from the others? Their diaper features a unique envelope design, similar to a pocket diaper, but with NO NEED TO TOUCH THE DOO-DOO. The absorbent inserts come right out in the wash!

Or, try this example. Suppose you've had a great idea for a product, something that is so amazing it's bound to capture the hearts and wallets of consumers everywhere. You've designed a children's pant that "grows" with the child's age. The goal here: determine whether there really is a market for your design.

Not only do you need to prove there is a market, but the product itself may also need fine tuning. Perhaps you may need to use a closure that the child him/herself can alter without the help of an adult. You may also need to research both the child as well as the person with the wallet: the parent.

2. After establishing your goals, the next thing you've got to figure out is who you're going to study. Are these current, prospective, or past clients? You may choose to select people in a specific group of consumers, age, sex, or other demographics.

Going back to the example of the eco-moms, you would choose to not only to gather information on the moms but on their nannies as well. Women based in higher income areas are the focus.

3. Develop a strategy and select techniques you will use to gather data. Gathering a sufficient amount of both types of data will give you a better overall insight to the market and to verify if there is indeed a market for your product. You may not only need to use multiple methods but also several reiterations of one method. For example, you may decide to hold focus groups, conduct surveys, and talk to both group members and survey respondents in person. Make sure to include sales reps in your conversations.

Interviews And Surveys

Both a mixture of questionnaires and interviews is the best way to go to gain insights. In the research phase of any design, product or business idea, one skill that's paramount is crafting good questions for your user interviews.

Keep your research goals at the forefront of your mind as you craft your questions – what do you want to know, or what are you trying to prove/disprove?

Surveys have proven to be vital in gathering useful information. Although it seems simple enough, it's important that you craft a well thought-out survey to ensure you don't waste precious time and money.

Face-to-face interviews with your current and potential customers are also critical to gaining the deepest insights to inform your design, and the questions you ask must be carefully staged in order to get to them.Unlike surveys, you get to speak to them and hear what they have to say and how they feel. The more you understand how a consumer feels- the easier it will be to brand, sell and create a business that your target market will gravitate to.

Listen To Consumers

"Follow your passion and success will follow." Probably not the first time you've heard it, right? It feels so good to think about, doesn't it? A life spent doing what you love (and making oodles of money from it, if you're an entrepreneur).

Well, it is the worst business advice I have ever heard! And it's particularly disastrous in the fashion world, where designers tend to create products that they think everyone will buy, but are actually just products they would want for themselves. Being able to do what you love requires developing products that sell.

Lululemon is an athletic apparel company that focuses on high-tech quality yoga clothing. Back in 2000 when the company opened for business, no one offered quality products for active women. The company has achieved success using a niche marketing strategy, targeting a narrowly-defined market segment: a mid-30s, high income, health conscious yoga practitioner. Lululemon has expanded its business by understanding its target market values and providing customers with a strong sense of authenticity and community. The company began a movement in yoga clothing where the founder relied on feedback from yoga instructors to optimize Lulu's apparel. As of May 2016, the value of the company was at $1.15 billion dollars.[2]

Listening to and understanding your customers is critical. Solving problems is key. Your message will resonate with your chosen market and turn customers into fans who will ultimately buy products and rave about them. Just follow Lululemon's example.

Market Research Methods

Surveys: Uncover Answers To Specific, Important Questions

Surveys have proven to be vital in gathering useful information. Although it seems simple enough, it's important that you craft a well thought-out survey to ensure you don't waste precious time and money.

1 Going back to the first steps, ask yourself: what do I want to get out of this? What's more, conduct some preliminary research to help you come up with research questions that will give you insightful results.

2 Below are some tips on constructing the survey:
   > Keep it short and brief
   > Keep the questions straightforward and easy to understand
   > Make sure the questions are in the right order
   > Avoid using compound questions (two or more questions in one)
   > Make sure the questions can be answered
   > Keep it clean and visually appealing
   > Use open-ended (freely write) & close-ended (check mark fields) questions appropriately
   > Use clear response scales. (Response scales assess the level of agreement or disagreement with a statement, or their satisfaction with experience, using numbers or words)
   > Avoid using leading questions - a question that prompts or encourages a desired answer. This can frustrate respondents and skew your survey results. Some examples of leading questions include things like "You like wearing cotton to lounge in X, don't you?" or "Why do you like wearing cotton X more than polyester?"

3 Decide how the surveys will be filled out, for example, as a questionnaire (respondents fill out answers) or interview

(with an interviewer asking questions and recording the responses either in person or on the phone). Ideally, a mixture of both is always the best way to go. Online survey platforms such as SurveyMonkey are also great tools.

4   Always pre-test the survey to determine its effectiveness. Go through the survey with a non-biased person and ask them what they think the questions mean and how they feel about it. Do not tell the respondent it is a pre-test.

5   Offer an incentive. Offering an incentive can significantly increase your response rate, though it can also skew your data, possibly getting feedback from unqualified respondents and, of course, eating up your budget. But by choosing a relevant and enticing incentive, you can safeguard both your budget and your data quality. Make sure you consider your audience when selecting an incentive. Discounts, free shipping, gift certificates, and other items are a great way to promote future purchases, and get them excited for when the business launches!

6   Finally, review and analyze results to obtain amazing insights. You never know what information you will dig up and which way it might steer you!

Focus Groups: **Grasp Customer Needs & Insights With Physical Samples**

WHAT: Focus groups are a powerful means to evaluate services or test new ideas.Similar to a face to face interview, only you collect your research from a group of people who answer questions about their perceptions, opinions, beliefs, and attitudes towards a product, service, concept, idea, or packaging. Often, one of the best ways to get inside the minds of your consumers and understand their likes and dislikes is to physically show samples or pictures.

WHEN: You should hold your focus groups before you launch your business and before any other new product launches or concepts. You can conduct focus groups at any time during the product life-cycle.

WHY: Feedback gives vital insights into new product designs and solutions (especially before you invest the big bucks).

WHO: You should carefully select participants of the focus group for useful and authoritative responses. Typically, 6-8 people participate, but be aware: because they share their reactions in front of each other, dominant individuals within the focus group could skew the feedback you get. Somehow there always seems to be a diva in the crowd.

You remember that one smart-alecky kid in high school who would always ask annoying questions in class mostly for the attention? Or that one friend who has an opinion on everything no matter how little they actually know? Fun fact: focus groups can sometimes attract those kinds of people. They're actually being asked for their opinions for a change! If you can learn to manage the divas, you can limit their ability to sway the group.

HOW

1 Identify the primary objective of the meeting. What do you hope to learn?

2 Plan your session: date, time, place, refreshments, etc.

3 Carefully select and invite 6-8 persons that fit your target market.

4 Carefully develop five to six questions to answer over the course of an hour. Wherever possible, show and test physical samples or provide photographs. If you have nothing to show, store-bought samples may work. This is your opportunity to have people try on your products and provide real-time reactions.

5 Offer incentives, such as gift certificates, as extra motivation for people to come and participate.

6 Find a moderator with some experience in running and controlling group sessions - this is critical. If not you can always ask a friend for help but remind them that they should try to balance the feedback given by everyone in the group.

7   Plan to record the session with either an audio or audio-video recorder.

8   Set the tone of the session from the start, this is very important. Set the mood by introducing yourself, the objective, and the agenda.

9   Review and analyze the data for insights after your focus group sessions are complete. If necessary, hold another focus group. Some things to think about:

> Did you discover any problems customers face that you can help solve?
> What patterns emerge? What are the common themes?
> What new questions arise?
> What conclusions seem true?

Psychographics
Psychographics is the information on a particular group's social attitudes and values. In plain English: how people think. Psychographic information may include things like a person's hobbies, spending habits, and values. The most effective way to reach your target market is by understanding the psychographics.

Let's say your target customer travels on a regular basis. You may want to incorporate easy care, easy-to-wear fabrics in the design of your new product. Thoughtful use of psychographics will help you develop not only the messages and campaigns for your promotions but also products that specific customers want and need.

Beyond surveys and focus groups, interacting with customers is the best way to get "into" their minds. Once the business starts selling, engagement with social media has proven to be very useful. Right now, you're probably already following some of your favorite brands and makers on Instagram or Facebook. Look at what these brands do, and ask yourself: would that approach work for me and my target market? Which social media posts get the most comments? What are they saying?

Competitor Research
Now that you have a feel for your target market, you will also want a good picture of which companies offer similar products to you. The

number and quality of competitors are good indications of whether or not your niche could be lucrative. Why do they buy from your competitors? What's something that their favorite brands are *not* doing that they want?

Shopping For A Living

Everyone needs an excuse to go shopping, right? Well then, look no further! Understanding what's currently happening in the market as a whole involves shopping at a variety of retail stores and researching competitors. If you design for the baby market, find every possible outlet for a consumer to purchase babies' clothes.

Get inspired! Explore everything from vintage and thrift stores, chain stores, and boutiques to high-end stores and luxury brands. In doing so, you will discover unique construction details: trims, materials, prints for styling ideas, and other innovative products that can inspire you to design new products. Vintage and thrift stores are a great resource for finding unique details and cuts that can be incorporated into designs.

Shopping the market will help you to analyze trends, merchandise products, use colors, and explore new ideas. Shopping is research, and research, in case I haven't made this abundantly clear by now, is essential to the creative process, offering a wealth of free information on a market.

Let's talk about that word "market" for a minute. A market is a general category, such as men's, bridal, baby, women's fashion, etc. Industry professionals purchase products and take photographs as ways to research the market, get inspiration, and collect physical samples for reference. Designers compare styling, price, fit, and quality, tirelessly shopping both the domestic and international markets.

A target market is a well-defined customer group to which a business wants to sell. Keep in mind that consumers and markets are very different around the world. For example, New York styling is as different from Los Angeles as Tokyo is from Milan. Designers reinterpret these ideas to fit their target market.

If you see a product that sparks your interest, buy it to serve as a reference for materials, construction, fit, styling, and anything aesthetic. The apparel industry refers to these products as store-bought samples. The intention of buying samples is not to copy. If you're in it to copy a design exactly, you will come out extremely disappointed. Exact replicas almost never happen; and why would you want to copy? Your will profit by finding a niche. Sew, the point of buying a sample is to help communicate an element of your product to the factory.

Purchased samples can be:

> Used as inspiration for mood boards
> Used to aid in the development of tech packs for silhouette designs, stitching, or fit
> Given to factories, pattern makers, or sample sewers as a guide for construction or stitching details on a design
> Given as a standard for sourcing fabrics, trims, and embellishments

Below are some questions to consider to help better understand your competitors or the overall markets - strengths and weaknesses:

> What types of products are they offering?
> What types of fabrics are the products made from?
> What are their quality standards?
> At what price point are their products sold?
> Where do they market and promote their product?
> Which of their social media posts, showcasing a product, is the most successful?
> How is their customer service?
> Where do they sell their products?
> What products are selling fast?

> How big is the company? What are their general sales, revenues and employee figures?
> Check out the care label: where is it made?

Your Shopping Allowance

Ahead in Part 6, we will set aside a budget for sample shopping. Try to stick to it. You can easily get carried away with overspending if you don't set a budget before your shopping trips. If the product is out of your budget, take pictures. Remember these images can be added to tech packs and mood boards to help clarify direction.

Designers, Artists, & Stylists

Seek inspiration from others in the design community. My fave unicorn would have to be Tiffany Pratt (tiffanypratt.com). She is the colorful creator behind many projects. She is a designer, artist, stylist, author, HGTV host and much more. Tiffany is one of the most inspiring designers I have ever met. Her personality is as vibrant as her hair, her energy is infectious, and she gives the BEST hugs! If people could be a unicorn, she would definitely be one! And yes, I have a girl crush.

What's even more remarkable is Tiffany is self-taught. She started her line catering to artists and stylish makers looking for something fashionable for their side hustle. She created a line of minimalist pieces made of only canvas; initially it began with three garments and an oversized clutch, and since has expanded.

Analyzing The Market

Take a close look at your market and investigate consumers. What products do they want, but cannot find? What will they pay a premium for? Survival in business is directly related to a demand for that product.

Your product is likely to sell if you can answer most—if not all—of the following questions.

- Can you solve a problem?
- Can you design a product that fills a need?
- What is missing in your market?
- What can you do better?
- Why would someone give you money?

Organize your collected information on a spreadsheet using Microsoft Excel, Google Sheets, or another spreadsheet-generating software. I know, I know, you didn't get into design to do spreadsheets, but as with everything we've covered thus far, organizing your information in this way is super-efficient, allowing you to quickly add, alter, or refer to any of the information you've collected when you need to use it.

Also, scan your competitors on a weekly basis so that you can stay up to date on current events, changes, and innovative marketing initiatives. A better understanding of how your competitors market themselves can help you stay one step ahead with your own creative ideas.

❊ GOLDEN NUGGET

Don't just visit a competitor's website. Google the actual company name to see what comes up. You might be surprised at what you find.

Consumer Websites

Consumer sites such as Pinterest and Instagram offer some critical insights into what is trending. Let's say you're considering running a type of print, fabric, color, style, or garment shape. Just compare the number of images and repins that you find on these two platforms. What's more, you can make great use of Pinterest analytics to get a better understanding of your customers once you launch your products.Etsy is also an awesome website to scope out what is trending. Check out your competitors shops and see which products sell the most. Create a folder for all your product images in one place to keep you organized.

Here are a few other websites to check out:

Polyvore (polyvore.com)& Lookbook (lookbook.nu)
The Culture Trip (theculturetrip.com)
Cotton Incorporated (cottoninc.com)
Treehugger (treehugger.com)

Tradeshows - Walk The Show

If you've never been to an apparel trade show, then you're missing out on a veritable goldmine of information on what's happening in the industry. Trade shows are the foundation for apparel and wholesale buying. They are scheduled at specific times during the year for brands to sell to wholesale buyers. They happen all over the world and are usually organized by category: children's, men's, gift, women, etc. For example, the Dallas Market Center has the Gift and Accessories Show at the end of March. Most brands typically sell in January, February, the spring months, July and August, and the Fall.

The Holy Grail of all apparel trade shows is MAGIC, held in Las Vegas, Nevada. Brands from all over the world showcase twice a year, catering to over 14 categories, from footwear and women's to accessories and sourcing, and more.

Most trade shows offer educational seminars that are absolutely worth attending. Walking the show allows you to see what booths are hot, what's new, and what competitors are currently selling in the market.

Meet Your New BFF: **The Sales Rep**

Fashion isn't a desk job. Get out there and see the state of the world for yourself! While buyers and company executives will give you good intelligence, the retail sales associates who work on the front lines at the store, can also be valuable in painting a vivid picture of how your product performs on the shop floor. They are talking directly to consumers.

Another key individual is the person selling wholesale to shop owners. Wholesale reps take original pre-production samples to sell to retail buyers at major market centers in wholesale showrooms and trade shows and sometimes go on the road. They take pre-orders for all styles, typically only the styles that have enough quantity to move forward into production. Products that did not do well are cancelled.

Try to schedule a meeting to talk to a sales rep at their showroom. Tell them about what you are working on. Ask questions, seek advice. Encourage them to speak candidly about what is and isn't working (and also what's missing). They can give you invaluable information that could help you immensely with your new products. Be sure to start these relationships as often as possible.

Market Research Firms

Secondary research comes from third party market research firms. The information is already compiled and organized for you. While secondary research is less targeted than primary research, it can provide valuable information and help you answer your research question(s).It also enhances any primary research that you've already done supporting your idea.

Advantages

1 It can help prove that the business idea is viable.
2 Many providers offer accurate and detailed reports on consumer trends and competitors that can help you better understand your customer base.
3 Third party market research can look at all of those "impractical" questions that may not be specific to you but can provide greater context, such as assessing the economy as a whole rather than smaller groups.
4 The data can also lead to unexpected and new discoveries.
5 Taking this route involves less cost, time and effort.

Disadvantages

1 Secondary data sources provide a vast amount of information, but it may not all be relevant to what you're looking to have answered. It has been collected to answer different research questions or objectives.

2 The quality, timeliness and reliability of data provided are not in your control. You have to carefully evaluate the information that a market research provides, and determine how current and credible it is.

❈ GOLDEN NUGGET

Avoid making the mistake of conducting only secondary research and neglecting primary market research. Although secondary research is essential and time-saving, doing the legwork of primary research provides you with, up-to-date insights and also a better perspective of the market. Furthermore, primary market research is the only way to understand your customers' values, psychology, attitudes, lifestyles, and interests. After all, they're your target market and isn't it best to learn about them yourself? In any case, both research techniques are valuable, and you should make use of them.

Sources Of Secondary Data

If you're a startup, you will do well to seek out these sources, organize and apply the data to the specific project, and then summarize and analyze it all in a way that makes sense to you and your audience.

To get you started, I've compiled a few of my favorite secondary research resources and website addresses. Search online and visit your local library as well. Keep in mind: the Internet may not always offer reliable sources and complete information (I know what you're thinking: 'Thank you, Captain Obvious", but it's still worth remembering!). And, as they say, incomplete information is dangerous. Start by dropping by a local library and asking the business librarian who is trained in the use of research sources. They will be happy to get you pointed on the right path.

Government Guidance

Government agencies offer an invaluable source of market research and give most of it away for free. You will find information that can help you improve and make informed business decisions. Almost every country publishes population density and distribution figures in widely-available census tracts.

The government provides the following and much more:

> > Demographics & population censuses
> > Statistics
> > Trade data: Import/export & global trade data
> > Industry sector data
> > Trends in the industry

Demographics

Demographics explain "who" your buyer is, while psychographics explains "why" they buy. Demographics treat customers as a part of a larger group, whereas psychographic analysis views each one as an individual. Demographic information includes geographic area, age, income, race, gender, and education level. It also provides shopping habits, marital status, number of children, and other information about consumer characteristics.

Let's say your target customer predominantly lives in hotter climates. If that's the case, heavier fabrics such as wool won't make sense. You'll want something lighter that allows the wearer to stay cool.

Fashion startups gather demographic information on the target market, which affects all the choices an entrepreneur makes in developing a marketing and business plan. As a designer, the more you understand your customer, the more successful the outcome of the design (namely, the more units you'll likely sell).

The North American Industry Classification System (NAICS)

The NAICS classifies business establishments to collect, analyze, and publish statistical data. It was developed jointly by Canada, the US, and Mexico to describe economic activity. The NAICS industry codes define establishments based on the activities in which they are primarily engaged. You can browse NAICS by sector or use the keyword search to identify relevant industries.

For example, Women's, Children's, and Infants' Clothing and Accessories Merchant Wholesalers fall under NAICS code: 424330. For this specific category, it differs for Canada and falls under 414110.

IBIS Research (ibisworld.com) offers market reports by industry (NAICS).

Other sources where you can find valuable statistics:

Statistics Canada, Industry Canada and USA.gov and the U.S.Census Bureau & Department of Commerce's International Trade Administration

✲ GOLDEN NUGGET
Contact the government for support on collecting relevant data.

Trade Associations & Organizations

For the most targeted and current industry information, you cannot overlook trade organizations and trade associations. There are thousands of associations for businesses, and they have a vested interest in tracking their respective industries. You can find valuable information on what is and isn't selling, as well as trends in the industry that can further help you create a successful brand and business. Networking at events held by these organizations can also keep you on your toes and help build your tribe. Most have membership costs.

Just to name a few:

Fashion Group International (fgi.org)
Retail Council of Canada (retailcouncil.org)
Business Of Fashion (businessoffashion.com)
Canadian Apparel Federation (www.apparel.ca)
Council of Fashion Designers of America (cfda.com)

» BEST PRACTICE

Get onboard with all websites that cater to your market by subscribing to their newsletters and following them on social media. Doing so is an easy way to keep current in the industry. Create a separate email account, so you don't feel inundated with emails.

Incubators & Accelerators

Designers looking to start off on the right foot can turn to an incubator or accelerator for help. Most do not charge, but there is an application process. The main goal of both are to help grow businesses and and they often improve their chances of attracting an investor. Many government grants and funding can be best found through these.

So, what is the difference between the two? The primary function of an accelerator is connecting startups with mentors, guidance, resources, and funding.These tend to be more competitive to get into and only have a select number of slots. Applicants need a more thought-out plan and must demonstrate that they are investable and scalable. Accelerators operate for a shorter fixed duration as compared to incubators that operate on an open-ended timeline.

Incubators take entrepreneurs with promising ideas, and teach them how to run a successful startup.They support startups entering the beginning stages of building their company. The startups possess an idea to bring to the marketplace, but no business model and direction to transition from innovative idea to reality. Incubators do not traditionally provide capital to startups and are often funded by universities or economic development organizations.

Just to name a few:

Toronto Fashion Incubator (fashionincubator.com)
The Brooklyn Fashion + Design Accelerator (bkaccelerator.com)
Chicago Fashion Incubator (chicagofashionincubator.org)
Fashion Incubator San Francisco (fashionincubatorsf.org)
Trade Publications

Trade publications are geared to people who work in a specific industry. Magazines and newspapers provide media kits to prospective advertisers. Media kits offer valuable data and demographic stats and research as well as market calendars. Published articles give insights into the industry.

By now you should have a good idea of what your market is. Let's say you specialize in boys' clothing. Check out Earnshaws (earnshaws.com) trade publication catering to businesses in wholesale childrenswear.

Just style (just-style.com)
Fiber To Fashion (fiber2fashion.com)
Women's Wear Daily (wwd.com)
California Apparel News (apparelnews.net)
Apparel Magazine (apparel.edgl.com)
Eco Textile (ecotextile.com)
The Sourcing Journal (sourcinejournalonline.com)
Sportswear International (sportswear-international.com)

✳ GOLDEN NUGGET

To save time, scan the headlines of the industry newspapers, newsletters, and weekly news magazines to ensure that you stay current with national and international events.

Gazing Into The Crystal Ball: **Trend Forecasting Services**

A trend is a direction in which something (ideas, products, values) tends to move in a way that affects culture, society, or business. Tracking trends is not just about looking at fashion but also looking at demographics, behaviour, technology, lifestyles, and current events.

Forecasting services can be the eyes and ears of product developers. For a fee, Fashion Snoops, WGSN, Pantone, and other forecasting service companies perform much of your market research, such as travelling to out-of-reach retail outlets and attending trade shows, so you don't have to do the legwork.

Subscription-based trend forecasting services are typically costly for startups. You may need to be resourceful: again, subscribe to newsletters, visit blogs, follow social media or dig around the corporate brand websites to access free information.

Although these services can be invaluable to understanding what is "hot," consider designing classic pieces that have a longer shelf life. Trends mean that styles become outdated. As we talked about in Part 1, smaller orders with higher quality standards take longer to manufacture, and it's challenging to turn inventory around quickly. If your products become outdated, they will be harder to sell. Creating classic products with a longer shelf life will help grow your company.

For many designers, being eco-conscious also means designing quality-driven pieces that can stand the test of time. With that said, if you're more interested in making pieces that people will always desire and therefore live as staples in consumers' closets, then steering clear of trends or fads might seem the right way to go. Seasonless, year-round products will also give you the much-needed time to create and sell your products. You'll feel less pressure meeting delivery dates and deadlines.

Regardless, if the products are sustainable, it's important to understand the market's general direction. What is developing or changing to help ensure the best outcome of the design?

WGSN (wgsn.com) a free newsletter offering valuable information. Their Tumblr consists of a wide variety of images that are either re-posted or curated from their own forecasts. Students in fashion programs have limited access.
Trend Hunter (trendhunter.com)
NotCot (notcot.org)
EDITED (edited.com)
We Connect Fashion (weconnectfashion.com)
Fashion Vignette (fashionvignette.blogspot.ca)
Trend Stop (blog.trendstop.com)
Pantone Incorporated (pantone.com)
Promostyl (promostyl.com)

❋ GOLDEN NUGGET

Regular scanning of a variety of media and well-chosen trend forecasting resources helps to mitigate the risk of poor design decisions. Make it a daily habit to flip through these resources so you can stay up to speed.

Colleges & Universities

Check out local colleges and universities with fashion programs. Their libraries have valuable sources of information. You will find a large selection of reports, business plans, books and much more about the industry and information specific to your market. Speak to the librarian, they always have research tips up their sleeve. It may be possible also to access their online portal.

Analyzing The Research: **How To Think Like Sherlock Holmes**

SEW... let's take a quick breather. That was a lot. How are you doing?

By now, you should have gained an appreciation for the advantages of doing research. Maybe you've really taken it to heart and have already started some (or even all) of the steps that I've outlined up to this point. If so, that's amazing! Good job!

Now, once you've got your data, what's next?

When your research is done, the next step is to compile and review the information you have found. It's time to analyze and begin to formulate a plan for running your business. There are many ways to evaluate research. You may find it beneficial to perform a SWOT analysis for your business. You evaluate your current position and compare it to future opportunities and risks. It's worth taking the time to do this.

SWOT stands for "strengths, weaknesses, opportunities and threats." You can perform a SWOT analysis for any company, product, place, industry, or person.

Strengths and weaknesses are internal factors within an organization that you have some control over, whereas opportunities and threats are external to your specific business, usually coming from a community or societal forces.

> **Strengths:** characteristics of the business or products that give it an advantage over others. Competitive advantages, skills, experiences or other internal factors this is difficult to copy that you have some control and can change.
> **Weaknesses:** characteristics of the business or products that give it a disadvantage relative to others. What reduces your ability to achieve your goals? What improvements do you need to make?
> **Opportunities:** elements in the environment or larger market that the business or products could exploit to its advantage. What will help your business grow and be more profitable? What opportunities can you take advantage of?
> **Threats:** elements in the environment and market that could cause trouble for the business or products. Look at competitors and hazards.

Check our the example below. Make a list from your research findings; then take a look at it and analyze it.

> Use your strengths and internal strengths to take advantage of opportunities and minimize threats.
> Work to eliminate weaknesses to avoid threats. Can you take advantage of any opportunities?

It's an important tool to revisit every year.

Table | *Example Of Swot Diagram*[3]

	HELPFUL to achieving the objective	HARMFUL to achieving the objective
INTERNAL ORIGIN (attribute of the organization)	**STRENGTHS** >Provide products using a new sustainable fibre innovation >Fair trade & B Corp certified >Ability to trace entire supply chain >Only Canadian supplier of wholesale printable blanks >Ability to grow and produce larger quantities offshore >15 years' experience in sustainable product manufacturing >Give back program (diverting textiles from landfills)	**WEAKNESSES** >Do not have a patent for the new fibre innovation >Weak social media presence >Not in any retails stores >Offshore manufacturing has longer lead times >Lack funding for marketing (organic growth) >Lack funding makes it difficult to carry large inventory >Currently no distributors >Costs slightly higher since not buying large volume
EXTERNAL ORIGIN (attribute of the larger market)	**OPPORTUNITIES** >Growing demand for sustainable and transparent businesses >Government support for sustainable businesses >Target market growing (# of start> up businesses)	**THREATS** >Offshore manufacturing (fluctuating USD exchange rates) >Shortage of certified dying units overseas >Factory may not be able to purchase the raw material >Shopping malls and retailors struggle to operate

Find Your Purpose

"**TRUE HAPPINESS**… IS NOT ATTAINED THROUGH SELF-GRATIFICATION, BUT THROUGH FIDELITY TO A WORTHY PURPOSE."

- HELEN KELLER

Do you know your *why*? The purpose, cause, or belief that inspires you to do what you do? To really communicate your message to your customer, incorporate your "why" into your designs. As author Simon

Sinek says, "People don't buy what you do, they buy *why* you do it." I highly recommend reading *Start with Why: How Great Leaders Inspire Everyone to Take Action*. In his book, Sinek studies the thoughts, actions, and communication styles of the world's most influential leaders. Sinek concludes that great leaders "inspire people to act" by giving them a sense of purpose or belonging. In other words, a call to action.

Go Niche or Go Broke

You can't be everything to everyone. A niche market is a specific segment of a much larger market. Any market can be divided into smaller parts based on particular interests and demographics. It should be comprised of a tight, clear range of products sold to a tightly focused target group. Let's say your market is babywear, your niche could be socially responsible moms or working mammas to be. From there it is easier to design products specifically for their needs.

Seems counterintuitive, doesn't it? After all, wouldn't it make more sense to go for a significant, broad market share? That's what a lot of first-time designers do: they spread themselves too thin by trying to appeal to everyone at once. Unfortunately, you can't compete with Wal-Mart (at least, not at first). You are just not producing a high enough volume of product to justify buying and selling at lower prices. When you try to appeal to all consumers, you have no brand identity, and it's very likely you will fade into obscurity. When you try to be all things to all people, no one notices you. Period.

There are so many options of a product flooding the market. Every product category from sportswear to promotional products is brimming with options and choices. Why would someone give you money? Understand, and watch competitors very carefully, not only to seek inspiration but to carve a niche for yourself. If you're not offering something unique or doing it in a different way, your customers will have no reason to buy from you. If you give people enough reasons to buy your products, sales will flow. Think about what need or demand is not being satisfied. Where is the hole in the market, and can you fill it?

Narrowing your focus and not trying to be *all* things to *all* people can help you establish a stronger business reputation. When you have a tight niche, your outcome is more likely to attract consumer attention. A niche market allows you to define who you are marketing to, which makes it easier to speak to them. The media will also have a great angle for giving you press, in turn helping drive sales.

> "IN ORDER TO BE IRREPLACEABLE ONE MUST ALWAYS BE DIFFERENT."
>
> **-COCO CHANEL**

Standing Out In A Crowd

A narrow, tight niche sends a clear message about what your company does and represents. Consumers want simple, not complicated. Make it easy for people to understand what it is you do and why they might need you. Let's say you design unique aprons with funny quotes, customers might perceive you as "the funny apron lady." They will remember exactly where to go when they need an apron. Offering unique products will be what sets you apart from your competitors. Once consumers test your product and trust your company, it will be easier for you to introduce new products into the marketplace.

Examples of successful companies and their claim to fame:

> - Anyone can make a pair of blue jeans, but Levi Strauss & Co., founded in 1853, made the first blue jeans.
> - British Luxury Brand, Burberry - founded in 1856 - originally focused on outdoor apparel and is known for their trench coats.

The Number of Styles Offered Directly Impacts Your Budget

One of the top questions a designer entrepreneurs will ask is "how many styles should I start with?" Before you even begin to design, it might be worthwhile to plan how many products would work within your budget. The more styles you start with, the more money and time you will need. Check out Part 6, Budgeting, Pricing and Target Costs, to learn more.

Too Many Choices Create Confusion

Have you ever found yourself sitting down at a bar or restaurant and just staring at the menu options? All of your other friends have ordered drinks, and here you are, trying to pick between the vegan mushroom burger and the fish and chips. Maybe you'll get the salad instead? Wait, they've got avocado toast? OMG! Meanwhile, your friends sit around, hungry and annoyed, waiting for you to make a decision. Sure, you could just tell your server you need yet another five minutes, but to quote Sweet Brown, "ain't nobody got time for that!" You finally decide, but somehow you've lost your appetite.

And do you know the main reason why you can't pick? "There's so much good stuff here!" Too much choice is your problem, and it's a problem you don't want to inflict on your customers.

I strongly recommend when you first start manufacturing to keep the product assortment to a minimum. You don't need to launch a large collection using various materials. A whole mix of pants, skirts, tops, dresses, handbags, and so on is risky to design, manufacture, and distribute successfully. Most importantly, too many choices overwhelm retail buyers and consumers.

There is something great about a clothing company that enters a market and says, "I do skirts, that's what I have." Then buyers know where to go when they need a skirt. Consumers will be clear with what you offer and remember you.

Customers Who Are Given Too Many Choices Are 10x Less Likely To Buy

Sheena Iyengar, a professor at Columbia Business School, has been studying choice for more than 10 years. She has spoken on the internet show, the Art of Choice, aired on TED Talks, a streaming video channel that broadcasts influential videos from industry experts. In her research, Iyengar has identified many factors that demotivate choice in consumers.

In one study, Iyengar's research team set up a tasting booth in a grocery store, offering consumers a selection of six different jams. Only 40 percent of the customers stopped to taste, and 30 percent ended up buying one or more of the products. A week later, the researchers set up the same booth in the same store, offering 24 different jams. This time, 60 percent of the store's customers stopped to taste, but only 3 percent bought any product.

Both groups tasted an average of 1.5 jams, the group with less selection bought more product.

Lessons learned from the study:

1 Offering many choices is appealing to customers
2 Offering too many options makes customers less likely to buy

In my opinion, startups that start out with too many options send the wrong message. "Hey, I have no clue what you like, so I'll design a bunch of products, and maybe there might be something you like!" Put more simply: it shows that you don't understand who your customer is. To learn more about customer choices, I recommend reading, "The Paradox of Choice," by Barry Schwartz.

Keep It Simple

Once more, louder for the people in the back, *there is absolutely nothing wrong with starting with just one type of product or product category.* It's good to become recognized for doing one thing really well, such as aprons, then expanding. At Source My Garment, one of our clients designs only kids' organic underwear. All the patterns and fabric are kept the same every season: the only change is the screen prints. The factory is acquainted with our client's product; hence the production process moves along a lot faster. Changing only print designs is enough of a business to make a living: it's simple, it's a niche, and it generates considerable profits.

Within one product category, you can have different subcategories. Underwear, for example, is a category that has many subcategories - or options - where designers can market niche products. For instance, you can offer boxers or briefs, printed, embroidered, plain, and so on. Even if you start with one product category, such as dresses, there is a multitude of versions: long, short, casual, dressy, embellished, printed, and the list goes on. You know you will only need same-length zippers, trims, and similar patterns for all styles. Working from one product category is not as exhausting and, from a production standpoint, is easier to manage.

Behind Every Successful Brand Was A Small But Smart Start

As the saying goes, "You never get a second chance to make a first impression." Launching a new business is a great way to grab media attention, so ensure that you make a positive first impression. The first styles and products you unveil to the world at your debut are how you'll be remembered for years to come. *Sew*, give the media and members of the fashion industry a debut to remember!

Bigger is not always better for your company and product debuts. This fact is especially true when it comes to big brands. Here are some examples of successful brands that made their debut with select products.

Merchandising Success Stories

Diane Von Furstenberg, more commonly referred to as DVF, first entered the fashion industry in 1970 with a suitcase full of jersey dresses. Four years later, she created the wrap dress, which came to symbolize power and independence for an entire generation of women. By 1976, Furstenberg had sold over one million dresses and was featured on the cover of *Newsweek*.

Eileen Fisher, an American fashion designer, started her brand in 1984 with only $350 in her bank account. Her first clothing line was based on simplicity: a pair of flood pants, a three-quarter sleeve top, a V-neck vest, and a sleeveless shell. She had four samples made and got pre-orders at a tradeshow. In 2005, Fisher sold the

$300 million company to her 875 employees through an employee stock ownership plan.

Club Monaco was established in 1985. Owner Joe Mimran saw the demand for tailored work wear for women and focused on that niche area. It was the search for the perfect white T-shirt that inspired his first major enterprise. By 1999, Club Monaco had 125 stores worldwide, and that same year, the company was purchased by the Ralph Lauren Corporation.

Ralph Lauren began designing neckties in 1967. The American fashion designer started his enterprise by developing his own line of men's colorful neckties with a wider cut, at a time when narrow and plain was the norm. Under the name "Polo," he made over half a million dollars. Today, the Ralph Lauren Corporation is a $10 billion enterprise.

Pamela Anderson, a long time activist for People for the Ethical Treatment of Animals (PETA), launched a vegan-made boots line in September 2015. The line, Pammies, has three versions: short, medium, and tall.

I can hear the wheels turning in your brain. What will *your* claim to fame be?

Computing Your Results

SEW... at this point, you should analyze all the research, data, and feedback you've collected. Once you have honed in on your niche, finalized your why, analyzed your market, researched your competition, identified your target market's need for your product, and listed your ideas for the types of products you want to develop, you move into the next phase of product development: choosing the materials you want your products to be made from.

In some cases, your target market may dictate what materials to use. For example, if your target market is eco-conscious moms-to-be, it's likely that they will opt for a sustainable and natural knit fabric that is soft for babies. Alternatively, your design may dictate the fabric. If you're a high-end dress designer, embroidered silks are a good starting point. If you're designing workwear, hand-crafted durable fabrics might be the right fit. Your research will guide you to the materials you might want to use.

The F Word (No, Not That One)

Cheers to you! If you've made it to the fabric selection stage, you've come a looooong way (and we're proud of you!). The fashion designer's relationship with fabric is at the heart of the creative process. Choosing the right material is fundamental to good design and is crucial to its manufacturing success.

Apparel design and garment production are lengthy processes, and likewise, sourcing your fabric is no quick task. The types of textiles out there are endless. Every garment begins with the material; it is the fabric that brings a design to life. You can dramatically alter your design's end result by merely changing the fabric. If you want to ensure that everyone is on the same page about your product, you need to be able to know how to precisely describe and classify it.

Sew, let's get you headed in the right direction by assisting you with things to consider before you get started:

1 It's critical to select your product's main material before you begin the design process. It will help you estimate costs and give direction on the functionality of the fabric with your design. Some things to think about: how does it hang or drape? Where and when will your customer wear the garment? How will it function or feel when worn? What fabrics do your competitors use?

2 Fabric price is the most substantial factor in the total cost of making a garment. Since the fabric is a product's biggest expense, the more you know about your material, the easier it will be to control costs.

3 Most factories overseas can source the fabric for you because they can easily access mills, receive better volume discounts, and most importantly, control the fabric quality. If you buy material from a retail or wholesale supplier, there

is little guarantee that you will be able to get the same quality of fabric next season.

Every Fabric Has A Recipe

The more you understand your fabric, the better the outcome of your design. It's worth your while to understand what it is you want. If you can show the factory you know what you are talking about, it will be a lot easier for them to address your needs.

You can research your fabric by attending trade shows, such as Textworld, participating in webinars, and reading industry literature. You can also meet with industry experts to increase your product knowledge about composition and properties that make up the material. Fabrics can be classified in several ways.

You should be able to convey the following information to the factory:

> Fiber Content
> Structure
> Construction Type
> Weight
> Count/Gauge

You should also be able to answer the following questions before giving any information to the factory:

> Are there any fabric enhancers or washes you need to be added?
> Do you need any test reports to maintain your company standards or ensure you are compliant with government laws?
> What handfeel would you like to achieve?

All of these ingredients form the recipe for that exact fabric. These details are part of the science behind creating the textile.

Providing a Fabric Standard to the Factory

Sew... If you've decided to let the factory source the fabric, you need to provide a standard. Where do you get the fabric standard? You can shop retail stores and buy products using the precise fabrication that you think may work. Try it, test it, and wash it. If the fabric is exactly what you want, cut it up and submit it to the factory as your standard. You can also buy fabric from suppliers. It's incredibly important to convey your fabric requirements to the factory and show you are knowledgeable about the composition and structure of the material. The more you know, the more you can direct and guide the factory to achieve what you want. If you are unable to provide all the information, that's okay, too: the factory can help you fill in the blanks.

Classifying & Measuring Fabrics

1. Fiber Content

There are numerous ways to classify and measure fabrics. Begin by determining the *fiber content* or composition: is it cotton, polyester, or a blend? Fibers are either synthetic (man-made) or natural. Fiber is the smallest visible unit of any textile product. Common natural fibers include wool, cotton, linen and silk. Synthetic fiber was introduced in the 1930s and 1940s. Most common synthetics include polyester, acrylic and nylon. Fibers are flexible and may be spun into yarn and made into fabrics.

It is essential to know how a particular fiber or fiber blend will impact the material's overall performance qualities such as drape, insulation and wash care.

Fiber content is a legal requirement in North America and must be disclosed to the consumer. This information must be labeled on all garments.

2. Structure

The second most crucial description of your product is the way the fabric is formed. It is vital that a designer understand the different types of fabric structures to be able to select the best fabric that will behave as needed for a particular design. There are many advantages and disadvantages to each structure, whether it be knit, woven or non-woven. When it comes to construction methods, weaving and knitting are the most common.

WOVEN MATERIAL   KNIT MATERIAL

Determining Knit Fabric
If you see loops, it is a knit fabric. Think of a T-shirt, Polo shirt, or leggings. Knit fabrics are made by inter-looping yarns and can stretch in different directions. Generally, knits are considered comfortable and wrinkle resistant. If the structure resembles more of a checkerboard, it is woven. Knits are faster to sew and shrink more than woven fabrics.

Products made from knitted fabrics may include:

> Products that you want to stretch and have some give
> Swimwear
> T-shirts
> Activewear
> Socks and undergarments

Determining Woven Fabric

Picture a weaver using a loom to create fabric, and you can kind of already visualize what woven fabric looks like. Think of a shirt, a trouser, a suit, or denim jeans. They are all made from woven fabrics. Woven fabrics are created by interlacing two sets of yarns. Yarn sets are known as *warp yarns* and *weft yarns*. The fabric manufacturing method of woven fabric is known as *weaving*. Woven fabrics are made on looms (handlooms or power looms) and are stiff and not stretchy. Woven fabric stretches only on the bias direction. It is possible to make stretchy woven fabric by using spandex (Lycra) yarns, as you may be familiar with in stretchable denim pants.

Products made from woven fabrics may include:

> Products that you don't want to lose their shape by stretching
> Dress pants
> Dress shirts
> Towels
> Curtains

Determining Non-Woven Fabric

The third, and least popular, method includes non-woven fabrics such as felting, laminating, and bonding, made by sticking fibers together using heat, glue, needle punching or felting. Bonded-fiber fabrics are made from webs of synthetic fibers bonded together with heat or adhesives. Non-woven textiles tend to be weaker, easily torn material, as the fibers are not held together in any structured, secure way. Wool felt is a example of non-woven fabric made from animal hair or wool fibers matted together using moisture, heat and pressure. Felt has no strength, drape or elasticity but it is warm and does not fray.

Products made from Non-Woven fabrics

> Often used to make disposable items such as surgical masks or menstrual hygiene products
> Cleaning cloths such as Jeye Cloths
> Support or strengthening for garments - interfacing
> Children's toys - fuzzy felt, finger puppets

3. Construction Type

Each structure can be further classified into construction type, or how they are knit or woven together. There are different ways of knitting or weaving that change the kind of fabric, altering its look, properties, and feel. Factories are set up by fabric structure, and determining the structure will help you select the best factory. Different sewing and manufacturing processes, machinery, and skill sets are needed depending on the fabric structure. I recommend choosing only one structure to start, to help make the production process more manageable.

❋ GOLDEN NUGGET

Since knits are generally quicker to sew, they provide cost savings.

Knit Construction Types

There are many variations of knit fabrics, all serving specific purposes and intended for specific uses on garments:

Interlock Knit: A variation of the rib knit stitch, resembling two separate 1x1 ribbed fabrics that are inter-knitted. Plain (double knit) interlock knit fabrics are thicker, heavier and more stable than single knit constructions. It also has more natural stretch than a jersey knit, is soft to touch, and is identical on both sides. It's often used in higher-quality babywear.

Jersey (plain knit/single knit): Single knit jersey is lightweight with one flat side and one piled side, most often used for T-shirts. Double knit jersey is two single knit jerseys, knitted together with two flat sides for added weight and durability. The difference is that it has a distinct front and back side.

1x1 Rib Knit: Commonly used for sleeve- and neck-bands because it is highly elastic and retains its shape. 1x1 rib knit construction is a pattern of one rib and one flat space, repeated over and over. Both sides of this knit fabric look identical.

1x2 Rib Knit: Also commonly used for sleeve- and neck-bands; highly elastic and retains its shape.1x2 rib knit construction is a pattern of one rib, two flat spaces, one rib, two flat spaces, and so on. 1x2 rib knit has a chunkier appearance compared to 1x1 rib knit.

Double Knit: Made with two sets of yarns, this double-constructed fabric has fine ribs running lengthwise on both sides. Because both sides are often identical, this fabric can be used for reversible garments. Heavy and firm, it usually has almost no stretch in either direction, but does boast good shape retention (cut edges don't curl). Best used for tailored garments, like jackets and suits.

Woven Construction Types
Like knits, there are several varieties of weaves. The three main weaves are plain, twill, and satin.

Plain weave: Plain weaves are the most simple of all weaves. Same-size warp and weft threads are woven together one by one. This is the simplest and tightest method of weaving. The warp yarn goes over and under each weft thread, creating a piece of fabric with two identical sides. Examples of plain weave fabrics are crepe, taffeta, organdy, cotton calicos, cheesecloth, gingham, percale, voile, and muslin.

Twill weave: Denim is the most popular twill weave fabric. Other examples include drill, serge, and gabardine. Warp and weft threads are interlaced, causing diagonal lines to appear on the fabric.

Satin weave: Examples include satin, sateen, duchess, and damask. The interlacing of the threads are never adjacent to one another. The repeat is usually over at least 4 threads, but the warp end interlaces over the 1 weft thread per each pattern repeat. Therefore, the back of the fabric looks very different from the front. Satins and sateens have shiny or lustrous surfaces.

4. Fabric Weight

Weight is an essential component when it comes to choosing the right fabric for your project. There are two systems of fabric weight categorization, imperial and metric. GSM or gm/2 is a metric measurement meaning grams per square metre - it is how much 1 square metre of fabric weighs. GSM is the most common method used in the industry. Ounce per square yard (oz/sq2) is the imperial measurement, used mainly in the US.

Lightweight fabric: 30-150 GSM
Medium weight fabric: 150-350 GSM
Heavyweight fabric: 350+ GSM

The larger the number, the heavier the fabric. Testing can be done in specialized testing labs, such as SGS and Intertek or measured on a GSM scale. The fabric's weight significantly impacts its drape, or the way it hangs, which ultimately informs where and how the garment should be worn. It also affects comfort, durability and usage. The weight of the fabric is particularly important when having to choose between two similar materials. Be sure that when you're ordering or even re-ordering fabric that you specify weight, so there are no issues. It is essential to document the weight of the material before manufacturing and after getting the finished fabric to ensure that you are getting what you expect.

It is easy to know the weight of the fabric by cutting the material with the GSM cutter. For measuring GSM, a GSM cutter is used to cut a specific diameter of fabric. After cutting the fabric, you can calculate the weight of the material using a scale.

Photo |_GSM cutter with scale_[4]

To achieve a certain GSM requires that the mill know the fabric structure, yarn count and **machine gauge**. Determining machine gauge is a vital ingredient to creating your specific fabric. It helps the supplier to recreate the fabric. Machine gauge indicates the fineness of the stitch. It is the number of needles in a specific distance on the needle bar. The higher the gauge, the finer the fabric. Finer gauges are around 28 or more; coarse fabrics are about 13 or fewer.

Let's say you need to make a 140 GSM single jersey. To produce a fabric of that quality, you would need to use 34's yarn and a 24 gauge machine. On the other hand, you may need a 160 GSM single rib which will require 40's yarn and 20 gauge machine.

5. Cotton & Thread Count

All yarn fibers can also be classified and measured. In the apparel and textile industry, yarns are the basic thread that make up the fabric. Yarn thickness is measured using various systems. We use different units for yarn count—like Cotton Count, Tex, or Denier.

Cotton Count

Higher Yarn Count = Finer yarn diameter and/or more tightly woven yarn

Lower Yarn Count = Wider thread diameter and/or more loosely woven yarn

For example, jersey T-shirts are typically made using yarns from 20s, 30s, 40s, and 50s count.

Thread Count

Thread count or threads-per-inch is a measure of the coarseness or fineness of finished fabric. It is the actual number of warp ends and filling picks per inch. It is measured by counting the number of threads contained in one square inch of fabric or one square centimeter, including both the length (warp) and width (weft) threads. The higher the number, the more densely the yarns are packed together.

Bedding is typically labeled with thread counts from 200 to 800. Thread count has come to be a primary factor of quality in customers' eyes. The quality of the cotton and the finishing process after weaving can often be more important to the soft hand and durability of fabric than a high thread count.

Fabric Quality
When manufacturing from scratch, many variables affect fabric quality: from the quality of the fiber, to the dyes and the treatments, to the quality of the machinery used to weave knit fabric. Many variables can affect the outcome of the finished material. It is almost impossible to achieve the same results from mill to mill. Creating textiles is a science. When submitting a fabric standard, keep in mind that duplicating materials can be a challenge.

The "hand" of a piece of fabric refers to the "feel" of the material against your skin, or in other words, the way the fabric feels when it is touched. Industry professionals may say something like, "that T-shirt fabric has a wonderful hand." (They're most definitely not implying that T-shirts have hands - that would be creepy). A fabric hand is everything you can tell about the material by touching it with your hands: texture, drapability, stretch, and wrinkle resistance. Terms like softness, crispness, dryness, smoothness, and silkiness are all used when describing the hand of the fabric.

Fabric washes, sometimes called finishing, are typically added to the fabric to achieve the desired hand feel or quality. Enhancers or garment washes are referred to as the mechanical or chemical treatment that modifies the performance, hand feel, or appearance of the fabric.

Fabric can be enhanced by softening, starching, polishing, and buffing it. Washing can be done at the fabric stage or after the garment is stitched. Stone washing, a current fashion trend, is an added wash to jeans, used to achieve a worn out broken look. Other examples include softeners and enzymes, which soften the fabric. A bio wash is commonly used to remove pilling on clothing. Silicone softener gives the material a silky feel. From flame retardants to wrinkle resistance, there are thousands of enhancers that can alter fabric.

Gathering all the "ingredients" to the fabric recipe will make it too much for a factory to provide a realistic first quote and help you achieve your desired quality standards.

(We'll talk more about fabric and tech packs in Part 3: The Product Development Process).

Selecting Fabric Colors

The longest part of the manufacturing process is dyeing the greige fabric. "Greige" refers to an unfinished knitted or woven fabric that has not been dyed or bleached. Dyers can only output a select number of colors each day. Typical wait times are 30 to 45 days for smaller product runs. Only one or two vessels are available for each dyeing plant. Lab dips are also created, and several options are submitted to the designer for approval before dyeing. A lab dip is a fabric test swatch dyed to hit a color standard. It is a process in which the designer's supplied swatch is matched with the varying dyes in the laboratory.

If you're starting out and at the point where you need to select fabric colors for your products, stick to one or two colors to keep costs down and save time. You can always play with colors in lookbooks to give your products the added appearance and feel you desire.

A Goal Without A Plan Is Just A Dream

Vision boards, mainly in collage form, have traditionally been used by people to set goals and create their dream life. It is a simple yet powerful visualization tool that activates the universal Law of Attraction to begin manifesting dreams into reality. If you are a designer entrepreneur with an idea, a similar board can be made for your brand.

Much like a business plan, the vision board visually showcases the target market, mission statement, corporate culture, products, and showcases where you want your company to be five or ten years from now. You align your artistic direction with company goals and objectives, including achieving a company mission and balancing marketing goals with product theme and inspiration. You can add words to describe the brand to give a clear message to accompany images.

Creating a mood board is the same concept as a vision board. It's a design tool that will help you remain focused and consistent as your line develops. Even with one or two styles, it will help clarify your direction to bring ideas to life. It's also a great communication aid when explaining your vision to others (retailers, media, etc.). The board also helps your team understand in a snapshot the target market and your overall vision. This will carry you through design and production development, all the way to marketing and sales. Designers should create a mood board for each new order or every season.

You can use any image editing software such as Photoshop, or use photographs, text, as well as your own scanned, hand-drawn sketches to create the boards. You can use the images from shopping the market, inspiration, as well as take photographs of stitching details, trims, colors and fabric swatches. Adding text helps convey your marketing and product direction. Words like "new", "cutting-edge", "modern"— or my fashion favorites — "edgy", "romantic", and "sexy"— mean different things to different people. You can search on Pinterest to help you find images of your target market or theme. The processes of adding, removing, and editing images on the board help designers create a focused plan.

You can make small changes or completely change direction before spending a lot of time and effort on the actual design work. Furthermore, the mood board can help you stay in line with the original concept as you move into the project, thus saving money on revisions if you were to drive too far off track.

❋ GOLDEN NUGGET

By putting a vision board somewhere you can see it every day, you will prompt yourself to visualize how to bring your ideas to life and do it almost subconsciously.

Sew... that was Part 2. I know, there was a lot to think about.

In Part 3, we are going to get to the product development process: that is, actually taking the concepts and ideas and bringing them into physical samples. There will be a lot of blood, sweat, and tears, but fear not. The good thing is you won't be doing it yourself. Product development involves a tribe, a team of people that help you carry out the vision. Onward bound!!

NOTES

1. Griffith, Erin. Why startups Fail, According To Their Founders in <u>Forbes Magazine</u>. Online: http://fortune.com/2014/09/25/why-startups-fail-according-to-their-founders/. Sept 25, 2014
2. "Brand value of lululemon from 2012 to 2015 (in million U.S. dollars)" in <u>Statista</u>. Online: https://www.statista.com/statistics/238666/brand-value-of-lululemon/. Accessed July 5 2018
3. SWOT en.svg. (2018, April 12). *Wikimedia Commons, the free media repository*. Retrieved 22:12, March 3, 2019 from https://commons.wikimedia.org/w/index.php?title=File:SWOT_en.svg&oldid=296712661
4. Textile Learner Blog https://textilelearner.blogspot.com/2014/03/fabric-weight-measurement-technique.html

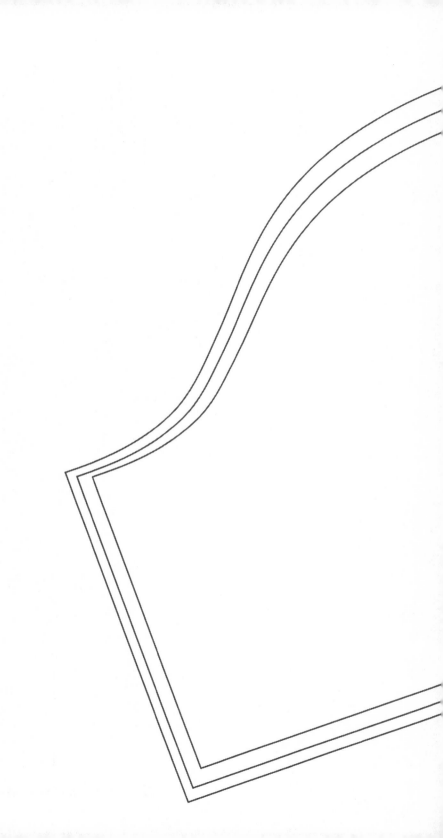

PRODUCT DEVELOPMENT

OVERVIEW

I don't know about you, but I'm super excited to start getting these ideas made! But before we begin, do you have everything (and everyone) in place that you need?

In spite of what you learn or the information you gather from industry experts, your first season can be quite confusing until you've experienced the entire process. Every business process is unique.

Beyond design, there are many steps and people involved in building a fashion business. Apparel design is more creative, setting out the overall picture of the creative direction, while product development involves working through a process to realistically create something physical.

Just remember that product development is an organic process that involves everything beyond creating sketches and mood boards. You are still using your creative skills but in a different way. I'm talking about things like building a team; legal compliance; creating tech packs, patterns and prototypes; pattern revisions, fit comments, and sample making; more revisions and second samples; requesting quotes, and more, all encompassing the entire process before a product is ready to get manufactured.

In this chapter, I'm going to go over all of the aspects of product development to help you get off to a running start. There are a lot of moving pieces, but my goal is to help you understand every step involved, and what you need to do to ensure a smooth, successful process.

Many designer entrepreneurs are really surprised when they learn just how long product development can take. It's usually much longer than expected and relies on a lot of people to achieve the end goals. You should know up front that whether you're an industry professional or a newbie designer, it can take up to a year to properly get a new design pre-production ready.

That's right, *a full year*. Let that sink in for a moment.

It may seem like a long time, but if you do everything that I'm going to teach you in this chapter, it'll be time well-spent, setting you up powerfully for success.

Learn from the big guys. You may have noticed big-box retailers like H&M keep all the latest styles at the front of the store. If you look closely, you'll see that new styles only account for 5-10% of the products sold. The rest of the store has styles that have been slightly tweaked or modified. Hemline lengths change, as do fabrics, colors, and prints, to create an entirely new look and feel in the eyes of a consumer. No one is reinventing the wheel. Large corporations understand that it takes a huge amount of capital, risk, and time to invest in "new" products. They are very careful in selecting the number of styles from which they will create from scratch.

Remember: creating one piece is very easy. Creating a product that can be manufactured to scale takes a considerable amount of planning and flexibility.

Sometimes a design aesthetic may need to change in order to achieve your target costs or what is actually possible within the factory limitations. Being flexible with the final outcome of your design is a part of the product development process. Contrary to what people think, creating an exact replica of any sample is extremely difficult.. Just look at Louis Vuitton or similar high end luxury brands that get knocked off. To a trained eye it's pretty easy to call out a fake. It's difficult to source the same materials and match quality.

The initial prototyping process or product development should be done locally. Face to face meetings are effective in order to get your design right. This is important in order to get the product right before manufacture. Ironing out design issues should be done before a factory sees your prototype. You must work through product development locally to understand every fine detail of the product so that you can more effectively communicate your needs to the factory. Without precise communication, a lot of time and money can be lost.

You will need to assemble the following into a package for the garment manufacturer: prototype(s), a line sheet, mock PO, tech pack(s), reference sample(s), and pattern(s). If that seems like a lot, but don't worry. I will discuss each of these in detail below. As a startup, the ultimate goal of this package is to make things as easy as possible for the manufacturer.

Small orders are much more difficult to manufacture and process compared to larger orders. Surprisingly, most startup companies invest a lot of money into manufacturing products, yet have no clue what is involved in creating the product. If you don't know the specifics of your product or what it entails, how can you expect the factory to know what you want?

Build Your Tribe

An old African proverb says "It takes a village to raise a child." Now, obviously, your design-business is technically not a human baby, but for most of us who have brands, we really feel like our businesses are our babies. In any case, the principle is similar enough: it takes a team, a community of devoted individuals, to build a successful business.

Success begins by being extremely organized and understanding your strengths and weaknesses. Successful entrepreneurs often say that being aware of their weaknesses is critical to their success. By definition, this is a requirement for being able to collaborate and reach out to the people who do know how to do the things that you otherwise can't. Share your vision with them, and get them on your side.

Lose your fear of sharing ideas and spending a bit of money for better returns. Admit it, some of you reading this right now are worrying about someone you bring onto your team stealing one of your visions and running with it themselves. That's okay. What you're experiencing is a fear common to many creatives, especially those who are just starting out. However, in the vast majority of cases, it is completely unfounded. It just doesn't happen. Point blank, you need people who are professionals and experts in specific areas of production to put together a top-quality product. It feels risky, and professional expertise comes at a professional cost, but it'll be worth it in the long run.

Starting a brand requires many people throughout the entire (cyclical) manufacturing process. You need to bring in the key people with the right skill sets and industry expertise to ensure the product is perfected. It may save you money to do certain things on your own, but it is virtually impossible to do everything yourself and expect to keep up with re-orders or growth. You need a tribe, period.

What Is A Tribe?

Simple: it's your team.

In a tribe, everyone has their own sphere of responsibility. Each role is required for the well-being of the community (company), and each person must be attuned to the well-being of the community. A true team is a group of people who, given the structure of the situation, win or lose together. They have emotional ties with the rest of the community and they care about how everyone else is doing.

Your tribe members begin with you, designers, sample makers, pattern makers, and sales staff, and extend to your factory: the many groups of people who execute the creation of your product. Your factory is an integral part of your tribe, and building that relationship is key to your growth.

You need people that will have your back. As a business owner you will find yourself having to continually put out fires. Problems often arise requiring someone to deal with them. For most, finding the right people can be challenging. For example, in order to work with a factory, you need a prototype of the styles you want it to produce. Who specifically do you need to create the prototypes? Depending on your skills and requirements, most startups require a skilled technical designer, sample sewer, pattern maker, and fit model. Here is where you need to get creative. Contact schools or associations to get referrals. You can also advertise a job posting online.

Better yet, visit www.sourcemygarment.com, my shameless plug (you'll thank me later!)

Over time, and assuming it all goes well, your tribe will become like your family. People from all walks of life, of different talents, will come together to create beautiful garments, helping to bring your vision to life. Tribe-building is a difficult, but ultimately rewarding part of the product development process, so choose your tribe members wisely.

Sketches

Okay, *sew*... let's do a quick checklist:

You've come up with an epic idea. Check.

You've collected and analyzed extensive research data. Check.

You've shopped the market (check) and created a mood board (check), both of which have given you a very clear picture of what you want your products to look like. (Check).

Now it's onto detailed design sketches (that is, if you haven't already done it for your mood board). Even if you aren't an artist and lack drawing skills, just give it a try: it's important to work out ideas on paper.

The design process parallels all the research you have done thus far: competitors' analysis, shopping the market, gathering reference samples, and conducting inspirations. Every designer entrepreneur has their own process of translating research into a product. Your ability to communicate your creative ideas will ultimately contribute to the success of the product.

Product development, as we talked about in the previous chapter, requires you to decide upon the finer details which will go in each tech pack. Your product will evolve as you perfect the design. Through this process, you can better guide your factories with extensive information in order to manufacture the design to the best of their production capabilities.

In the previous chapter, I suggested starting with a limited number of colors and styles. Picking only one to six products and a maximum of two colors will save you much grief. I also highly recommend designing for a year or two (typically three orders) in advance. This will save time and ultimately help streamline the process for growth.

Photo | *Comparison of a Fashion Illustration, Design Sketch & Technical Flat*
Photo Credit | *Lauren Kemp*

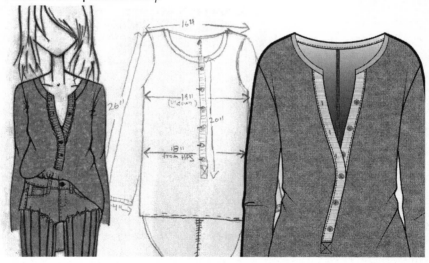

Okay... ready to put pencil to paper? Let's start sketching!

A design sketch differs from a fashion illustration; it's easy to confuse the two. A fashion illustration isn't always made by designers. It showcases a model, as well as colors and a more artistic approach to a garment, creating mood and fantasy. This goes on your mood board.

On the other hand, a design sketch is a starting point, all about the technical details, not the art. The technical flat, a CAD (computer-aided design) typically made using Adobe Illustrator, clearly illustrates design requirements. The beauty of developing vector-based flats is that you can modify them over and over again to create new styles and make revisions.

An illustration is very different to a technical flat and is used for a different purpose. **Illustrations** can be over-stylized and artistic, mostly to show presentation and mood as opposed to something you can use for manufacturing purposes.

When a garment is on a figure in a pose, it may be hard to see all the details of the garment. The factory, buyers, pattern maker, and sample sewer all need to be able to "read" what the design entails and the technical flat is the end result they need to achieve. It's essential that you have a complete garment or product design sketch that you can provide to the technical designer with some direction. He/she then creates a polished technical flat. The technical flat is your starting point for creating your tech pack, the blueprint and assembly instructions for your design.

The design sketch is very straight forward. First, draw out the front and back of each design similar to a technical flat or line drawing. A well-drawn design **sketch** has simple lines, with no shading or coloring. It's important to have a clear outline of your silhouette as if it were laying flat. Once you've finalized your designs, the next steps are to convert them to technical (CAD) flat.

What The Tech! Technical Flats Explained

A technical designer is kind of like your voice: he/she will figure out how your design sketch can be brought to life. A tech designer is needed to help put together all the assembly instructions, the blueprint of the design, also known as the tech pack.

To start with, if you're not able to do computer-aided drawings yourself, you can hire a technical designer to draw a technical flat of the front and back of all the finalized technical design sketches. A **technical flat** is a black and white computerized line drawing that shows a garment as if it were laid flat, in order to communicate all seams, topstitching, hardware, and any other design details. The purpose of the flat(s) is to form a basis for further product development. They are used for many purposes including tech packs, specifications, line sheets, cost sheets, pattern-making, and more.

For a single basic garment, it's typical to have just a front and back view, but remember that you may need to create additional flats to show the inside of the garment and/or how parts of the garment function. For accessories, it is common to have multiple views to give the viewer a better understanding of the design. For example, if you're creating a technical flat for a bag, you'll need front, side, inner, and sometimes even a top and bottom view.

❊ GOLDEN NUGGET

Ask the technical designer for the JPEGs for both front and back view as separate images and one with both images together. These images can be used for marketing and other materials. You can also ask for colorized techs. That being said, remember that your designs may change as you work through product development. In fact, revisions are inevitable, so be sure to request the finalized flat.

Editing Like A Boss

Even though you may develop several designs for each season, they may not all make it into your final order. After all of the design ideas are sketched out, you may realize some pieces are much "stronger" than others. Feedback from your tribe and target market will also give you some clues. You might also find that a particular sketch's requirements may push you over budget. As a result, you may need to edit or remove one or more of your styles. A successful designer entrepreneur designs to balance creativity, costs, and saleability.

Never assume everything you like will sell. It's a common mistake that even big players in many different industries make from time to time (remember New Coke? Or Cosmo Magazine's yogurt brand? Yeah, neither do most people).

Analyzing feedback is critical. Lay out all the products on one board. Show color options, inspirations, details and so on, as discussed in Part 2. Take the mood board and get feedback from your target market. Show them the fabric and get feedback. By speaking directly to your target market, you'll gain invaluable insights. As a result, you'll end up tweaking or weeding out some of your styles, which will leave behind only the most successful designs.

Sew, what's your goal? Simple: that every style you offer your customers sells.

Ensure all the styles work together but are different enough that your customers want to buy all of the pieces. For example, if you are selling bags, select three different types, such as a backpack, a weekender, and a crossbody. A customer is more likely to buy three different types of bags as opposed to three backpacks. You are able to get more money from one customer (because, really, who wouldn't want to get a matching set, especially if the bags are gorgeous?).

Referring back to your budget, you should have planned out the number of styles that you are able to order. Ensure the number of styles you pick is in line with your budget and plan. The final selections are then ready for you to develop further with a technical package.

Line Sheet

Once you've created all of the styles into technical flats, the next step is to create a line sheet. A line sheet gives the factory a single snapshot of what is being ordered or sampled. It's also used as a sales tool once you've finalized your styles. It helps you better communicate to retailers, pattern makers and everyone you work with.

The line sheet contains colorized front and back technical drawings of all styles on order. It also references every style number, the fabric structure, fiber content, colorways, brand name, date, and size range. If you don't have all the information to start, you can add what you're missing after everything's been finalized, but make sure you give as much data as you can up front.

A style number should be assigned to each design to help identify it. When you're starting out it may be easy to keep track of styles, but as your brand grows it will get harder to manage, and a clear system for everyone to quickly identify them will be necessary. Avoid using names because it is hard to track internally. Start by creating a numbered system that makes sense as you grow. Consider fabric, product type, color and season in your system. Don't forget to also share the numbering system, so it makes sense to everyone. For tracking inventory and sizes you can add SKU's (stock keeping units), which we get into more in Chapter 6.

Factories work on many orders at any given point in time and the line sheet is an easy point of reference for all departments. It also helps factories to provide a quote. Keep in mind, as with everything else, the product development process involves many changes. You must update the line sheet with every change that you make.

P.S. You can also use the line sheet as a sales tool for when buyers place their orders.

Photo | *Line Sheet: To learn more about these sustainable basics that #dogood www.thegoodtee.com*

Technical Sketch Steps

Once you've finalized your styles you can get into the nitty-gritty.

Specify as many basic measurements as possible for the base or sample size. Basic measurements typically include length, waist, hip, cross shoulder, chest, sleeve length, inseam, etc. If you have store-bought references for fit or style, this would be a good place to gauge rough specifications and measurements. Remember: the design sketch is just a starting point and guide for the technical designer, which will be revised down the road.

Important Sample Measurement Guidelines

> All circumference measurements are taken on the half, with the garment laid flat.
> Give all measurements in inches.

- Record measurements to the nearest one-eighth of an inch.
- All measurements are to be taken with a standard tape measure. Over time, the tape may stretch, so check it periodically for accuracy against a steel ruler.
- The tape measure must be held flat against the garment, not held on its edge.
- All measurements are to be taken with garments laid on a flat surface, in a natural position, free of tension and with wrinkles smoothed out. Where crinkle type fabrics are used, do not stretch out the crinkle.
- All measurements should be taken on the front of the garment with buttons and/or zippers fully closed, unless otherwise stated.
- For all buttoned garments, the button should be at the end of the buttonhole for any circumference measurement.
- Button spacing should be measured from center of button to center of the next button.
- Specify how or from what point a measurement is taken, eg. length from CB (center back) or HPS (high point shoulder). When measuring waist, specify from HPS to what point down the front the waist measurement is taken.
- When measuring from center back, fold garment in half to establish center back.
- All extended measurements should be the minimum stretched measurement. All elasticized stretch measurements are done until the fabric lays flat. The fabric should not be distorted, nor should the elastic be extended to its ultimate width.
- When measuring pleats, specify if the measurement is taken with pleat closed or open. In general, the high hip is measured with pleats closed and the low hip is measured with pleats open.
- Neck point is where the shoulder seam meets the neck seam.
- Regarding High and Low Hip: Depending on the style, it may be necessary to use alternative measurements from waist to hip (Eg. 3" down instead of 4" down).

❇ GOLDEN NUGGET

If you need help taking measurements, meet with the technical designer and ask for help or provide them with the garment to take the measurements.

» BEST PRACTICE

1 Always, *always* note how you are measuring each point so the next person that is taking the measurement is on the same page as you. These instructions must be conveyed in the tech pack to ensure everyone is on the same page. It's very easy to take measurements differently and think that you are doing it right, and it creates bigger, more frustrating problems later on.

2 Typically, the base (sample) size is the most medium size of the size range. For example, if you offer sizes 2, 4, 6, 8, and 10, the sample size will be a 6. Mention the sample size on the drawing.

3 If any part of the design is more detailed, complex or difficult to understand, "zoom into" that area of the garment, to clearly illustrate with a POM (point of measure(s)). For example, the product might have a unique side slit that has several measurements and may be complicated to construct.

The design sketch should be easy to read without any confusion. See the below example of a front sketch. The sketches should be drawn "flat" without a body.

Photo | *Initial Design Sketch With POM*
Photo Credit | *Maureen Bradshaw*

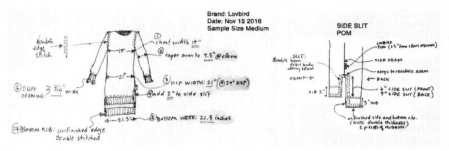

Put On Your Hard Hat And Grab The Blueprint(s)

The most important document given to the factory, aside from the purchase order, is the technical package, commonly referred to as the tech pack. As already mentioned earlier, a tech pack is an information sheet that designers create to communicate with the manufacturer with all the necessary components needed to construct a product. Similar to the blueprints home contractors use throughout the building process, your tech pack is a blueprint for assembling the garment. This document is your safety net to ensure that the factory executes your design as specified. The more thorough the tech pack, the faster the manufacturing process. It will ultimately help to minimize costs by mitigating any issues during sampling and production.

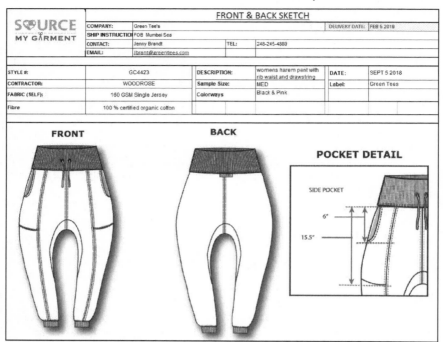

FRONT & BACK SKETCH					
S◊URCE **MY GÂRMENT**	COMPANY:	Green Tee's			DELIVERY DATE: FEB 5 2019
	SHIP INSTRUCTION FOB Mumbai Sea				
	CONTACT:	Jenny Brandt	TEL:	248-245-4889	
	EMAIL:	jbrant@greentees.com			

STYLE #:	GC4423	DESCRIPTION:	womens harem pant with rib waist and drawstring	DATE:	SEPT 5 2018
CONTRACTOR:	WOODROSE	Sample Size:	MED	Label:	Green Tees
FABRIC (SELF):	160 GSM Single Jersey	Colorways	Black & Pink		
Fibre	100 % certified organic cotton				

FRONT   BACK

POCKET DETAIL

SIDE POCKET

6"

15.5"

The anatomy of the tech pack should contain technical product descriptions, technical flats, photo references, measurements, all materials (fabrics, trims, colors, thread color, etc.), and artwork (for prints, labels, and packaging information), to a section that tracks comments and approvals with the factory when working through sampling.

Many people involved in the manufacturing process will have access to the tech pack. Every department in the factory, as well as any subcontractors they may hire, will refer to the tech pack. You may be surprised to learn that a factory manages many other subcontractors in order to execute your order. A simple T-shirt can involve more than eleven departments and subcontractors to produce, including the cutting department, fabrics department, merchandiser, production floor, fabric dyer, knitter/weaver, hang-tag printer, labels maker, screen printer, the customs broker, and many more.

Without a tech pack, no department would know the information they need to produce a garment. It also helps the factory estimate the resources required for construction of each style. This further enables them to allocate manpower and equipment for the completion of the order and decide whether certain value additions need to be outsourced to other subcontractors.

As a designer entrepreneur, you'll work with pattern makers and technical designers to produce tech packs. It's critical to hire an experienced technical designer to create the tech packs to prevent costly mistakes. The tech pack must contain complete details pertaining to the style such as grading, fabric, embellishments, trims, closures, labels, artwork, and packaging. Photographs from store-bought samples and reference samples can be included.

You need to give all of this information to the tech pack designer so they can create the tech pack. A thorough and detailed tech pack results in better first sample results with minimal errors. Remember: tech packs are the key to bringing the best end results in a finished product and most of the finalized information for them will come from your pattern maker.

Also, don't forget to give a store-bought, medium-size sample to the tech pack designer to use as a guide for fit measurements. The fit sample should be in a similar body from a brand that has a fit you would like to mimic. In addition, if you have a fit model, those actual body measurements should be provided as well. That helps them gauge fit (which we'll discuss further on in the chapter). Be sure to ask if the technical designer has any pattern-making or production experience. It's always best to hire someone experienced because one tiny small mistake in the tech pack could jeopardize production.

No matter how experienced you are, putting together a good tech pack takes time. Obviously, a more complicated style can take longer to complete than a simple style. This document isn't done in one sitting, nor by just one person; it evolves, and you'll update it regularly as you move through product development.

Getting Technical With Product Descriptions

You may have heard of product descriptions, which are more creative and used for sales and marketing. Product descriptions are ultimately derived from the technical garment descriptions. The garment description should be simple and include only the necessary words to help describe and identify your product quickly. It's the first thing everyone on your team reads and if it's done right it can save you time and money in the long-run.

As the designer, you need to be able to articulate the technical garment description and be fully versed in all of the correct terminology to avoid complications later on. If you're having trouble writing the descriptions you can always ask the pattern maker or technical designer for help.

Technical descriptions should begin with the target market and include product and fabric information and then proceed to finer details.

Below is a general guideline that you can use to help create a technical description:

1 Intended Consumer (ladies, men, children)
2 Fabric: Fiber content (cotton, polyester)
3 Fabric: Construction Type (Jersey, Interlock, twill)
4 Product Category/Type (skirt, pant, dress)
5 Sub-category/Finer Details (can include more than one word) (asymmetrical, briefs, mini,)
6 Product Basic Silhouette (overall shape/fit of the garment) (A-line, semi-fitted, wide-leg)
7 Closure type/value additions (zipper, elastic and/or printed, embroidered)

"Ladies' cotton twill corduroy A-line mini skirt with seamed pockets and invisible back zipper"

Photo | *Above example of the technical description*

Style Numbers

Style numbers help you and everyone in your supply chain keep track of your designs. Can you imagine a Chinese factory trying to read *"The Green Emily"* or *"Hot Kitten Pant?"* Or what about a boutique calling to order a few *"Delicious Pink Cozzies?"*

Sew, you will also need to assign style numbers to each design. The style numbers help you identify the specific garment. It's easy for a small company to keep track of every style, but as your brand grows, you add more styles, create carry-over styles, new collections, and new team members, you will need a system for everyone to easily identify all different garments.

Create a system

Start by creating a number system that is consistent and that will function for you when you grow and expand your product offerings. It is your brand, so guess what! You can create any number system you want! Your the boss, however it's best for it to be simple and easy to reference. There are no industry rules you have to follow but it is important that you create a thought-through system early on, so that you don't have to go back and change everything as you grow. . Avoid using names because it is hard to track internally. Consider fabric, product type, color and season in your system. Don't forget to also share the numbering system, so it makes sense to everyone. For tracking inventory, colors and sizes are called SKU's (stock keeping units) will be created once styles and production is finalized.

Here is an example system that you can use. Feel free to tweak as you see fit for your product offerings:

Season (Fall=F, Spring=SP)
Last two digits of the year
Gender (male=M, female=F, unisex=U)
Category (tops=T, pants=P, dresses=D, skirts=S)
Style # (01- 100)

An example for the skirt above is #SP19FS01

Getting Really "Spec"ific: **The Specification Sheet**

Contained within a tech pack is a specification sheet (spec sheet). A garment spec sheet is a technical document that contains a technical diagram/sketch of the garment, and all the measurements including grading (measurements of all sizes). These measurements are presented in an easy-to-read chart along with illustrations called specs. The measurements are taken on the "half" of the circumference. The sample maker and pattern maker both need this information to create the patterns and sew the samples.

Initially, with the help of the technical designer, you will provide the pattern maker with a measurement chart containing only the rough measurements based on a sample size. The patternmaker will use these specs as a guide for the general size and fit of a finished garment. The actual pattern piece measurements will be different due to the necessary adjustments needed to achieve the proper fit and balance of a garment. The actual numbers need to be documented so that the information can be added or updated to the tech pack.

As you work through product development, fittings, and revisions, you'll find that you'll be continuously updating the specs. The garment factory uses the final measurements for checking sewing quality and accuracy.

Photo | *Illustration of a specification sheet*

MEASURING POINT AND DESCRIPTION	XS 6	S 8	M 10	L 12	XL 14	TOLERANCE + / –
1	Front Neck Drop				4"		1/8"
2	Back Neck Drop				1/2"		1/8"
3	Neck Rib Width				5/8"		1/8"
4	Neck Opening (point to point)				6"		1/8"
5	Armhole length (point to point)				10 1/4"		1/8"
6	Front Length from HNP				29"		1/8"
7	Back Length from HNP				29"		1/8"
8	Sleeve Length (Shoulder Point to Hem Edge)				9"		1/16"
9	Sleeve Cuff Hem Height				3/4"		1/8"
10	Sleeve Cuff Extension Height				1 1/4"		1/8"
11	Across Shoulders (point to point)				18 1/4"		1/8"
12	Across Chest (1" from under arm)				20"		1/8"
13	Across Waist (15" from HNP)				20"		1/8"
14	Sweep (Bottom Opening Edge to Edge)				20 1/4"		1/8"
15	Bottom Hem Height				3/4"		1/8"
16							1/16"
17							1/16"
18							1/8"
19							1/8"
20							1/8"
21							1/8"
22							1/8"
23							1/8"
24							1/8"
25							1/8"

Still with me? There's a bit of a way to go, so have a quick stretch, refill your tea or wine, and let's keep going!

The specification sheets may likely include a technical POM similar to the hand-drawn POM but it is created as a vector. The POM is a technical flat with elaborate measurements and call-outs. These call-outs provide additional sewing information and point to the specific area of the design.

POCKET DETAIL

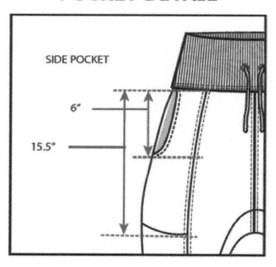

Important details that may not be included in the spec list, are shown as POM (point of measure) in a close-up illustration of part of the garment, using arrows and detailed technical drawing. Call-outs or codes are used to specify the measuring points of a garment or product.

Call-outs should include the information that the patternmaker will need to create the pattern for the garment. Specifically (and especially), any complicated sewing areas on a garment must have a POM illustration to clarify how a garment is constructed and measured. All important elements of the POM should remain visible and all measurements and descriptions should be clear. More complex designs may require several POM illustrations.

Let's talk about measuring for a moment. It's very important that you learn how to accurately measure, both for giving measurements for fit as well as checking samples when they come back. Both you and the person on the other end need to be measuring the "same way." For example, when measuring length, it's important to state how you are measuring. Are you measuring from high point shoulder (HPS) or back neck? These are actually two different ways of measuring the length and if you and the other person are not on the same page, things can get really messed up. We'll cover more on how to measure later in the next chapter.

Below are some general measurements for a shirt:

HPS: (High Point Shoulder) The main reference point located at the highest point of the shoulder, where the shoulder seam meets the neckline. Many measurements are given in relation to the HPS.

HIGH POINT SHOULDER (HPS)

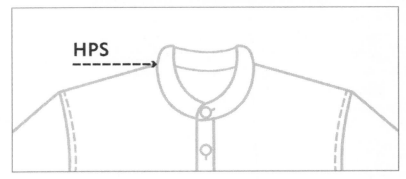

Length: Usually measured from the back side. HPS or Back Neck-Measure from HPS to the bottom of the seam.

Across Shoulder: Measure from the back. Measure from top of shoulder seam (HPS) to the other side of the shoulder seam.

LENGTH

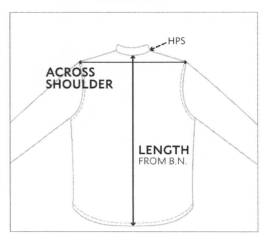

Chest: Usually measured 1" below armhole horizontally from edge to edge.

Across Chest: Measured horizontally from armhole to armhole at a specific distance below HPS, which will vary depending on sample size and company standards. Example: For a ladies t-shirt, across chest spec is taken from 5" below HPS.

CHEST

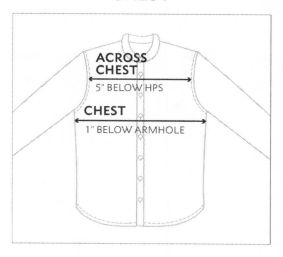

ACROSS CHEST
5" BELOW HPS

CHEST
1" BELOW ARMHOLE

Waist:Measured horizontally from edge to edge at a specific distance below HPS, which will vary depending on sample size and company standards. Example: For a Junior size 9, waist spec is taken from 15 ½" below HPS.

WAIST

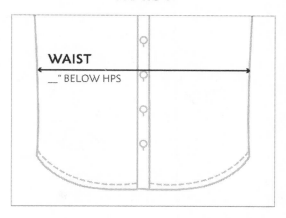

WAIST
__" BELOW HPS

Hip: Measured horizontally from edge to edge at a specific distance below HPS, which will vary depending on sample size and company standards. Example: For a Junior size 9, the hip spec is taken from 24" below HPS.

HIP

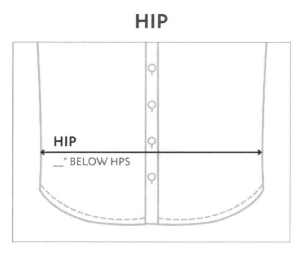

HIP

__" BELOW HPS

Bottom Sweep: The bottom edge of the garment measured horizontally straight across from edge to edge.

Slit: Measure from top of the opening to bottom edge.

BOTTOM

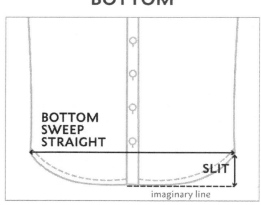

BOTTOM SWEEP STRAIGHT

SLIT

imaginary line

Sleeve Length: Distance from the top of the sleeve at the shoulder seam to the sleeve opening.

Bicep:Measured 1" below the armhole, perpendicular to the length of the sleeve.

Armhole (Curved): Measured along the curve of the armhole seam where the bottom armhole meets the side seam to where the top of the armhole meets the shoulder seam.

Shoulder Drop:From HPS to the shoulder seam at armhole.

ARM MEASUREMENTS

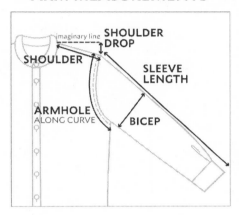

Neck Opening:Measured from neck seam to neck seam at HPS.

Front Neck Depth: Can be measured edge to edge or seam to seam. Must be specified in tech. Measure from back neck to bottom edge.

NECK MEASUREMENTS

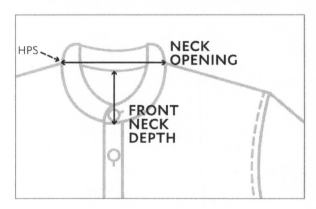

Construction Details

Sew... let's talk about sewing... (See what I did there?)

You may not know how to sew, and that's perfectly okay - some of the most talented musicians don't know how to read or write sheet music. Talent is talent. However, it very important, as a designer, to understand how a garment is constructed, even if you yourself aren't doing the sewing. Every seam and stitch requires a special technique, needle type, or piece of machinery. **Stitches** are loops of thread or yarn resulting from a single pass or movement of the needle in sewing or knitting. A **seam** is defined as a line where two or more fabrics (or other material) are joined together by means of stitches.

The factory will analyze every part of the design and what types of machinery they'll need to execute the sample. The factory arranges machinery requirements of the stitching and garment construction instructions provided in the tech pack. If they do not have the right machinery, they may need to outsource part of the manufacturing process.

It's extremely important to be clear on what you require the manufacturer to produce for you. If the prototype you've given the factory doesn't match the tech pack, make sure you note any deviations from the tech pack directly on the sample. For example, let's say you require a type of decorative seam, but don't have the machinery to make the sample, make a note of it directly on the sample with masking tape - "missing flatlock seam." Remember your selection of the stitching and garment construction details form the final look of the garment styling. The fit and durability are also determined by the types of seams and construction used on the garment. Therefore, your understanding of both seams and stitches becomes a very important factor in the success of the product. Every detail matters, and knowing what you want and how to explain it to others will only help improve quality and aesthetic, which in turn will help saleability. Remember: knowledge is power... and profit.

In mass production, garments are made in assembly lines. In the assembly line, workers perform only one specific operation throughout the day. Operators are only trained on specific processes to improve their skill on the job and eliminate the variation between garments of the same design. This is mandatory in mass production. An operational breakdown is the sequence of assembly of the product, usually written down as a list of steps for the production process. The merchandiser (the coordinator for production) must fully understand the tech pack and trust that everything on it is correct and that everything they need to do their job is present. Prior to manufacturing, during the counter sampling development, the sampling department is responsible for not only recreating your prototype but also accounting for the operational breakdown to get the cost, and fully understand the process. The sampling department is the only place where one operator works on the entire garment.

Construction methods, seams and stitches, and operational breakdowns can get very complex and intricate. For the sake of everyone's sanity (just kidding... okay, maybe not), I'm just going to give you some basics for now. For further details, again, consult people in this area of expertise or read up more on sewing construction and seam types. You must also consider sewing line efficiency and productivity improvement. The more you know, the more control and understanding you have over your product.

ASTM Textile Standards

ASTM is globally recognized as a leader in the development of standards in many industries, including fashion. Standards are used to improve product quality, safety, and build consumer confidence. ASTM's textile standards provide the specifications and test methods for the physical, mechanical, and chemical properties of textiles and fabrics. Committee D13 is dedicated to textiles, and has been in existence for over 100 years. The Body Measurements for Apparel Sizing, demanded by consumers, was created to ensure that whatever garment size they require despite the manufacturer, brand or type of clothing, the fit will be consistent. Depending on your consumer, you can purchase standards of body measurements and apparel sizing to help create your patterns and garments.

He Had Me In Stitches

Seriously though, stitches are no laughing matter. Every stitch has a different purpose and function in a garment.

Photo | *6 Classes of Stitch Types*[1]

Stitch Class	Name	Typical Uses
100	Single Thread Chain Stitch	1. Decorative, western wear, used at hems
200	Hand Stitch	
300	Lockstitch-variations include-plain,zigzag,	1. Plain- used to set pockets,zippers 2. Zigzag- used for athletic wear, decorative, buttonholes, bar tacks on jeans
400	Multi Thread Chain Stitch	1. Decorative stitching on belts. 2. Parallel rows of stitches for lapped side seams of woven shirts and jeans.
500	Overedge and Safety Stitch	1. Shirts, jackets, blouses and jeans.
600	Cover Stitch or Flat Seam Stitch	1. Knits and lingerie

ASTM D 6193

Common Industrial Sewing Machine Stitches

1 Chain Stitch

Stitch that interloops the needle thread(s) with a bottom looper thread on the underside of the seam. This stitch is used on most seams in woven apparel. **Single needle** stitching is the most common stitch used on a sewing machine. Clothing manufacturers use this in operations where the fabric is stiffer and stretches less. Back tacking is needed here as security at the start and end of the stitch.

2 Lock Stitch

This is the most common stitch formed on industrial sewing machines. **Lockstitch** is so named because of the two threads, upper and lower, which "lock" together in the hole in the fabric through which they pass. The stitch appears the same on the top as well as the bottom. This stitch is more secure.

3 Cover Stitch

A cover stitch is a professional-looking hem.It has two rows of stitching on the top and a serger like stitch on the back.

4 Overlock Stitch (Sergers Stitch)

This is a stitch that sews on the edge of one or two pieces of cloth to prevent unraveling of raw fabric edges and to neaten the inside of garments. The main purpose is to make the joined seams stronger and protect the edge of the cloth after cutting. Overlock stitching also protects the cloth and helps it last longer, even after several washes. Whether it's a woven or knitted fabric, overlock stitch is a must for durability. Take a look inside every garment you wear. Every seam has been sewn and requires the overlock stitch. You get three different varieties of overlock sewing machines with threads used from 3 to 5 spools.

Above are some of the most common stitching methods. Apart from these, there are many other sophisticated machines that manufacturers use. A good tech pack designer must know the methods of stitching in order to convey the stitching and construction details in the tech pack. The job of the tech pack designer is to mention the right stitching and garment construction details to plan the style. When in doubt, you can also consult your pattern maker or sample sewer.

Life Is Not What It Seams

Sew, it *seams* like we have something more to discuss.

How do you want the garment sewn together? It's important to determine what types of seams you want. How do you want the two pieces of fabric to be joined? For example, do you want a pleat? What type of pleat? Princess? Boxes? Inverted? Seams can serve both decorative and functional purposes. The seam length, width, and depth affect garment quality performance (and costs). Because of language barriers, the sewn sample helps clarify the instructions on the tech pack, along with the POM.

Seam Classification

Note:There are various types of seams within these classes

Photo: *Seam Classification* [2]

Class of Seam	Name
SS	Superimposed Seams
LS	Lapped Seams
1. BS	Bound (Binding) Seams
FS	Flat (Butted) Seams
EF	Edge Finished Seams
OS	Ornamental Seams

ASTM D 6193

Flatlock Seam

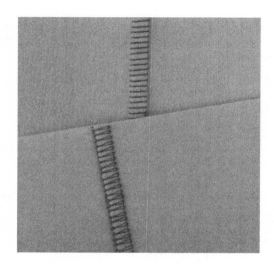

A flatlock seam is often used in jersey and stretchable fabrics. Unlike single needle lock, it has the capacity to withstand the stretch of the fabric. The stitching often resembles an overlock stitch on both sides of the fabric. Unlike an overlock, there are no layers to the underside, typically the seam is butted together. It creates a seam that is flat. It is often used as a decorative stitch and for performance garments.

Track All Comments and Revisions In The Tech Pack

Hopefully by now, you're not falling apart at the seams, and instead feel you have been reinforced with information that will give you the confidence to press on.

Just to recap very quickly: a tech pack is usually set up by you, the designer, as the initial source of development. During the product development process, changes are continuously made to the design, which affects the tech pack. It should (and will) be continuously updated with these revisions as you work through sampling and fitting issues. When a sample is made, comments and issues are addressed and should be noted directly in the comments section of the tech pack. At the same time, the technical specifications or drawings may need to be revised.

Assume the admin role: it's tedious, but *sew* very important.

For example, let's say you make the first sample, only to notice that the arm is too wide on the fit model. With the pattern maker's help, make a point form list of all the issues in the comments section of the tech pack. Highlight any measurement changes and update the specification chart and POM illustration of the tech pack (you may need the help of the technical designer to do this). For an additional reference, you can mark comments directly on the sample with a pen and masking tape. The comments will be used to revise the pattern and the second sample. Once you've made the revised sample, you can look back on the comments to ensure that your requests have been dealt with properly.

It's absolutely critical to track all required changes and have a paper trail so that both the pattern maker or tech pack designer know what needs to be revised. A tracking system is crucial: your tech pack serves as the master log of all edits, revisions, and comments. Relying on tracking comments verbally or via email is both insufficient and inefficient. It's also crucial to track and note the date of all changes made to your garment or comments on any development samples in the tech pack so that you can reference these changes throughout the production process. Having all notes, comments, changes, and edits tracked and dated in one place will prove to be tremendously helpful when questions arise about when or what changes were made and what samples were or weren't approved and why. You will need to go back to ensure that your changes were addressed, because if you don't have something to fall back on... well, you can guess what the consequences are gonna be.

The tech pack must always have the most current information. If the tech pack is not updated with accurate measurements and information, it causes huge problems during the manufacturing process and will alter the cost. Most importantly, when it comes time to reorder a style, all the information will be current and correct which will allow a smoother manufacturing process.

What Is Fabric Ease?

You know that great feeling when you're getting set to go on a night out and you've got a fantastic outfit laid out on your bed, ready to go? That sensation when you pick it up, lift it over your head, and in a single, smooth, flowing movement, pull it on and feel it just flow over every contour of your body like a warm hug?

You know that feeling?

Yeah, that's... not fabric ease. (Though there is something called "wearing ease", which I'll get into shortly. Still, it's a great feeling, though, right?)

Understanding how you want the garment to fit and sharing this information with the tech pack designer and patternmaker is especially important. This will help guide them in achieving the right fit. This is where ease comes into play.

Fabric ease is the measurable difference between the measurement of the body and the measurement of the garment. It is a sewing term used in pattern making. Every garment must have a certain amount of ease: in other words, a larger measurement to allow for movement and comfort. The amount of ease required depends on the design of the garment, the fabric, the body type, the end use of the garment, and of course, personal or design preference.

Wearing ease follows the basic rule that the wearer must be able to move, bend, breathe, sit, raise arms, and walk without the garment pulling, pinching, bending, stretching, or straining beyond a natural relaxed position. Fashion trends will affect the accepted amounts of wearing ease, but regardless of design, it's imperative that the garment both fit and hang well on the body.

The following chart lists accepted wearing ease for five different types of fit for womenswear: close-fitting, fitted, semi-fitted, loose fitting, and oversized. Close-fitting measurements are used for extreme or fashion-forward styles. Fitted and semi-fitted measurements are used for basic styles; loose-fitting measurements are used for garments or styles with gathers or excess ease. Oversized measurements are used for garments that appear to be larger than usual sized. You may need to refer to these measurements when evaluating fit.

Photo | Missey Ease Allowance Chart

Missy Ease Allowance	Close-fitting	Fitted	Semifitted	Loose fitting	Oversized
Bust	1/2"-2"	2"-4"	4"-5"	5"-8"	over 8"
Waist/Hip	1/2"-2"	2"-3"	3"-4"	4"-6"	over 6"
Waistband	1/4"-1/2"	1/2"-3/4"	3/4"-1"	1"-2"	over 2"
Crotch Depth	3/4"-1"	1"-1 1/2"	1 1/2"-2"	2"-2 1/2"	over 2 1/2"
Armhole	1"-2"	2"-3"	3"-4"	4"-5"	over 5"
Upper Arm/Sleeve	1"-2"	2"-3"	3"-4"	4"-5"	over 5"
Elbow	1/2"-1"	1"-2"	2"-3"	3"-4"	over 4"
Wrist	1/2"	1/2"-1"	1"-2"	2"-3"	over 3"
Thigh/Knee/Leg Opening	1"-2"	2"-3"	3"-4"	4"-5"	over 5"
Shoulder Seams	0"-1/4"	1/4"-1/2"	1/2"-1"	1"-1 1/2"	over 1 1/2"
Across Back	1/2" - 3/4"	3/4" - 1 1/4"	1 1/4" -2 1/2"	2 1/2" - 3 1/2"	over 3 1/2"

Note: Blazer/Jacket ease minimums should use the semifitted measurements, and coat/outerwear ease minimums

Trims, Closures, Labels, Embellishments, & Packaging (Oh My!)

The tech pack includes every detail and component of the product, everything from trims, closures, and labels to embellishment, packaging, and the fabric recipe. Wherever possible, provide the tech pack designer with a sample reference. You must also supply all the information, from the quality of materials to be used, Pantone number(s) (a universal system for matching ink or dye colors) and the dimensions. Additionally, include artwork created from the labels, screenprints, packaging and more.

The difference between "trim" and "embellishment" can be a gray area.

Now, let me be clear - by "embellishment", I DON'T mean something ridiculous. We're not talking about things like diamond necklaces on poodles (adorable, if a little bougie) or even ordering gourmet gold wrapped sushi (who does that?!). So, what *do* I mean by "embellishments?"

An **embellishment** is a decorative detail or feature added to a product to make it more attractive. It's anything that enhances the appearance of clothing or fashion accessories without actually having any functional purpose. A very common use of embellishment is the utilization of embroidery, printing, bows, beading, or rhinestones. In addition, you'll often find beads, buttons, toggles, tassels, zippers, appliqué, piping, or lace used to embellish garments. Some of the trimmings manufactured today are works of art in themselves.

Trims, on the other hand, are used to enhance the aesthetic and/ or functionality of a garment. Trims are required for the proper construction or fit of a garment. Trims are items that are more of a necessity to the garment (for example, thread, labels, binding, ribbing, grommets, rivets, zippers, and buttons etc.). Zippers can either be functional or decorative.

» BEST PRACTICE

Be sure to break down and list every component of the product. Does it have zippers, printing, or ribbing on the cuff? Make sure to supply a reference sample for each trim or embellishment so that both the factory, and everyone you collaborate with, has an understanding of your requirements and standards.

When You Need Closure

The human body shape requires certain garments to separate or expand so that the person can wear them with ease but also be able to take them on and off. Closures or fasteners are mechanical devices, such as zippers, buttons, snaps, elastics, and hooks and eyes. You can use them for aesthetic value or function.

"Zip"-lining Your Way To Success

The zippers, invented in 1890 by Whitcomb L. Judson, is an important component to a garment. It may seem like a small detail in the grand scheme of things, but it keeps your client's clothes on (well, when you put it that way...) and can make or break your garment (literally). *Sew*, it's crucial to know the multitude of options out there and to be able to specify the most appropriate one for your design.

There are thousands of styles and sizes of zippers, and you've got to make sure you choose appropriate ones for your garment. Selecting the right zipper requires close attention. For instance, there are invisible zippers, reverse coil zippers, two-way closed-ended zippers, and magnetic zippers, just to name a few. Zippers can be non-separating or separate.

ZIPPER TYPES

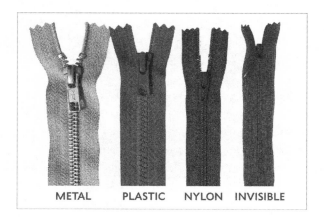

QUALITY:

There are many different styles and sizes, which can be sorted into four broad categories:

1 Metal
2 Plastic
3 Nylon (coil)
4 Invisible (Technically still a nylon coil zipper, but gets a special mention due to its unique design and functionality)

Zippers with the most common types of teeth include **metal** teeth, **coil (polyester)** teeth, and **plastic** teeth. Plastic-moulded zippers are identical to metallic zippers, except that the teeth are plastic instead of metal. Coil teeth are the most commonly used zipper, where the slider runs on two coils on each side.

Each differs in quality, function and suitability, so choose wisely!

FUNCTION:

Zippers can be non-separating or separating. Non-separating, also known as closed-end, is linked at the end and when fully unzipped does not come apart (such as a zipper on a backpack closure). In contrast, a separating zip can come apart, separating two elements of a garment (think zip-off pant legs like the ones your dad wears, but probably shouldn't, wink wink).

SIZE/GAUGE:

Typically, the size or gauge of a zipper is an approximation of its teeth width in millimeters when it is closed. While working with zippers, you'll hear the terms #3, #4, #5, etc. This is a direct reference to the zipper gauge (these numbers determine the size - the higher the number, the wider the teeth!). #3 or #5 gauges are most common, but gauges range up to #20.

It is pretty easy to measure the zipper gauge. Place the garment on a horizontal surface, zip it up and measure the teeth width from left to right with the help of a ruler or a tape.The measurement should correspond to those numbers, like 3, 4, 5, 7, etc. For example, the teeth width of a #3 gauge zipper amounts to approximately 3.1-3.5 millimeters. #3 or #5 gauges are most common, but as mentioned, gauges range up to #20 (for those who want that wider teeth).

WEIGHT:

Don't forget to choose a zipper according to the weight of your fabric. Always consider the weight of the zipper with the weight of your fabric – if the zip is too heavy for the fabric, it will cause the garment to sag and not hang right.

LENGTH:

A zipper is measured from the very top of the zipper pull to the bottom of the zipper stop. It does not include the tape. Remember that once your pattern gets graded into different sizes, the factory will have to determine the correct length of zipper for each size.

Photo | *Anatomy Of A Zipper*
Photo Credit | *Do It Better Yourself Club*

COLORS:

> You can order ready available stock (ensure you're getting the correct lengths for all your sizes)
> To ensure that zippers match the body of a fabric- order dyed to match (DTM). Order times can be lengthy (up to 45 days), especially when they're dyed to match or a custom length, so be patient and order ahead!

A zipper costs relatively little, but if it fails, that spells trouble, because the garment then likely becomes unusable until the zipper is repaired or replaced, and that can be quite difficult and expensive.

Problems often lie with the zipper slider: when it becomes worn, it doesn't properly align and join the alternating teeth.

Ordering zippers can require long lead times, especially when they need to be dyed to match or made to a custom length; which is the norm. In fact, it can take up to 45 days for the factory to receive them.

Zippers are an integral part of the apparel product development process. Keep your target market in mind when choosing your zipper, as well as your garment type, and what the zipper is actually connecting.

ZIP TIPS:

> YKK is the most reputable brand for zippers, known for its unrivaled quality, and supplies over HALF of all the zippers around the world - that's over 7 billion (yes, *billion*) YKK zippers manufactured each year! (Check the zipper of whatever you're wearing right now- chances are, it says "YKK)

> Advertise your brand's unique identity and customize your garment's zipper by adding a custom zipper pull, (ribbon or brand name monogram)

> Invisible zippers aren't as strong in a stress point as other zippers are, so use them for parts of a garment that require less strength, such as the half-zip on the neck of a sweater

> To save you time, choose from the zipper lengths that are in stock.

> When in doubt, ask your pattern maker - they know best.

When Someone Pushes Your Button

Has anyone ever accused you of being too "buttoned up"? Well, guess what?

In fashion as in life, there's always someone who knows how to push our buttons. Family, colleagues, romantic partners - you name it. Now, I can't help you with the button-pushers, but when it comes to the buttons themselves, that's another story. Knowing your stuff when it comes to buttons and other closures is invaluable to excellent design.

Closures are objects secured to a garment with thread and paired with buttonholes to fasten shut. As with all trims, these may be decorative, functional, or both.

Button styles include 2-hole and 4-hole sew-through buttons, shank buttons, and tunnel buttons. They can be attached via hand or machine.

Button sizes or diameters are specified in lignes. This term derives from the French system of measurement that predated the metric system. Button sizes range from 14L to 60L and up. 40L (the "L" after the number stands for ligne) is a button that is 1 inch in diameter. Regular shirt buttons are typically 18L (just less than ½ inch), and the button on a shirt collar is typically 14L or 12L. On an irregularly shaped button, the measurement in lignes signifies the distance between the two widest points.

Photo | *Button Ligne Measurement*

BUTTON SIZES

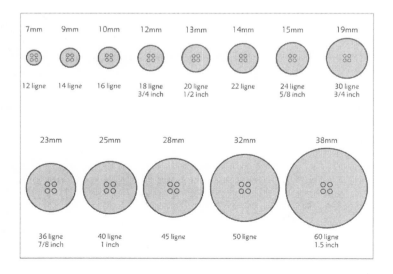

Buttons are made from many types of natural and synthetic materials. Polyester plastic buttons are most common. They are durable, easily dyed to any color, and can be made shiny or matte. Bamboo, wood, coconut, and seashells are some eco-friendly options that are all milled into buttons. Beware: some natural materials are difficult to dye and are not reliably color-fast. Buttons are most commonly dyed to match the color of the fabric if a Pantone number is provided.

Hanging By A Thread

All right, let's take a breather. We've gone a long way in a short span of time, and I'm sure that many of you are just hanging on by a thread.

Speaking of thread....

A thread is a yarn that is used to stitch garments together. The thread type must be compatible with the garment and selected with great care. Thread has a strong impact on the quality and durability of the product. Besides color, the thread is selected based on fiber, size, strength, elasticity, and colorfastness. Choosing the wrong thread can result in issues during construction.

Threads can be made from a single fiber type such as cotton, linen, silk, rayon, nylon, polyester, or rubber, or from a combination of fibers such as cotton and polyester. The most common natural fiber used for threads is cotton. They have excellent sewability with little kinking or skip stitching. Although cotton is most common, it can shrink and is weaker compared to synthetic yarns. Cotton threads dye well, and they mould to the fabric better than other fibers and are particularly attractive for topstitched elements.

The most common synthetic threads, polyester and nylon, were developed to perform well on synthetic fabrics and withstand the chemicals and heat of durable press treatments. Compared to cotton threads of the same size, they are stronger, more resistant to abrasion, mildew, and ultraviolet radiation, and have less shrinkage.

If in doubt, the merchandiser at the factory can give you the best advice on which thread to select.

» BEST PRACTICE

Initially, you may be unsure of which thread is the most suitable for your product. After consulting with the factory, be sure to add the thread type to the tech pack so all the information is conveyed for current or future orders.

Put A Label On It

Let's talk labels. No, I don't mean the bad kind: you know, like when the kids at school called you "Spilly McGee" for months because you got hot chocolate all over your new white pants (c'mon, that was one time!). I mean real, actual labels that you put on your clothes.

Labels are printed or woven attachments to garments that give consumers information about the product. They can be in the form of hang tags, brand labels, stickers and care labels. The government requires specific labeling information, and specifies where labels must be located, whereas some decisions about labels are at the discretion of the designer.

Printed labels are the least expensive and are coated to improve print durability. Labels printed on synthetic paper are the most cost-effective, but wear out over time. Woven labels are the most costly, especially with low quantities, and take the longest time to manufacture. Woven labels, however, are the most durable and indicative of a higher-end brand.

Labels & Legal Compliance

Ensure that the information contained on your labels protects your brand name. It is important that you understand and adhere to all labeling laws and regulations that apply to your business so you are fully protected. No matter who is involved in the design process or helping manufacture your products, at the end of the day, you are distributing the products and are responsible for complying with all laws and regulations.

Each country operates under a different set of rules and regulations regarding the transfer of goods entering or leaving their borders, as well as those sold within a province or state. Products must be labeled correctly and are inspected by customs. Customs regulations and laws concerning the import and export of goods are constantly changing all over the world, sometimes even on a daily basis.

Businesses that don't comply with the provisions set forth in the laws can face monetary penalties. If goods are not marked properly, the improperly marked goods can also be seized or destroyed. Laws regulated in the U.S. are enforced by the Federal Trade Commission (FTC) and U.S. Customs and Border Protection. Laws regulated in Canada are enforced by the Competition Bureau Of Canada and the Canadian Border Service Agency. Unfortunately, not all labeling requirements are found in one single place.

Set aside a fair amount of time to research and understand your responsibilities as a designer entrepreneur. Research the mandatory labeling laws, product testing requirements, recordkeeping protocols, and customs and marketing issues that apply to the specific product category of each design created. If products are being sold in other countries, make sure you understand and adhere to all applicable laws. Word of caution: childrenswear products are heavily regulated.

To learn more visit:

USA: Federal Trade Commission (ftc.gov)
USA: RN#
Registered Identification Number Database
Consumer Products Safety Commission (cpsc.gov)
Canada: Competition Bureau Of Canada (competitionbureau. gc.ca)
Canada:CA#
CA Identification Number
Consumer Product Safety

Disclaimer: The content in this book should not be considered legal advice nor as creating an attorney-client privilege between you, the reader, and the author. If you have questions, consult with your own licensed attorney.

Marketing Claims

Intellectual property is the legal right to ideas, inventions, and creations. It prevents competitors from copying or closely imitating your products or services. You can choose to trademark or copyright logos, brand names, and so on. On the flip side, if you are using someone else's logo, you should also ask for permission. Regardless of whether you've received a certification for fiber such as GOTS (Global Organic Textile Standards), or your factory is fair trade certified, you are using their brand to help you build trust and will need to ask permission. Some organizations request payment for logo use and some have guidelines to follow. Any artwork that is also used for your product should only be used with the consent of the artist. This includes fabric prints, screen prints, and so on.

Choose your words wisely. Are you telling the truth, *the whole truth and nothing but the truth* when it comes to your product descriptions, whether made in advertisements, print or online?

Truthful marketing statements and non-deceptive advertising are highly regulated practices.

Where To Start With Labels

Nobody likes being labeled. Okay, I suppose maybe some people do, depending on the label (I wouldn't mind "hustler", personally). But as far as garments go, you really do want to make sure you label, and label properly.

After you've registered your business and obtained all of the licenses and permits that you require, you can start your labeling with the information below.

1 Contact the government and apply for a manufacturer's identification number. The government requires all businesses that manufacture, import, or distribute goods made of textile fiber to register with them in order to easily identify companies. Brands in the U.S register an RN# and Canadians register a CA#. Costs may apply.

2 Research requirements for care labels and brand name labels. In most instances, depending on the product type, brand labels will need to be placed in a particular location, with the country of origin and fiber content. A second language may be required.

3 Find out whether or not your packaging needs to adhere to additional labeling laws and requirements.

4 Contact your customs broker for any additional information on import/export requirements.

General Labeling Requirements

Critical business data must appear on the labels of all your products. Requirements vary depending on the type of product. Remember that the major intent of labeling laws is to inform and protect consumers. A helpful way to work toward this goal is to put yourself in the position of an uninformed consumer. Consider the questions they might have, such as: Do they (the company) avoid certain materials? Do they prefer to buy from one country? Have they had a bad experience with a manufacturer?

Labeling involves the data or information that you're required to disclose on each product.

General Labeling Requirements:

> Fiber Content
> Manufacturer/dealer Identity
> Country of Origin
> Care Instructions

Laws pertain not only to the information disclosed but also the placement of information. Some products must be labeled in certain spots on the product. Typically, a label must be applied to a product in such a manner that the label is legible and accessible to the consumer at the time of purchase. Most laws require the labels to be permanent. Other products may only require non-permanent labels such as a hang tag.Some States or Provinces may require labels to be bilingual.

Testing and Record Keeping for imported consumer products are heavily monitored to help ensure the quality and safety of their products, processes and systems. Depending on the type of product, you may be required to provide test results from a third party. Product testing and certifications can be done locally or offshore. For example, some childrenswear products require tests to ensure there is no lead content. CPSC, Consumer Product Safety Commission, provides oversight in the U.S, while Health Canada monitors Canadian products.

» BEST PRACTICE

Testing requirements should be stated on both the tech pack and the purchase order. Ensure that all products are legally compliant for all countries that they are distributed to. In the U.S., the governmaent may require tracking labels so they can identify certain batches easily if a recall is made.

(Tender Loving) Care Labels

A garment's care label is often a deciding factor for customers. While some consumers look for the convenience of dry cleaning, others prefer the economy of washable garments. Labels for clothing must have washing or dry cleaning instructions. Ensure the care label information meets legal compliance: as I mentioned, most apparel labels require, by law, that they are permanent, and in some cases, that they are fixed in an easy-to-find location, and legible for most of the life of the product.

Pass the label information onto the tech pack or graphic designer to lay out all artwork for labels. You will need to provide the material used for the label, the dimensions, ink colors, and all information for the label. The exact location for the tag placement is also required. Care labels are normally printed on cotton or satin and can be woven as well. Care labels in North America should have either an RN or CA number depending on where it is from. You can also use the care symbols from the American Society for Testing and Materials (ASTM) to help with the wash care instructions.

✳ GOLDEN NUGGET

Ask the fabric supplier for the care instructions. Then test it yourself by following the instructions given. Be sure to check for shrinkage, pilling, color fastness and any changes that might occur to the overall appearance and quality.

Brand Labels

Never underestimate the power of a brand label. It's so much more important than just a brand name. Brand labels or main labels are usually large, colorful, and affixed in a prominent location. They help the consumer quickly identify the product, and typically include company name, country of origin, fiber content, and the size. Sizes are generally printed on the main label. In some cases, it can also be attached as a small flag inside the seam separately or on the brand label. These are generally in black and white. (Remember!

Make sure the information is legally compliant or it can result in fines or penalties.)

Photo | *Methods of attaching labels*

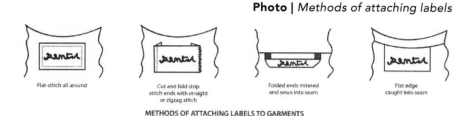

Flat-stitch all around	Cut and fold strip stitch ends with straight or zigzag stitch	Folded ends mitered and sewn into seam	Flat edge caught into seam

METHODS OF ATTACHING LABELS TO GARMENTS

Tag! You're It!

Hang in there, the labeling part is not over yet. Hang tags are like business cards that are attached by a string to your product. They are one of the first things a consumer sees, possibly before they even fully inspect the garment. They relay important information, conveying the branding and message you want to send to your customer.

Hang tags are typically printed on paper, and you must specify on the tech pack the paperweight, ink colors, dimensions, and the string and fastener used to attach it to the garment. Also, provide the exact location for the tag placement and artwork to be printed. Supply a paper quality reference or sample for the factory to source. If you can, opt for recycled paper to help the environment.

Hang on! Are you using someone else's certification logo or artwork? If so, be sure to ask for permission.

Photo | *Hang tags printed and cut*

Packaging Dem Goods

You're amazing, have all the ideal qualities - sexy, funny, intelligent, kind. You're the whole package. But for now, let's concentrate on your products, and how to best package, protect, and brand them.

Packaging has become increasingly connected to the success of a product. Take a second and think about the last blouse or pair of shoes that you bought. Why did you choose that one over the others? Even over one that looked very close to the one you bought? It may have simply been the packaging.

Packaging can be your easiest marketing tool and can play an integral role in building your brand. Making sure your product stands out is just as important as what's inside the packaging. In today's marketplace, it pays to be different.

There are endless creative ideas for packaging that can help give your product a better presentation and added value. Some brands use fabric bags, whereas others may use cardboard containers. Your unique brand messaging should align with your package design. Remember that packaging adds costs and should be accounted for in the price of your product. In fact, you should factor in packaging costs as part of your initial budget. Also, consider the weight and dimensions of the package: Do they make it more difficult to transport and ship the product to your customer? What impact does the packaging have on the environment, and how can you minimize waste?

In most cases, specialty packaging will not be the factory's area of expertise. It's best to source, purchase, and deliver packaging to the factory. A quick online search on specialty packaging will turn up thousands of suppliers. Supplying the materials will allow more control over quality. In addition, it will help the factory focus on the quality of the product and production efficiency.

Packaging The Shipment

Packaging goes beyond improving the aesthetic and promoting the brand. How the goods are shipped to you is often overlooked. Your products need to reach you from thousands of miles away and must be kept safe from damage. Packaging is a form of protection and serves as a barrier against damage. Garment packing is not only the final step in the production process, but a very important one.

Packaging can also communicate how to use, transport, recycle or dispose of the package or product. When transporting and packing products, most brands use poly bags to ship each individual item. To reduce negative environmental impact and reduce costs, bulk pack as many products as possible to fit in one bag. Providing the factory with packing instructions and including photos is extremely helpful. This information should be included in the tech pack.

Production orders are shipped in paper cartons and packed according to size, color, and style. Boxes are clearly marked indicating their contents. Again, you can provide the factory with carton markings or packing instructions to help process orders when the products arrive.

Common Information Found On Cartons:

> Carton/box number
> Order number
> Style(s)

- > Color
- > Number of pieces in each color and style
- > Total number of pieces
- > From address and To address
- > Company and contact number
- > Net weight of the box
- > Dimension of the box

Many designer entrepreneurs often forget there is a cost to having workers offshore pack and package the products. When factories quote prices, they also account for bags and cartons in the cost.

Sew, you have decided on all the elements of your product and detailed them in your tech packs. These elements include the design, specifications, fabric, the thread, the closures, the labeling, the packaging and more. What is your next step? It's time to put everything all together.

Creating Prototypes

Prototypes are the heart of the apparel manufacturing process, and they lead to the perfect fit, instruct production, and act as the "showpieces" that bring in business. Arguably, they are the most essential part of apparel production. The first sample created from a pattern is your prototype. Typically, this is done locally. The factory requires prototypes to help analyze costs for sewing efficiencies and serve as a guide to recreate a counter sample & production-ready sample. Essentially, the process involved in creating a prototype is to give the factory a guide for what you want your final product to look like.

Once you've created the initial tech pack, you're ready to move onto sampling: creating a prototype with the help of your tribe. Your next step will be to find and hire your tribe, an expert dream team specializing in making apparel. Beyond a graphic designer and technical designer, it's likely you will need a sample maker and pattern maker to create the prototype.

Share the samples you bought earlier from the store, as well as the mood board that you made with your team.This will help them understand your vision, reference fit, fabric, rims, stitching, and/or any type of quality standard.

The pattern maker will create a pattern for the sample sewer to stitch up the prototype. The prototype is cut and sewn from the first pattern to evaluate fit, functionality, and styling. Multiple revisions and experiments may be needed from both the pattern and prototype until a perfect sample is created. You might need several rounds of sampling as you find issues in functionality, fit, and styling.

It is important that you refer back to your budget to see how much you can spend on prototyping. Your costs will include paying the sample sewer, pattern maker, technical designer, hiring a fit model, and purchasing material. The budget will be the ultimate guide in determining how many rounds of sampling you can afford. Refer to Part 6: Budgeting, Pricing and Target Costs, for more information on creating a Budget.

» BEST PRACTICE

Never purchase black or white material to create prototypes. Mistakes will be hard to see, and the samples will not photograph well.

Pattern Makers

Pattern makers are the technical backbone of the manufacturing process. In India, they are actually called "masters", and for good reason. They have more control over the outcome of producing a quality product than any other single person. Most pattern makers use computer-aided designs (CAD) software. The most common software used are Gerber, Optitex, Tukatech and Pad.

A good pattern maker, your ride or die, must have a solid background in designing for manufacture. Always hire a pattern maker that has sewing and construction expertise. Find an experienced pattern maker who has experience working with similar products. If the pattern maker typically works with childrenswear, they may not be the best person to produce a technical outerwear.

Provide the tech packs, the fit sample, and any other sample references as guides for the pattern maker. It's very important that the pattern maker has a clear understanding of the fit you want to achieve and the target market. If it doesn't fit, it won't sell. When you find a perfect fit model, provide the pattern maker with their measurements. Again, these measurements should reflect the same measurements of the sample size on the tech pack and the target market. If you're having trouble finding a fit model, you can post an ad on Craigslist or even go through a modelling agency to find the right person that embodies the perfect fit. Your pattern maker will use all of the provided material to draft the first pattern. The first pattern will be used to create the first prototype.

The pattern maker can recommend the amount of fabric that you need to purchase to have the prototype made. Be sure to purchase at least enough fabric and trims for two to three samples because you will likely be making revisions. You can buy materials from retail or wholesale fabric suppliers. The material that you buy must also closely resemble the structure, fiber content, and weight of the production fabric, or it may cause issues in fit and functionality, resulting in serious errors in production.

Together, discuss all the style requirements and create a prototyping plan to meet deadlines. Keep in mind that patterns may have to undergo several rounds of changes. The clearer the direction the pattern maker has up front, the easier the prototyping process will be.

Your pattern maker will use all of the provided material and information to draft the first pattern. The first pattern will be used to create the first prototype.

Pattern Making Costs

It is not recommended to get the factory to create the patterns. Instead, have the patterns made locally. Not only will you have greater control over managing them yourself, but it will save both time and money. Depending on the complexity of the design, it may cost anywhere from $150 to $400 and up. Patterns should be made in a medium sample size.

The Sample Making Process

Once the pattern is made, the next step is sewing the prototype. The sample maker collaborates with the pattern maker and designer to sew the sample. Find a skilled seamstress or sample sewer with the appropriate machinery to stitch both the outside and to finish the inside of the garment. For example, if your product is a T-shirt then an overlock machine will be required. Typically, pattern makers have a sample sewer that they prefer to work with. If the sample sewer is unable to use the right machinery for a certain stitch or construction, the final prototype must be clearly labeled with the issue. It should also be clearly specified on the tech pack.

Provide all the materials, trims, and accessories to the sample maker. The sample sewer will sew a first rough sample to check for fit. Once it is made, you are ready for the fit session. designer entrepreneurs often make the mistake of putting on the garment themselves expecting to see all the issues.

As mentioned above, you will need a fit model. The fit model will try on the garment, while you and the pattern maker discuss any fit issues and adjustments that need to be made to the pattern.

The sample must be worn by a fit model to critique and test functionality.

A pattern and sample may go through at least two revisions before an almost perfect fit is achieved. Ensure the tech pack lists all the comments and issues for each round of sampling. All revisions to the pattern must be updated in the tech pack accordingly. It's crucial for the sample maker and pattern maker to have open communication with every revision.

The final prototype and tech pack should closely resemble an almost perfect production garment. As mentioned earlier, any critical issues concerning how the sample should be duplicated for production must be mentioned directly on the sample with masking tape. The factory will closely follow and use the prototype and the tech pack as a guide. In some cases, a store-bought sample may work as your prototype, which means you won't need to sew a sample, but a tech pack is always required. For example, standard styles such as bedding sheet sets, aprons, or pillows can work in this circumstance.

Work with both the sample sewer and pattern maker, and take any advice they have for improving the design for production. Strive to create the final sample with all the finishing details. Does it closely match a finalized product that you wish to achieve with the manufacturer?

➤➤ BEST PRACTICE

Always remember to have an extra finalized sample made to keep for yourself.

Fit Models

When starting an apparel business, perfecting the fit of your brand is a major piece of the sales puzzle. As your company grows, you will begin to better understand the target market's average body shape and size. Typically, a designer can reference an ideal brand or competitor and purchase a similar style to help the pattern maker and tech pack designer understand your fit standards. Understand your sample size body measurements, and find a model that would best reflect a typical target customer.

In addition to gauging your fit with other brands, hiring a fit model is a must. A fit model is a live model used to check how a garment fits. Beyond merely wearing the garment for inspection, a fit model can serve an integral role in the process, commenting on garments and materials with regards to fit, movement, and how the garment feels on the body. Everyone's body is different, however, an ideal target customer is what you aim to find in a fit model. Ensure the fit model is an average age and height within your target market, in addition to his/her build and body shape.

Cutting the cost for a fit model is a bad idea. Trying on your own products will not allow you to critique your product. Body forms or mannequins cannot replace a fit model. They do not move, are not able to zip up jackets or put their hands in pockets. They cannot tell you how the garment feels, moves, or if the neck is too tight.

Before you start the tech pack, it's helpful for the technical designer to have all the measurements of the fit model. The pattern maker will also need these measurements to help gauge the fit. Fit (body) measurements are not the same as your clothing specs, but knowing how the body measures underneath your designs will give you a better idea of your clothing measurement. A size chart will reflect body measurements, whereas the measurements on the tech pack will reflect a garment's measurement. Keep in mind that not all size six garments fit the same way. Understanding your brand's definition of that size is important to your brand identity as well.

The Fit Session

The fit session is the main point of evaluation for a garment during the product development process. During the meeting with the pattern maker and possibly the sample sewer, samples will be tried on by the fit model. Issues are recorded in order to make improvements.

Fit Issues: Garment fit is as important (if not more so) as the design itself in terms of the product's wearability and saleability. You will be doing fit sessions with both the prototypes you make locally as well as the counter samples made offshore.

1 Arrange a meeting with the fit model, pattern maker, yourself and, if possible, the sample sewer. If this is not your first meeting, be sure to keep the previous sample version and notes handy.

2 Have the model try on the garment. Ask her/him if there was any problems putting it on or taking it off. Address any issues at this stage.

3 Take a full photograph of the front and back view of the garment.

4 Make a numbered list of all issues regarding fit, design, and/ or construction. Take close up shots of any issues that you can see at a glance.

5 After the session, be sure to send an email regarding all issues to the pattern maker. (Establishing a paper trail is important) You may go through two or three rounds of the aforementioned steps before achieving the perfect sample.

6 Once the final prototype has been approved, you will need to update the tech pack. If the design has changed, for example, a pocket placement, all images on the tech pack will need to be revised, not just the text.

Commenting and Approving Fit

Unfortunately, it's not always possible to correct every issue, but the idea is to make sure the garment is suitable for your customers. You're not only looking at the styling to see if it appeals to them, but also at things like the fit and how it feels when it's worn. If it's supposed to be for work, can you sit down in it comfortably? If it's meant to be for travel is it stretchy? Can you move easily? Is the fabric pulling and creating crease lines? Can the model get in and out of the garment easily? Essentially, you are looking for anything that will either affect the performance of the garment (such as neck openings that are too tight, or seams that are coming apart), or things that will stop your customer from buying it (like movement restriction or discomfort).

Wrinkles can indicate a fit issue. In general, diagonal wrinkles tend to point to areas where a garment does not fit well. If unintended wrinkles appear in the garment, typically this indicates it is too small or too large in the area where the fabric sags or pulls.

Below are a few examples:

Tight bustline: Wrinkles tend to form in the side seams and point to the crown of the bust.

Snug crotch line: Pair of pants is too snug in the hip or rise. Wrinkles will form across the lap or in the back thigh area and point toward the crotch.

Snug Top: Horizontal wrinkles across the back into the armhole reflect too tight a fit.

A savvy pattern maker can identify problems in fit by observing the direction of the wrinkles. These fitting problems can then be corrected while the garment is in the sample stage before it goes into production.

Sometimes these fit sessions go beyond addressing the actual fit. A pocket placement might be off and require design adjustment.

Sourcing Fabric

Selecting a fabric supplier can be, in a word, overwhelming. Most new designer entrepreneurs are unsure of how to navigate their options. Every fabric supplier offers different benefits, from high-speed shipping to different minimum orders. So how do you know which assets are the best fit for your apparel brand? It all depends on the way you manufacture your products.

It's crucial to understand that there are many different types of suppliers. While some suppliers custom-make orders and may take time to get the product into your hands, others offer ready-to-ship stock that will arrive sooner, but with fewer customization options. Let's explore some of the fabric supplier types to get an idea of what's the best fit for your fashion brand!

Fabric Suppliers

Mill: A company that manufactures textiles and other fabric products using raw materials. They do so by spinning, weaving, knitting, and other methods. Some mills have made-to-order fabric options, and typically have high minimums of at least 1000 - 5000 yards.

Converter: A person or firm that purchases unprocessed goods directly from a fabric mill, and then dyes, finishes, prints and/or washes them to create finished fabrics. They generally offer current fashion colors, prints, unique finishes and specialty effects for fabrics. Their minimums are lower than dealing directly with a mill, too.

Jobber: A person or firm that purchases excess finished fabrics from mills and converters (called overruns), leftover goods from manufacturers, and seconds (fabrics with manufacturing flaws). They flip and sell wholesale fabric with lower minimums to new designer entrepreneurs and smaller fashion firms, as well as retail fabric stores. However, keep in mind that most of their fabrics cannot be reordered, so this solution is better for one-offs or for limited edition garment pieces.

Sales rep: An agent that shows and sells fabrics for companies and works directly with manufacturers and other textile customers. If you plan to work with mills overseas, or if you plan to work with several different companies for sourcing your materials, working with a sales rep may make the process faster and more efficient.

Wholesalers: An umbrella term that relates to any secondary fabric sources (meaning anyone who purchases from mills, converters, manufacturers, or jobbers and sells fabrics to smaller manufacturers). Their prices tend to be cheaper than if you go to the stores they sell to, as they up the price to make a profit.

Retail Stores: A store that sells directly to consumers. This is an obvious choice - you get instant access and are able to touch, drape and feel the fabric against your skin. Typically designers need to buy for sampling purposes. But this is never purchased for bulk or to fill large orders - it is not cost efficient, and definitely not your best choice.

When it comes to offshore manufacturing, if the factory works directly with mills and is capable of sourcing it for you, let them do it. In most cases, they purchase the yarn, work with the knitter or weaver, finishing, and dyeing mills to create the fabric. The factory can also handle certification requirements, such as the use of organic yarn.

They take care of it all.

Asking the factory to source for you is convenient but it does require some level of patience. It saves you the headache of running around and handling any defect issues. They will also manage logistics of the material. If anything goes wrong with the fabric, the factory will handle it. Less work on your plate. Another benefit is that, since most factories work directly with the mill, your customized fabric can easily be reproduced. What happens if your wholesale supplier runs out of the fabric stock you want? Well, that can be a big problem if you need to reproduce that style. When you have the factory work directly with the mill you have more control over the material and reproducing it is much easier. Most importantly, the factory has a bigger buying power, allowing them to negotiate better prices for you.

How do you get the factory to source the fabric you need? All you have to do is provide the factory with a fabric cutting to use as your standard. They use the fabric swatch or standard as a guide for sourcing the right fabric. You should prepare a fabric swatch, or at least 10" by 10" size. Keep one piece of fabric for your own reference. The factory analyzes and checks the weight of the swatch in GSM (grams per square metre).This way, they can get an accurate idea of what hand feel you are looking to achieve. Next, the factory sources material options from various mills and suppliers and will send back fabric swatch options for you to approve. Once you receive the fabric, you can select the fabrics you desire and provide comments. At that point, with your feedback, they have a better understanding of how to cost your product. Keep in mind, it is extremely difficult for factories to duplicate an exact match to your fabric standard. Multiple factors, such as different yarn qualities, types of equipment, and chemicals go into processing the fabric and affect the final results of the material.

To create the fabric the factory will work with several mills or suppliers to procure the yarn, have it sent to the weaver/knitter, dyed, washed, and printed if need be, to your specifications. Various washes can be added to produce the hand feel you desire.

Selecting Fabric Color(s)

After you have selected the fabric you will need to determine the fabric color(s). Remember, for lower volume orders, select no more than two colors. In order to dye the fabric, the factory requires a color standard. Collect a fabric in the exact color that is required to be dyed. The color standard must be in the same fiber and structure of fabric selected for production. Cut and provide a minimum of 5" by 5" square of material.

Once a product quote has been agreed upon, the factory will begin counter sampling. During the counter sampling process they will provide color options, called "lab dips." From the lab dip options provided, you will select one for approval to proceed for bulk dyeing.

Pantone is a universal color system, but it's not an exact science. If you are not very picky or care too much about variations in the shade of the fabric, you can provide Pantone numbers. Referencing paper swatches from a Pantone, then trying to match dyed fabric can alter results. Paper chips are also so small that it can be very difficult to visualize what an entire garment would look like. Submitting fabric swatches are more favourable to the factory over Pantone numbers for matching colors and dyeing the fabrics. However, Pantone's numbers are critical to use when matching other components of your design such as artwork for prints, hang tags, packaging, and trims.

Lab dips are created in what looks much like a science lab. To recreate a single Pantone, or color recipe, takes lab technicians over nine hours. It is extremely time-consuming, and only a limited number of lab options can be produced per day. If you submit a Pantone and it does not turn out to your standard, asking the dyer's to remake lab options is both a costly and a challenging process. Be very sure of the color you have selected prior to asking for lab dips. Again, if you are not flexible with shade variation, submit a physical fabric color swatch instead of a Pantone number. Your chances of getting what you want will be much greater.

How To Get A Rough Cost Estimate For Your Product

Now, let's talk numbers. You may want to get a rough idea prior to actually moving forward with creating counter samples.

A factory can only provide a very rough estimate after physically seeing samples. To get this rough estimate, the factory can use a mock purchase order, a line sheet, tech pack, and fabric details. You must supply the weight, structure, and fiber content of the fabric.

How To Get Firm Price (Quote) For Your Product
The Pre- Production Package

There are a few necessary tasks that must be undertaken before working with an offshore factory. To request an official quote, you must put the following package together and submit it to the factory:

1 **Tech pack(s)** with supplemental artwork files for any printing, embroidery, labels, etc.

2 **Fabric swatch(es)** Provide the fabric standard. Mount a 10" by 10" fabric swatch to cardboard. Label the cardboard with the fabric's corresponding date, brand name, and style numbers. Mention all fabric content and any other fabric details. Note any additional quality expectations that the factory needs to have.

3 **Color standard(s)** If the factory is sourcing the fabrics, provide a fabric color standard, so the factory can reference and match the exact shade.

4 **A Line Sheet** Provide a one page visual of all the styles and colorways to accompany the purchase order.

5 **Quality References** Various materials and samples collected from shopping the market, supplemented with the written materials that communicate quality to the factory. Label or mount each reference sample (style number, brand name, date, and any other notes to help the factory address your quality expectations). Make sure to provide a standard for packaging, embellishments, label qualities, and trims. Label and keep one set of each reference sample. Take a high-resolution photo of each reference sample.

6 **Prototype(s)** Mark comments directly on prototypes, using masking tape. Label each sample with date, style number, size, and brand name. If the sample is not exactly as required for production, call out any errors on the sample or measurement expectations that aren't reflected on the sample. For example, "add print here" or "add rolled hem" are instructions that can be marked on the sample with a

label. After labeling each sample, take a high-resolution photo of the front and back of each style.

7 **Pattern(s)** CADS (computer-aided design) should be emailed, and a printed copy of them is always helpful. Be sure to ask the factory what software they use so you can send the right file format. Paper patterns should be sent in the package and a duplicate kept on hand.

8 **A Mock PO** Purchase order, outlining the styles, targets costs, colors, and the quantities for each size. Delivery date and testing requirements should be included.

Request For Quote (R.F.Q)

Combine the aforementioned components into a package that will be sent via courier, and make sure that you keep a copy of all the contents of the package for yourself. Once the factory receives the package, they can start sourcing fabric from the textile and yarn mills. Keep in mind that they are sourcing fabric within your target cost. The larger the budget you give them, the better the quality of the fabric. Provide the factory with your courier account number. In turn, they supply fabric options from which you make a selection. The selected fabric allows the factory to confirm a product quote. It's critical to confirm a fabric for approval as costs vary according to quality. Again, the fabric is the biggest expense to the product cost. The factory provides a quote for all the styles based on the approved fabric. A counter sample is also made in available fabric. Once a counter sample has been approved by you, they're able to confirm a cost. Remember, though, that there is a charge for creating samples, even if they are using the fabric they have in-house.

Purchase Order (PO)

The factory will provide finalized quotes once the counter samples have been made. With an official quote, you can proceed by submitting a purchase order for sampling, production fabric (sales samples), or an actual production order. Your purchase order acts as a legal contract and agreement to purchase materials. Your time frame, sales plan, and budget all play a factor in the purchase order you want to write. The final delivery address must be agreed upon and mentioned in the PO. Production starts once the factory receives the deposit, which is typically 50%, or alternatively once a letter of credit is opened with the bank.

In Part 4, we are going to get you organized! There are numerous details in the pre-production process that need tackling. *Sew* for the next chapter, I've mapped out a handy checklist that will get all of your ducks in a row prior to approaching the manufacturer. Feel free to tweak wherever you need to in order to adapt it to your business.

Buckle up. Things are about to get real - real organized, that is!

NOTES:

1. ASTM D6193-16, Standard Practice for Stitches and Seams, ASTM International, West Conshohocken, PA, 2016, www.astm.org
2. ASTM D6193-16, Standard Practice for Stitches and Seams, ASTM International, West Conshohocken, PA, 2016, www.astm.org

THE ULTIMATE PRE-PRODUCTION APPAREL -MANUFACTURING STEPS AND CHECKLIST

CHAPTER 4

Sew, are you excited to get this party started?

Before you start working with an offshore manufacturer, or even so much as request a quote, you've got a few necessary tasks to undertake. One of them, which you've already started working through, is product development. As we've talked about in previous chapters, you will require a substantial amount of time and a considerable number of people to build a new design that will produce optimal success. If you really want to work effectively with a manufacturer, you need to get all your ducks in a row. The goal is giving them everything that they need so they will have little to no questions of what it is you want. Leave no stone unturned.

To help you with the stone-turning part, I've created the Ultimate Pre-Production Apparel Manufacturing Steps and Checklist. This is it: every task that you need to have done in advance so that you can actually get started with a factory. This is a winning recipe for success, and I've taken care of the prep for you because, well, you're awesome and I want you to win!

Your checklist is divided into three main phases, each of which contains smaller tasks for you to complete, in order, from the conception of your idea to submitting your completed pre-production materials to the factory right before starting your overseas manufacturing.

Here is the summary:

PHASE 1: CONCEPTION

- ❑ Research and Analyze the Market
- ❑ Shop the Market
- ❑ Select Fabric
- ❑ Color Standard(s)
- ❑ Initial Sketches
- ❑ Mood Board & Vision Board
- ❑ Legal Compliance
- ❑ Target Costs
- ❑ Mock Purchase Order (PO)

PHASE 2: TECH PACK, PROTOTYPE CREATION AND TESTING

- ❑ Courier Account
- ❑ Artwork Sketches
- ❑ Technical Packages
- ❑ Pattern(s)
- ❑ Purchase Sampling Materials
- ❑ Prototype
- ❑ Fit Session
- ❑ Update Teck Pack
- ❑ Line Sheet
- ❑ Update Mock PO

PHASE 3: FINAL FACTORY PACKAGE

- ❑ Preliminary Estimate
- ❑ Request for Quote
- ❑ Courier

Phase 1 - **Conception**

❑ **Research & Analyze The Market**

Find your niche. Discover products people will pay a premium for. Research target audience and competitors, collect statistics and read trade publications, engage in trend forecasting, and more.

❑ **Shop The Market**

Physical examples are king. Gather and purchase several samples for inspiration and referencing styles. Aesthetic and quality details can get lost in written translation. The samples supplement the written material to help communicate quality standards. The more references you can provide to the factory and all the people in product development, the stronger your outcomes will be. Some quality references to look out for are:

- > Features/functions
- > Stitching/construction details

- Trims and embellishments (prints,embroideries, beading etc.)
- ackaging Fabric & colors
- Hang tags
- Labels
- Fit Samples
- Anything else that inspires you to create

If the fit is a crucial element of the design, find a brand that has a similar fit and style that you want to achieve and purchase it. The store-bought sample will help guide the technical designer and pattern maker with reference measurements. The purchased sample should be a size medium.

Shopping the market will help you design a better product. Shop a variety of retail outlets: online, vintage/used, chains, local boutiques, and cross-border stores. The sample purchases help communicate your quality standards to whoever is involved in helping you build and produce your design.

❑ **Select Fabric**

Determine the type of fabric your product is made of. Find a perfect piece of fabric for your product, and one that meets your target market's standards.

Keep a large cutting as a backup for yourself and supply a 10x10-inch piece of fabric to the factory. The material you provide should reference weight, hand feel, structure, and fiber content. The factory will analyze the fabric cutting and source similar options for you to select from, for bulk production. A similar, available fabric will also be used to create the counter sample.

Take the time to understand the recipe of your fabric. What are the composition and properties such as content, weight, structure, construction type and count/gauge? Is the fabric structure a knit, woven, or non-woven? The structure will help determine a suitable factory and what machinery is required.

❏ **Color Standard**

Determine the exact color(s) you want the fabric to be dyed. Next, collect a color standard in the same material you want for production. Cut a minimum of 5x5-inches of material, for the factory to match or reference. Alternatively, you can provide a Pantone number. Remember that referencing the paper Pantone and achieving exact matches to a dyed fabric can cause shade variation.

❏ **Initial Sketches**

Put pen to paper. Draw a rough, flat sketch - front and back view of all your style(s), calling out as much detail on trims, label placements, measurements, stitching, and other items as possible. The technical designer uses this sketch as a guide. If the design has a print, gather artwork samples or drawings to guide the graphic designer.

❑ **Mood Board & Vision Board**

Hash out your ideas in a visual plan. Create a vision board for your company and mood board for your designs, to help create a cohesive plan.

❑ **Legal Compliance**

Research mandatory labeling laws, product testing requirements, record keeping and marketing issues that apply to your specific product category and design(s). If you are selling products in both the U.S.A and Canada, as well as other countries, ensure that you adhere to all applicable laws.

Below are some excellent places to start:

1 **Product Labels:** Register for a manufacturer's identification number RN# (U.S. residents) or CA# (Canadian residents). Research and ensure you adhere to labeling laws pertaining to your product.

2 **Testing & Record Keeping:** Research testing certification requirements for importing your products. Some product categories require tracking labels.

3 **Intellectual Property:** If you're using any logos or artwork that is not yours, seek permission from the organization and follow any guidelines for the use of the artwork.

4 **Business Registration:** Register your business and obtain all required licenses and permits.

❑ **Target Costs**

Determine the retail prices of each style. Knowing your retail costs will help you establish your target costs. You determine what you want to pay for your product, and the factory works around those numbers. (a more complicated style divide by 2.5)

Retail cost / (2 or 2.5) to get wholesale cost/ 2= target cost
Eg. Technical Jacket
Retails at $400
Wholesale Price $160
Target Cost: $80

The less you spend on the product, the lower the quality, especially when ordering smaller quantities. Knowing your target costs will help you determine and work within your total order budget. Please note target costs vary depending on many variables, this formula can be used as a starting point.

❑ **Mock Purchase Order (PO)**

A mock PO helps determine the budget for the production. Create a mock purchase order, which identifies the colors and styles. Estimate how many pieces you want to order of each size. Input your target cost—give yourself some buffer—and total your quantities. You will quickly find out how much you will need to budget for.

》 BEST PRACTICE

Ensure you are meeting the minimum order quantity (MOQ). Average minimums are 1,000 pieces in one color and can be broken into four styles.

Phase 2 - **Tech Pack, Prototype Creation and Testing**

❑ **Courier Account**

Set up a courier account with FedEx, DHL Express, TNT Express, or another reputable courier company. This process may take time, so start this process now so you can negotiate the best prices.

❑ Artwork Sketches

Collaborate with a graphic designer to create artwork—including logos, hang tags, packaging, prints, and embellishments—using computer-aided design (CAD) software. The graphics files are given to the technical designer to create production-ready artwork.

» BEST PRACTICE

Ensure production artwork calls out dimensions, size, placement, Pantone colors, the quality of material/print, and other necessary details.

❑ Technical Packages (The Blueprint & Assembly Instructions)

Find an experienced technical designer to create a technical package for each design. Work with the designer to ensure every detail of the product is covered.

1 Provide your design sketches and fit samples.

2 Provide artwork files, including all details for packaging and labels (care, size, brand, and hang tag).

3 Provide photographs or physical store-bought samples referencing trims, stitching techniques, or product features that should be included in the tech pack. The images help illustrate details that may need clarification. A physical sample is very helpful with measurements.

❑ Pattern(s)

Find a reputable pattern maker with experience working with your type of product. The pattern maker should be proficient in computer-aided design and sewing, regardless if they are stitching the actual garment.

1 Provide the tech pack to the pattern maker. Work with him or her to create a first pattern. If necessary changes need to be made after analyzing the first prototype, create a second pattern.

2 Print one copy of the final pattern using CAD software, or keep two copies if you are producing a manual pattern.

☐ Purchase Sampling Materials

1. Ask the pattern maker how much fabric you need to create the samples. Buy enough fabric to make the prototypes. The fabric must closely resemble the weight, structure, and fiber of the fabrics you've selected for bulk production. Also, purchase all trims and accessories, as close to your quality standard as possible.

☐ Prototype

Find a skilled sample sewer with the appropriate machinery to stitch the garment. The pattern maker may be able to refer you to a sample sewer that he/she has worked with.

1 Give the pattern, fabric, accessories, and trims to the sample maker, who will stitch the samples from the pattern.

2 The sample sewer will sew a first rough, quick sample to check for fit. A pattern and sample may go through at least two revisions before an almost perfect fit is achieved. Work with both the sample sewer and pattern maker, and take any advice in improving the design for production.

3 Create two final samples with all the proper finishing details. The factory uses one prototype sample as a guide to produce a counter sample. The other sample is kept for you to reference.

❏ **Fit Session**

Find a person that is an ideal size or shape of your brand and target market. That is your fit model. A fit model is a person who is used as a live mannequin to check the fit, drape, functionality and visual appearance of a prototype.

1 After the garment is sewn, have the model wear the garment and inspect for any issues. Document the problems.

❏ **Update Tech Pack**

1 Finalize all measurements with the pattern maker and update the tech pack accordingly.

2 Ensure that every detail of the design, from pocket placement to thread color, matches the tech pack.

❑ **Line Sheet**

Create a single line sheet that showcases all the styles (technical flats), style numbers, and colorways. If possible, showcase each style in every colorway. Specify the size range, fabric detail, and brand name. The line sheet is a single "snapshot" of your purchase order.

» BEST PRACTICE

Working through the design, product development, and costing process might mean having to remove, add, or alter designs. Feedback from consumers may also affect final outcomes.

❑ **Update Mock PO**

Finalize the mock purchase order, making changes to style numbers, colors, target costs, sizes, and quantities if necessary.

Phase 3 - **Final Factory Package**

By this point, you should have the following just about ready to ship:

❑ 1. **Tech pack(s)**
❑ 2. **Fabric swatch(es)**
❑ 3. **Color standard(s)**
❑ 4. **A Line Sheet**
❑ 5. **Sample references for quality standards**
❑ 6. **Prototype(s)**
❑ 7. **Pattern(s)**
❑ 8. **Mock PO**

If you are missing anything from this list, go back and make sure you have it physically ready before continuing.

❑ **Preliminary Estimate**

Send the factory an email with the following information: a mock purchase order, the line sheet, and the tech pack(s). The tech pack(s) must convey weight, structure, and fiber content fabric details.

❑ **Requesting A Quote**

To get an accurate quote, the factory must see a physical sample - most importantly the fabric swatch.

The following information is required in order to receive an actual quote.

Put together the following pre-production package:

❑ **Prepare Prototype Sample(s)**

1 Quality or measurement expectations in production that are not reflected on the prototype sample must be stated directly on it. Using masking tape or sticky labels, call out any differences that should or should not appear on any production sample. For example, "add print here" or "add rolled hem" are instructions that can be marked on the sample with a label.

2 Label all prototypes with style number, date, size, and brand.

3 After labeling each sample, take a high-resolution photo of the front and back of each style. Remember to keep one sample aside for yourself.

❑ **Print the line sheet, mock PO and tech pack(s)**

Print two copies: one set for you and one set for the factory.

❑ **Trims, Labels, Packaging**

1 Label or mount each reference sample with the style number, brand name, date, and any other notes to help the factory address your quality expectations.

2   Keep a sample of each reference for yourself.

3   Take a high-resolution photo of each reference sample.

❑ **Fabric**

The factory analyzes your fabric swatch and works with the textile and yarn mills to find a close match to your standard. It is challenging to achieve exact fabrications due to the many variables such as the quality of machinery, quality of fibers, finishes, dyes, among other things. The factory will send fabric options for you to select. If you are confident about your decision, you can proceed with sending the sample.

1   Staple a 10x10-inch fabric swatch of the fabric(s) that you have selected to cardboard. Label the cardboard with the date, brand name and the style number(s) the material corresponds with. Any additional quality expectations should also be noted.

2   If you are providing a fabric for color reference, mount a 5x5 fabric swatch (in the same fiber) to cardboard. Label the cardboard with the color name, date, brand and the style number(s) the fabric corresponds with.

3   Keep a sample of each reference for yourself.

4   Take a high-resolution photo of each reference sample.

❑ **Courier: Assembling The Package**

1   Combine the components mentioned above into a package that you will send via courier. If your pattern maker is not creating the patterns using CAD software, you can send a paper copy.

2   Ensure that you keep one copy of all the contents of the package for yourself.

» BEST PRACTICE

When filling out the commercial invoice, state that the products are samples with no commercial value. Value of samples should be one dollar each.

All right! It took a while to get here, but all the work you've put into creating a great sample will only help ease the process of having the factory re-create the prototype for the manufacturing process.

In Part 5, we will finally get to work with an overseas manufacturing partner. Let's get this party started!

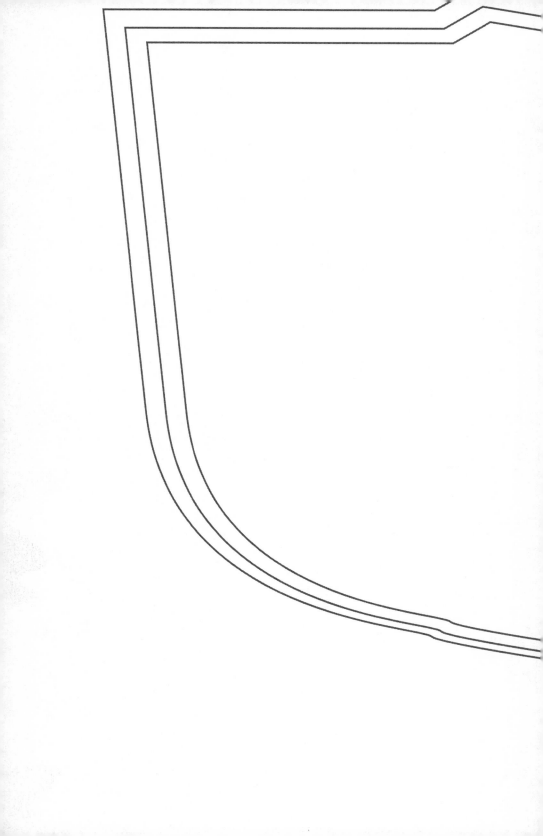

CHAPTER 5

COUNTER SAMPLING COMMENTS & APPROVALS

OVERVIEW

The idea of counter sampling may seem intimidating, but think about it this way: you've made it to this point, embracing and overcoming every challenge along the way so far. This is just another mountain that will bring you closer to the end of your journey, and if I can do it, so can you! What was that thing our friend Miley Cyrus said? "It's the climb."

Counter sampling is arguably the most time-consuming and challenging part of production. The sample approval process contains necessary steps to ensure that everything meets your expectations, and that there are no surprises for either you or the factory. (Especially in offshore manufacturing - no one likes surprises, the factory in particular.)

The process certifies that the factory understands and will adhere to the specifications established for a particular product. For the factory, the challenge will always be two-fold: staying true to the initial design and being able to deliver your prototype into something scalable (that is, manufactured in higher quantities), while meeting your target costs. This is all worked through in sample approvals.

Bulk production is the very last stage, during which the product is manufactured to the actual order requirements. Before starting bulk production, the factory requires approvals and comments from you on samples at various stages in product development to ensure that everything is to your liking. Various sampling stages may include the counter sample, sales samples, and the pre-production (PP) sample.

Every sample you receive is checked for fit, construction, and quality. Approvals on the components will accompany the actual garment. These may include print strike-offs, lab dips, fabric quality, embroidery, trims, embellishments, and so on. Only when working through the approval and commenting process, can a factory begin to learn your brand's standard for quality. Every brand has its own unique tolerances and quality standards, which can only be truly understood over time, working through orders.

Any delay in a sample approval, on either the factory or designer end, pushes your delivery date further out. For this reason, it is critical that you take no more than 24 hours to give comments or approvals. Beyond establishing approvals for production and quality, the factory is working through counter sampling to determine costs.

We know that fabric is the most significant cost in production, so consumption must be treated with great care. Fabric cost is subject to many variables, and sampling allows the factory to estimate the cost before processing the order. Fabric efficiencies can be analyzed according to different size combinations and shrinkage standards established by the designer and the type of fabric.

By providing them with a mock purchase order, you help the factory get estimates from outsourced suppliers such as tags, trims, thread and so on. This will require the factory to produce a bill of materials (BOM). From the itemized list, they typically contact a few suppliers for each component to establish estimates. This can take time, as they are likely relying on many suppliers to get back to them.

The sampling department sews a sample to figure out time efficiencies. They will also assess what machinery and equipment may need to be outsourced. Different fabrics require different machine settings, and all may need to be adjusted according to every sample and manufacturing run. It is critical that the factory understands every design made as a sample and how it is manufactured to scale.

As designers, we have a vision, a desire to see our magic manifested. For most of you who pretty much consider yourselves control freaks (you know who you are), I bet there is a desire to want to watch and see the sewers in a factory make each piece precisely as you envisioned. Everything from the idea, to the sampling, to the production is part of an entire process to which everyone contributes. There is no such thing as perfect. The ideas that you start with and how it will end up will never be the same.

Heads up! As you work through product sampling comments and approvals, please keep the following in mind: What you need to do is focus on the idea of a product being saleable, not this "perfect" thing that you can picture in your mind's eye. Your comments are not about samples being right or wrong. There is likely a very good reason why a sample has come back "different" from what you envisioned.

A good rule of thumb is this: when samples come back to you, only ask for a revision if you believe the product will not sell. That's it. The magic word when doing approvals is "saleable." Sampling is not about achieving a perfect sample that you envision - it's about creating a sample that will sell. Too many designers get super attached to their vision and then ask for revisions for needless reasons; often for things like shade variations or changing a stitch technique that has zero impact on saleability. Rejecting a sample because it's not "perfect" will cause delays and possibly more issues. Letting go of control will help you as you move through this process. Always look at the big picture.

✽ GOLDEN NUGGET

Offering different prints on a single style is an easy way to offer another SKU. For example, two identical black short-sleeved shirts (body) with two different prints are considered two different styles. Keeping bodies and styles the same while offering different prints is an easy way to offer more product choices to your customer. At the same time, the production process is easier to handle and faster to process.

Your Go-To Person: **The Merchandiser**

Meet your new BFF! Your main point of contact through this phase of the process will be your factory merchandiser. It's their job to coordinate and carry out your order as instructed. In a typical factory, merchandisers have several roles in product development. They work with all departments within the factory: accounting, logistics, sampling, production, materials sourcing, CAD (computer-aided design) department, and all the suppliers in the supply chain. Merchandisers manage sampling as well as production orders. Their role mostly covers the following responsibilities, but is not limited to what is mentioned below.

RESPONSIBILITIES OF A MERCHANDISER

1 Prepare the materials requirement sheet and source all fabric from local and imported suppliers.

2 Manage logistics for all components and materials to the factory.

3 Oversee quality standards of sourced material and trims.

4 Arrange approvals of lab dips, trims, packaging, labels, and samples.

5 Work with suppliers on value-added processes like printing and embroidery that are outsourced.

6 Prepare the time-and-action calendar (refer back to Chapter 1).

7 Communicate with sampling and CAD department about the design and order requirements mentioned in the tech pack(s).

8 Communicate with all suppliers and departments, including accounting.

9 Approve each stage of sampling development and communicate designer comments to sampling team and pattern maker if there are any pattern changes.

10 Check finished sample and arrange to send the samples to the buyer.

11 Prepare quotes and costs of developed products, prepares bill of materials.

12 Schedule and execute meetings and activities.

13 Responsible for inspections

14 Manage logistics and shipping wherever required.

The below diagram illustrates the steps and the entire process that a merchandiser of a full package manufacturer will manage:

Photo | *Steps in the manufacturing process*

STEPS IN THE MANUFACTURING PROCESS

Sampling Process

The Pre-Production Meeting

Once the factory receives the pre-production package (which includes the fabric standard, tech pack, prototype, line sheet, reference samples and mock purchase order), the sampling department holds a meeting to review the package. Typically, the general manager, merchandiser, sampling manager, materials manager, production and CAD manager are present. Together, they examine the pre-production package and discuss the program.

Below are some key areas that they address in the meeting:

> Reviewing the bill of materials (BOM) and requirements.
> Examining the package to understand the fabric details, accessories, styling and garment construction requirements.
> Examining all garment details for process requirements, like printing or embroidery and if they are needed before or after stitching.
> Checking the tech packs and comparing and/or matching them with the prototype sample for possible questions on points of measurement, etc. The pattern maker's method of measuring specific specs can vary from person to person.
> Specifying sewing threads (thickness and variation).
> Examining the garment to identify operation sequences, noting if any of the operations can be started simultaneously. They access all seam types and stitch classes, and accordingly think about machine requirements or attachments. They note sewing operations that look difficult and may need extra attention for quality stitching.
> Identifying finishing processes.
> Identifying any testing or certification requirements noted on the tech pack.
> Identifying machinery requirements.
> Reviewing target costs.

Sampling involves a great deal of coordination amongst many people. Every department is responsible for its part in processing the order. The merchandiser ensures that all his/her responsibilities are carried out. For example, the materials department orders all trims based on the reference samples and tech packs that they are given. The sampling department arranges the sampling fabric and waits to receive trims to make the counter sample. They also create a plan for machinery and manpower requirements before carrying out the sampling program. If there are issues with the pattern, the CAD department gets involved. Everyone has their own tasks, but still works closely together.

Fabric Approval

Next up? The fabric department sources fabric based on a budget that you provide with your target costs. Using the fabric sample supplied as the reference, the fabric weight is verified. In some cases, the fabric standard may need to be sent to a testing lab to test fabric properties, fiber content, and so on.

Remember: giving the factory higher target costs will allow them to provide better quality and help improve service from suppliers. Cutting costs on production usually isn't the best strategy.

Next, fabric options and trims, including other component options, are sent to you via courier for approval. The factory cannot provide you an official quote without selecting and approving a fabric option. That's why it's a good idea to confirm all the approved fabric details, including weight, with the factory so they can update all of the tech packs. Are you happy with your design requirements? Hopefully so, because any significant changes during sampling can alter costs.

Purchase orders can be placed for sales samples, counter samples, or bulk production. Samples are not free; there is a cost for all samples that are produced. **Counter samples** are the first to be made, using available fabric to help establish costs and verify sewing capabilities. **Sales samples** are like a mini production run: the fabric is manufactured and dyed for sales samples. When you write a purchase order, you should receive **pre-production samples** in the exact fabric order before production starts. The pre-production sample costs are incorporated into the bulk production orders.

Counter Samples

The counter sample is made by the factory in an available fabric. Using your prototype, reference samples and tech pack as guides, the factory works on a first sample to get sewing efficiencies, understand machinery requirements, and calculate an accurate cost. Sampling charges are billed separately, and prices vary according to design complexity. Two samples of each style should be made, with the factory keeping one for reference.

Along with the counter sample, options for fabric, tags, lab dips, packaging, print approvals (more commonly known as "strike-offs"), trims and accessories are provided for your approval. Color options submitted by the dyers are called "lab dips." Because the factory is working with many suppliers, this will take time.

The counter sample should be made in a fabric similar to the weight, content, and structure as the fabric standard you provided in order to ensure proper fit for production. Samples created in different weights or structures affect fit and may not establish correct machinery settings for the factory to follow. As mentioned in previous chapters, samples should never be made in black fabric, as it is difficult to detect flaws. If a black fabric is required for production, it's still a good idea to check in a different color.

Counter samples may likely go through a couple of revisions before a final sample is approved for production. It takes an average of six to ten weeks to work through revisions and finalize a counter sample ready for production. Every change or revision request may take the factory two to three weeks to re-submit a sample for approval (setting back your delivery date - if you've placed the order already). Remember, the transit time for a courier can take three to five days, with an additional day to respond to the resubmission. It's critical that you take no longer than *48 hours* to make your comments to the factory, or it will further delay your order.

Being flexible and tolerant with approvals is the key to saving both time and money. A factory may be submitting a sample in a certain way to help them move through production easier. Keep in mind that every revised sample is also an additional courier charge. Ask yourself if the revision is really required, or if perhaps a photo approval would suffice. No more than two rounds of sample revision requests should be ordered. It's important to be flexible and work within the factory's capabilities.

>> BEST PRACTICE

If the factory cannot achieve a counter sample close to your standards, after two revisions, drop the style. Increase the order quantity in another style to maintain the total target budget given to the factory.

Counter Sampling Challenges

Let's talk about commitment for a moment... Too personal? Don't worry. This conversation won't have anything to do with our exes, our current partners or really any of our relationships that are no one else's business but our own.

However, production commitment is our business (or, at least, a huge part of it). Sampling with a factory involves a production commitment; that is, the intention to order. Several factories and suppliers are involved in the development process, and it's a massive loss to them if an order is not placed after samples have been produced. For a single t-shirt, quotes can come from several subcontractors, including but not limited to: labels, hang tags, packaging, screen printers, trim suppliers, yarn, washer, dyeing, weaving/knitting mills, and ultimately the logistics of materials being delivered to the factory. Developing samples takes a considerable amount of time, resources and labor.

As I'm sure you're starting to see by now, sampling is hugely time-consuming and costly. Once you've gone through a round of prototyping, you will truly appreciate the amount of effort that goes into creating a new style. Counter sampling is no different for the factory. Just like you, the factory is working with many partners to orchestrate the whole re-creation of the product. When working with partners, they are at the mercy of the person that they are waiting on. Quite often, suppliers are located in a different country. Even dyed to match(DTM) zippers take anywhere from 30 to 45 days to receive in-house. Typically, delays are not their fault.

Things go wrong with your counter samples. I get it. Every time you ask for a revision, it costs the factory time and money. Not only are the sewing and CAD departments involved, the factory sources from multiple contractors to provide you with options for trims, screen prints, lab dips and more, also come into play. Coordinating with subcontractors can be challenging, especially for lower volume orders. Most suppliers are so busy they don't care to provide samples for approvals. Remember that couriers and component samples also cost the factory moola.

Pre-Production (PP) Samples:

The factory prepares a PP sample once the fabric is procured and in-house. The PP sample is made from the production fabric. Depending on what other orders or programs are running in the factory, the PP samples are generally ready to deliver 30 days before the complete order is ready to ship from the factory.

For every order placed, a pre-production sample is given in the procured fabric, trims, labels, etc. before manufacturing in bulk. The PP sample is what the total product will look like when being processed in bulk production and used as a guide. Production commences with the approval of the PP sample. The entire PP sample must be checked for any discrepancies against the tech pack and the approved counter sample.

» CRITICAL BEST PRACTICE

Because the PP sample is made in the actual production fabric trims, embellishments and so on, you must wash the product at home. Check to ensure everything is intact and washed as directed on the care label. Be careful to wash as the label instructs, or it will affect the outcome. For best results, most fabric products should be labeled and washed in cold water on a low heat setting.

Sales Samples

Sales samples are samples made in the exact approved fabric and colors, using all trims and labels approved for production. Costs for sales samples are typically very high and billed separately. The yarn must be purchased, made and dyed, and washed no differently than a bulk order. The turnaround time to create these samples is almost as fast as the time it takes to manufacture a bulk order. Ordering a sales sample is like doing a mini production run. If you place an order for sales samples without a purchase order, it will push the delivery date further out. Make sure you plan accordingly.

When Should I Place Purchase Orders and Sample Orders?

Ready to rock and roll? The best way to ensure that the factory meets your quality and sewing standards is to place a counter sample(s) order before you go ahead with production. The first sample was meant to get a rough estimate and is likely not ready to go to production. You will also have to finalize a firmer cost and improve the sample, as there will likely be changes during the counter sample process.

Since you know that you will receive PP samples, you can use them as your sales samples. They can be sent out the same time that PP samples are sent out, approximately 30 days before bulk production is ready to ship from factories. You can order a sample of each color, in each style, which can be used for photo shoots. Typically, the factory will only send one PP sample in each style for approval before they start cutting; however, it is likely that if you offer other colors, you may want to photograph each product before delivery. Placing sample orders with PP orders will help save the factory time, which means you save on sampling costs.

Alternatively, if you've worked with the factory in the past, you can place bulk purchase orders once a quote is given (based on your approved fabric) to save time. This is only suggested if you have manufactured similar styles with the same factory. While you work through counter sampling approvals, the material will be produced, saving you some time. The factory can provide an estimated delivery date when the goods will be ready to ship at the time you place the order. Keep in mind: working through sampling revisions can affect delivery dates.

After the factory receives a deposit and a PO, fabric production begins, and components are ordered. Typically, the factory purchases the yarn and has it sent to the mill for knitting and weaving, and then sent to the dyeing plant. After the counter sample is approved and the fabric and components are delivered to the factory, the PP sample(s) can be made. This sample is made with actual production fabric, trims, and accessories, and is stitched by sewing line tailors. Production only commences once the PP sample is approved.

>> BEST PRACTICE

Remember to get the time and action calendar from the factory, so you can stay on top of key dates in the process to ensure that production remains on schedule.

❊ GOLDEN NUGGET

Counter sample approved? Check. Once you're ready to place a bulk production order (PO), a sales sample order can be placed at the same time as the bulk order.

The Art of Communication

Communication is everything. Don't think so? Consider the following scenario (which may or may not have actually happened, and I'm not naming names in either case):

There was once a factory that was working with a new designer. The merchandiser had a question about how the garments were measured for each size. It seems the fields were left blank on the tech pack, so he emailed the designer the following: "Any chance you could provide the grading for each style?"

He received back an email from the designer: "Here you go! I'm pretty sure the styles will sell – 90% of the feedback I got was Grade A!" Attached to the email was the research that the designer had collected from both the questionnaires and the focus groups.

The merchandiser, after showing the email to his colleagues and having a good laugh, responded, "That's wonderful! However, I was talking about the measurements for each of the sizes."

Within an hour, the designer replied with, "Oh! Why didn't you just ask for that in the first place?"

It seems the designer in question did not use that particular abbreviation in his own work. It just goes to show that even when you speak the same language, things can get lost in translation (especially where jargon is involved). I'm sure you don't want to end up like that guy! Sew, make sure you take a look at the glossary so you can quickly get up to speed with industry terminology.

No matter the relationship, be it personal or professional, communication is the key to success. Like many other designers, including industry professionals, "getting things right" is an ongoing challenge. If you are manufacturing offshore, communication is even more challenging, as are time differences and language barriers, and most designers have not met the merchandiser in person. The loss of one or two senses certainly can further impair communication.

It may be hard to believe, but the merchandiser and the team both feel equally frustrated. The emails given to the factory are like playing the game 'Telephone.' The message may get passed from one person and possibly a chain of people. At the same time, merchandisers are dealing with several clients who also have deadlines. Their job is no easy task.

Clarity and simplicity are vital to good communication. Below are some guidelines to think about when sending emails.

9 Tips For Effective Email Writing

1 Do not use any slang, abbreviations or figures of speech.

2 Use simple words and grammar. (Grade 7 English level)

3 Keep subject headings clear, and change them if it's a chain so you can search through emails quickly.

4 For every point or task request, separate paragraphs with numbered points.

5 Use bulleted lists or numbers wherever possible.

6 Use spacing in emails wherever necessary to make them easy to read.

7 Always ask the person you are dealing with to "confirm by return and confirm understanding." Microsoft also has a confirmation for receipt button. They should reply directly to each point (highlighted in another color) and reconfirm that they understand. When you respond, you can also do the same.

8 Have someone else who is not involved in the conversation read it over. If that person understands the email, it's likely the recipient will too.

9 Read over the email three times. Think about your messages before you press send. Wait at least 15 minutes. The worst thing you can do is send several follow up emails because something was forgotten.

This may seem obvious, but above all, be polite and assertive. I've heard first-hand accounts of many instances where people don't speak to factory liaisons with respect and react out of stress and lack of understanding. Even an email matters. If communicating via email becomes an issue, consider a video conference via Skype.

The Sample Approval Process

YES! The first package from the factory has arrived! Upon receipt, you have 48 hours to make comments, approvals, and address any issues. The comments should be made by you, along with a fit model and pattern maker. You got this. If you require advice from the pattern makers or sample sewer during counter sampling be sure to make arrangements before or during prototyping.

Below is a guide to help ensure you conduct a thorough sample review and help get your comments across. On average, expect to spend three hours on each style. Yes, three hours, folks! Compare your prototype, sample references and tech pack with the counter sample and approvals you receive.

Sew, let the fun begin! Below is a guide to follow when going through sample approvals.

1 Hopefully, you have kept a duplicate of the prototype and everything that was sent to the factory. The first thing you should do is gather the original prototype and reference samples sent to the factory.
2 Grab a plastic measuring tape, masking tape, notepad and permanent pen.
3 Make a list of everything that is in the package. Make a note of anything that might be missing. The last thing you need is to realize you lost something and have no recollection of it. (Trims, embellishments, lab dips, etc. may also be in the package for approval-procedures below.)
4 Insert a date in the document.
5 Take a picture or everything the factory sent. Take a full shot of both front and back sides.
6 Counter Samples: Inspect both the front and the back of the garment and the inside and outside. Remember to ensure that the fabric is in a similar structure, construction, and weight as

the one you approved for production. Initial observations can be made flat on a table.

7   Not all products are made for the body, such as home furnishings, for example. However, you will require a fit model for garments. Make sure comments are made while a garment is on a fit model.

>> BEST PRACTICE

Design changes should only be reserved for prototyping. You should be very clear on your design before you start sampling. Making design changes can cause significant problems for the factory. The purpose of counter sampling is to prepare the design for production, not work through design.

Stitching, Workmanship and Construction Issues

Group all the comments regarding workmanship and stitching and make a point form list of any and all issues. Photograph each issue to help further illustrate what you are saying. Are the seams sewn as per the spec or tech pack? Is the sample sewn with the correct thread tension or thread quality?

Make sure to photograph all of the issues. After the images are uploaded to the computer, use editing software such as Microsoft Paint to add comments and use arrows to point to the issues or to show measurements. Taking photos of the garment with measurement tape can also be very helpful in conveying measurement issues. To ensure they understand what product you are commenting on, add the style number directly on each image.

Try to use industry terminology for seam classifications. If you are unsure of the correct industry terminology, use/find a photograph of the right seam and supply the image to the factory.

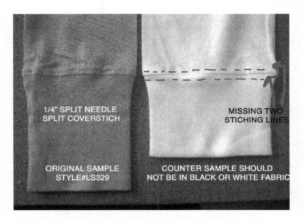

Photo: *Example making fit comments on a photograph*

Quality Issues

Quality standards and workmanship, such as loose threads or pressing, are tough to convey with words. Quality issues should be photographed.

When Your Sample Just Isn't Right...

As mentioned earlier, the factory may make minor changes on the sample to help move through production easier. For example, the machine settings for hems are set at 1", but your tech pack and sample requested 1.5". Try to be flexible. If approved, ensure the tech pack is updated, so the information matches the counter sample.

"IMPERFECTION IS FINE"

- ANNA WINTOUR

Checking Measurements Against The Tech Pack

After inspecting the counter sample, review the measurements against the tech pack. Make a note of any measurement discrepancies from the counter sample to what is written on the tech pack. Allow some tolerance for slight variations, as sewing garments is a manual process and measurements can vary slightly. Make a point form list of any discrepancies and circle the spot on the tech pack that will need updating at a later point.

» BEST PRACTICE

Ask your pattern maker for guidance on measuring. It's critical that you are conveying how each point is measured on the tech pack. Measurement instructions must be stated, so the factory and everyone involved with the production are on the same page. Point of measure (POM) illustrations on the tech pack are an additional guide. Refer back to Part 3 on guidelines for measuring samples.

Photo | *Measurement chart and a POM illustration within a tech pack*

	POINT OF MEASUREMENT	XS	S	M	L	XL	TOLERANCE + / −
1	Waist band rib height	2					1/4
2	Distance between button/eyeless holes (for draw cord)	3					1/4
3	Waist Circ-nce (rgt at top of rib waist band)	13					1/2
4	1/2 Hip Circ-nce – 6" down from waist band	18 3/4					1/2
5	Outseam excl. waist band and cuff from gusset seam	32 3/4					1/2
6	Inseam excl. waist band and cuff from gusset seam	19 1/2					1/2
7	Front rise – from gusset seam excl. waist band	7 3/8					1/4
8	Back rise – from gusset seam excl. waist band	12 1/8					1/4
9	1/2 Upp. Leg Circ-nce – measure from side seam to gusset end	9 5/8					1/4
10	Pocket Height	10 1/4					1/4
11	Pocket Width – at widest point	6					1/4
12	Pocket Opening	7 1/8					1/8
13	Cuff width – at folded edge of rib	4 1/2					1/4
14	Cuff rib height	3					1/4
15	Length of exposed draw cord relaxed	20					1/4
16	Width of the gusset at the widest part	12					1/4
17	Height of the gusset	4					1/4
18	Width of the turned over hem at the pocket opening	1/4"					1/8

Waist · Hip · Knee · Ankle

The Fit Session

Fit Issues - Commenting On Counter Samples

As mentioned earlier, garment fit is as important as the design itself, (if not more so), in contributing toward product wearability and saleability.

Make sure to use the same fit model during this stage that you worked with during prototyping. Body forms or mannequins cannot replace a fit model. They do not move and are not able to put their hands in pockets or zip up jackets. They cannot tell you how the garment feels and moves, or if the neck is too tight.

Referring back to Part 3, the fit session is conducted precisely the same here. The only difference is that what happens during the fit session needs to be meticulously documented and communicated in a way that the person on the other end (who reads the comments) is crystal clear on what the issues are. If it's not communicated well, issues will likely not be resolved. Giving clear instructions to the factory is essential, so make sure you're very specific about what you want.

1 Arrange a meeting with the fit model, pattern maker, yourself and, if possible, the sample sewer.

2 Have the model try on the garment. Ask her/him if she had any problems putting it on/taking it off. Address any issues at this stage.

3 Take a full photograph of the front and back view of the garment.

4 Make a numbered list of all the problems regarding fit, design and/or construction. Take close-up shots of any issues that you can see at a glance.

5 Ensure that when you upload the pictures, the style number is referenced with text directly on the image. Use simple language and arrows and measurements to describe issues.

6 Update the tech pack, with any issues you find.

Submitting Comments for a Sample Revision

As mentioned earlier, sample(s) may need to be revised. After you have listed all mandatory issues that need correcting, they should be put into the tech pack on a separate Excel page. Insert the date and point form list the issues, and supplement the issues with the photographs into the comments. Once you've emailed the comments, ask the factory for the send date for the revised sample. On average, it takes two weeks. No more than three revised samples is considered acceptable by the factory, as there is a cost to each sample produced. Taking more than 48 hours to reply with comments can drastically impact production turnaround times. To save time, you can ask the factory to submit a picture that shows the revision for approval.

>> BEST PRACTICE

Review your list of issues. Are the "errors" okay to approve? In other words, if the garment issue does not affect saleability, you should approve. Omit the issue and move on.

Photo | *Designer comments on a counter sample*

Grading: **It's Not Just About Getting the Answer Right**

If you've come this far, you are *sew* deserving of an A+. Your garments are also graded, just not in the same way.

The process of scaling the sample size to the range of sizes is called "grading." Grade rules are the difference in measurements between each point of measure on a garment. After the final counter sample is approved, the pattern maker can grade all other sizes. The tech pack must be updated accordingly. The amounts that are added (or subtracted) from each measurement, as a garment changes from one size to the next, are referred to as "grade rules." Most brands develop a set of grade rules that they routinely apply to the new styles they produce. Grade rules are referred to as the set of measurements that reflect the increments between sizes.

Some measurements on a garment don't require grading. Examples of some non-graded measurements include buttonhole placements, dart lengths, placket width, hems, cuffs, depths and belt loops.

Understand Tolerances (In other Words- Nothing Is Perfect)

The POM diagram above shows the measurement chart on a tech pack. To the far right is a column labeled with "+/-" followed by a small measurement, such as 1/8". This is the tolerance. This means that any given post-production measurement should come within the tolerance (it should be x, give or take y). That also means that one size may have one garment measure at 27-1/8" and another at 27-3/8", and both pass tolerance. An example of this is when you shop at a retail store and try on two pairs of the exact same jeans in the same size – one may fit slightly better than the other. From the fabric(s) to the cutting, sewing, or even pressing, deviations can happen. Although machines are used to make the garments, manufacturing is very much a human-based activity, and numerous factors contribute to creating mass-produced clothing. Deviations are to be expected. A good factory will do everything within its power to limit deviations from each SKU (stock keeping unit), but it is impossible to make everything perfect.

Organizing Development Samples

Sew... I get it, you're excited and things are humming along. You might feel tempted to do what many designers do at this stage and show off your creations to the people in your life. While showing them your sketches and pictures of the designs is fine, whatever you do, please don't give away your prototypes!

Development reference samples and prototypes should not be given to friends or donated to a charity until after production is delivered. The same goes for all samples made by the factory. Often, these samples need to be referenced throughout the development and manufacturing process. Ensure changes are correctly implemented from one sample to the next. Date each sample and keep them organized, and preferably hung up. Keeping all of these items creates a tracking system to ensure edits and changes are made correctly and that what you've signed off on and approved is actually implemented in final production. After the goods are shipped, keep at least one or two of each style to reference for any future reorders.

And rest easy: your friends and family will have plenty of time to enjoy your designs when they hit the retail racks.

Fabric Dying Approval Procedure

After sending the fabric color standard or Pantone number, the factory will supply lab dip options for each color. A **lab dip** is a swatch of fabric test dyed to hit or match a color standard. Lab dips are created with a purpose: to provide a visual guide to how a color will look when it is dyed. Numerous variables, including the light source, dye types, fiber type and fiber quality can all affect the outcome of the dyed fabric. When the goods are dyed in a real production run, the conditions are different from the laboratory, so final production fabric may vary from the approved lab dip. No two dye lots are exactly the same.

First, select and supply a fabric swatch or Pantone color, such as (19-3418 TP) Chinese Violet. Also advise on the light source for the color standard, such as indoor lighting. Light sources such as sunlight, ultraviolet, tube (fluorescent) and indoor lighting all affect how a color is perceived. In return, the factory will provide three to five lab dip options of each color for you to select and approve. The lab dips must be viewed and approved in the same light source that was provided to the factory.

The dyeing lab uses a fabric color matching cabinet machine, also called a **lightbox**, to help evaluate color samples under different light sources. The fabric on which the lab dips are dyed should be dyed on the same fabric content and structure (knit or woven) as for production.

Photo | *Lab dips options*

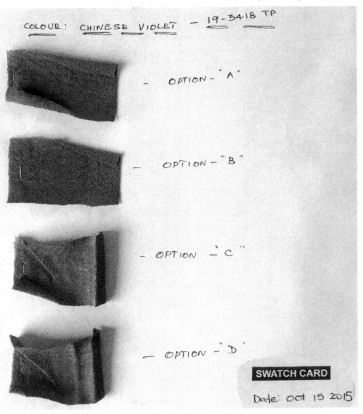

The Dyeing Laboratory

If you're like me, a laboratory (probably filled with bubbling beakers and crazy-haired scientists) isn't the first thing that comes to mind when you think about garment manufacturing. Still, even if the only experience you've ever had with a lab was that awful science class you had to take in high school, it's important to understand the vital role that lab dips play in the manufacturing process.

Creating lab dips is indeed a science, and no easy task. They are produced by engineers or technicians with an extensive background in dyeing. A series of tests and recipes are formulated according to your fabric quality and quantity. A single dye recipe and color option takes a technician, on average, nine hours to produce. The lab dips are made in a sample dyeing machine. Every dyeing mill has a capacity and therefore, only a certain number of lab dips and bulk order dyeing can be processed each day. As such, lab dips can take two to three weeks to complete. Unfortunately, this is one part of the process you can't speed up, as there is almost always a queue of other companies waiting their turn to dye their fabrics.

Dyeing mills contain dyeing vessels. Each vessel is equipped to handle dyeing based on order quantity. Typically, most mills have four to six dyeing vessels of different sizes. The other machines at the mill are used for washing and pre-shrinking fabric. Because only an "X" number of dyeing colors can be done in a day, the process takes a long time. Typically, the dyeing process can take anywhere from 30 to 45 days.

Color Approvals Gone Wild

Consider the following when artwork or lab dips are sent for you to approve:

1 The lighting conditions you are in can affect how the color appears. When submitting a color swatch or Pantone, always state what light source you will be using when approving tones. Under what conditions will you be making an approval? Is the product best judged in the store lighting? Is the light source fluorescent, is it indoors, or is it outdoors? Ensure you use the same light source every time a color approval is made.

2 The fabric is always treated, washed, steamed or pressed. The high temperatures and chemicals affect the color results. Several tests have to be run to try to hit the right color. Achieving a perfect match to a Pantone is a science and can be difficult for the factory.

3 Dyes and inks are absorbed differently into different fibers. It is next to impossible to get one dye lot to match another. Every fiber lot, such as cotton, varies in quality, affecting final dyeing results.

4 The base fabric color can affect how the ink colors appear in print. Accordingly, the ink colors within a print can change

how a base color looks. For example, a fabric dyed off-white can appear white once a pink color print is added.

5   Giving the factory a Pantone based on a paper quality is very different from matching the color to dyed fabric. Paper and fiber are two different qualities and are very difficult to match. Submit a fabric swatch in the same fiber for the factory to match dyeing fabric. Pantone numbers are best for matching inks.

6   Eyesight varies from person to person.

The key takeaway? Color matching is complicated. As with dyeing, it's a science, and numerous variables affect the output. Take the above points into consideration. Be flexible. Is your product going in a museum? Not likely. The main deciding factor in making color approvals is to determine if the product is saleable or not. Is a shade darker or lighter going to affect sales? Having the factory work on several tests, utilizing resources and time to send approvals, not only further delays the shipment – it frustrates the factory.

Or, to paraphrase a song from *Bride and Prejudice*, happy factory, happy life.

Value-Addition Embellishments

While embellishments are not functional they enhance the design, and in turn the desirability and value of your garment or product. They require extreme attention to detail on your part to ensure they are executed in such a way that they meet the expectations you have, stay true to your design, function well for the consumer, have durability, and do not drive up the price too excessively. Embellishment is an artform in itself with endless possibilities that can really set you apart from your competitor. Some of the most popular techniques include printing, embroidery and beading. I'll break down each of these ahead.

Printing Mills

Printing onto fabric is considered a value addition, and is one of the thousands of techniques and qualities on the market. Specific fiber materials and dye types interact with one another in distinct ways, and it is these interactions that determine the best printing method and composition of a printing paste or ink.

The most popular methods include screen, digital, rotary, heat transfer, pigment, discharge, and block printing. Within each technique, there are numerous further techniques and qualities available.

Keep in mind, as I mentioned before, the printing and drying process overseas is always affected by the weather, especially in countries with a monsoon season. Monsoon seasons last from July to September in India. During the rainy season, the high humidity in the air causes longer drying times. Fine lines and details are lost, which can create a blurry effect.

Artwork for all prints must be provided with the accompanying tech packs. The print can be submitted as a vector file, along with a PDF. A professional graphic designer or textile designer should be hired. They use either Corel Draw or Adobe to create the print and the layout. The printing mills use the file to recreate the design on their software. Each print must take into account fabric widths for rotary prints, as well as dimensions for the flatbed, given the entire size run. The factory takes your artwork and will recreate it on their own software. Details can get lost during re-creation; therefore, carefully inspect any strike-offs (swatches of the print/color approval) that are given to you, and compare them to your original artwork.

» BEST PRACTICE

If you're not confident about the industry terminology used in regards to print methods, it is best to provide a reference sample. This way the factory can determine the print method, and figure out the process and machinery involved. With the reference sample, they can further guide you.

» BEST PRACTICE

Make sure you provide a vector file and ensure the factory is able to open it on their computer.

Screen Printing

There are numerous types of screen printing techniques on the market. There are two basic ways to apply screen prints to garments: (1) single placement print, where a single design is placed on an area of the garment; or (2) all-over print, where designs are repeated all over the fabric. Screen printing is usually done at either during the fabric stage or after the garment is cut. It's harder to achieve finer detail that way, however, it's the most cost-effective technique.

Printing is done on flat tables, and the designs are printed on a screen. Each ink color requires a separate screen. Typically, a maximum of eight colors per print, and fabric widths up to 120" can be used. The fabric is spread out on a 20-foot table, and two people work down the table when an all-over print is required. A minimum for printing a placement print is typically 100 pieces per print. If you divide that by five sizes, you are left with 20 pieces per size, which is very manageable.

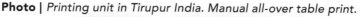

✿ GOLDEN NUGGET
To keep costs down, only use a maximum of three colors.

Photo | *Printing unit in Tirupur India. Manual all-over table print.*

Rotary Printing

Rotary screen printing is used for all-over prints. It is always done before the cutting stage. Costs are higher, with minimums starting at 5000 meters per print. In the roller printing process, a print paste is applied to an engraved roller, and the fabric is guided between it and a central cylinder. The pressure of the roller and central cylinder forces the print paste into the material. Because of the high quality it can achieve, roller printing is the most appealing method for printing designer and fashion apparel fabrics. The fabric is treated before and after the printing process. Close to 20 meters of material is wasted during initial set-up, to perfect the print quality.

Colors can be tricky to achieve due to the treatments, such as ironing and steaming post printing. Depending on the machine, minimum widths start at 42" to a maximum of 110". Every color requires a separate roller, and a maximum of 12 colors can be used in each print. As mentioned, the best way to keep your costs down, when working on minimums, is by using only three or fewer colors in a print. Every color requires a separate roller, thereby increasing costs.

Photo | *Printing unit in Tirupur India. Rotary Printing.*

Digital Printing

Digital printing is a popular method used for many brands, both small and large. Digital textile printing is the reproduction of digital images onto a textile substrate. Micro-drops of colored liquid ink is applied onto the fabric surface at precise points through tiny nozzles. These nozzles that are used to eject liquid dye and make the pattern can be controlled by computer to create intricate patterns and precise pattern repeats.

Designs can be created digitally with almost any graphic design software (Photoshop and Illustrator are the most popular) and exported as Tiff files. To help execute your design, textile designers can be hired to help create and layout the artwork. Remember: the quality of the file is an integral component of the digital fabric printing process. Alternatively, existing artwork or photographs can be scanned and then digitally manipulated to make a textile design. Usually, textile designs are created as a seamless pattern that is repeated (tiled or stepped) across the fabric for the traditional layout of continuous yardage. You can also create a textile design that is custom engineered to fit your products' cut and sewn pieces.

Comparing Digital vs Screen Printing

Digital textile printing is an expensive printing method compared to screen printing. However, with digital printing, there is no restriction on the number of colors you can use, and you can achieve very fine quality print, shading, and halftone designs. The inks in screen printing are applied much thicker than in digital printing, which results in brighter colors even on darker shirts. Digital printing can only print on fabric up to 60" widths. The inks used are more expensive than the dyes used in conventional screen printing.

Digital textile printing gives better quality print than conventional printing. When printing a repeated pattern, every print is the same, whereas, in traditional screen printing, slight variations can occur. Digital printing can be used for items that require high amounts of detail, allowing for a photographic print, which is not possible with screen printing.

Block Printing

Wood block printing is a technique for printing images, text or patterns on textiles and paper. It is widely used throughout East Asia and originated in China. The earliest surviving examples from China date all the way back to before 220 AD. The traditional process of hand block printing on textiles is deeply embedded in the Indian culture. The main areas of India known for their stunning block prints are Gujarat and Rajasthan. The art of block printing has been passed down for generations within families and communities.

Block printing is a great value addition to any garment. This kind of careful, labor-intensive work yields gorgeous results. Block carving is in itself an art requiring years of apprenticeship to gain mastery and is done entirely by hand.

A print starts with the design, drawn on paper and then carved into a wood block (the negative space (ink does not transfer) is removed). Designs are meticulously carved by hand into the blocks. The physical block is the design for a single repeat which is then stamped in rows across the fabric. Each color in the design is carved into a separate block. The outline block is the most intricate and usually stamped first. Next, the fill block, or possibly the ground color block depending on the color scheme used.

The block is then coated with dye, often vegetable dyes, and used to stamp a pattern right onto the fabric. Each color pattern is stamped individually onto the fabric. The process takes skill and time, as the pattern must be stamped repeatedly across the material, color by color. The slight human irregularities — inevitable in handwork — create the artistic effect of block prints. The final outcome of this meticulous labor is a unique garment made from a block printed fabric.

Despite being primarily overtaken by newer technology, woodblock printing still remains relevant in fashion and textiles. Whether a designer is using the technique as inspiration for a digital print or carving a stamp themselves, the look is beautiful and timeless.

Embroidery & Beading Embellishments

Embroidery and beading is a value-added process in garment manufacturing. Both involve the art of displaying adornments on the fabric or any other product with the help of needle and thread. These can be applied to the garment at the fabric stage or after the cutting or stitching. Embroidery is applied by hand or machine. Although most embroideries you find on the market are done by machine, they are still very labor intensive and require many people to set them up, as well as to check for errors. Operators are required to set up both the machines and each garment. Thread breakage during stitching is a common problem and a sewing operator must re-thread it. After the embroidery is complete, each garment must be checked, and the excess stabilizing fusing is removed, along with the frame.

The factory will send embroidery strike-offs (swatches of the print/ color approval) for feedback and approval before production. This is also done to check the accuracy of the pattern, quality and the associated stitches in it. When a strike-off comes back, you may need to ask the factory to either reduce or increase the number of stitches.

The quality of the embroidery is based on the design and execution of the product. Many variables can be evaluated: thread type and size, stitch count (how many stiches per inch) and size, stitch formation, stitch patterns, and material selection. All of these factors affect the aesthetics, performance, and quality. Thread considerations include colorfastness, strength, color range, and sewability.

The most common embroidery threads used are 100% rayon and 100% polyester. Cotton has a very limited use. If the fabric is thin, then heavy threads should be avoided. Embroidered designs must not cross seams and should be far away from them. Threads used must be compatible with the garment care instructions. You must also give some consideration to thread size; the finer the thread, the higher the price as it is considered higher quality.

In their simplest form, beads are small, perforated spheres and strung by hand. They can be made of metal, pottery, glass, or precious or semi-precious stones. There are thousands of types of embellishments such as sequins, pearls, rhinestones and much more.

> "TO CREATE SOMETHING EXCEPTIONAL, YOUR MINDSET MUST BE RELENTLESSLY FOCUSED ON THE SMALLEST DETAIL."
>
> **– GIORGIO ARMANI**

✽ GOLDEN NUGGET

A great way to find unique embroidery techniques is to ask the factory for images or samples they have made before. Using embroideries similar to what the factory has previously manufactured will help ease the production process, improve quality, and save time.

＞＞ BEST PRACTICE

Be sure to check the embroidery on the pre-production sample. Wash the garment to ensure that the thread color does not bleed or shrink.

The Printing & Embroidery Approval Process

Before bulk production, a strike-off test print, or embroidery, is created for approval. The strike-off represents a critical check before running production to ensure color, size and especially registration of artwork. Although the factory receives the artwork in Adobe Illustrator, almost every offshore printer recreates the design in their own software and format.

1 Once the strike-off is received, first inspect the scale, and ensure the design was re-created precisely like the artwork which was supplied.

2 The Pantone colors provided must be approved. The light source, ink types, ground fabric color and other variables affect the outcome of color. The designer must give comments such as "10% darker/lighter," "20% brighter / darker," and so on, to help the printer mixing the inks.

3 Check the quality of the print or embroidery. If it's embroidery, is the factory using the right thread quality, and are there enough stitches? Is the print ink quality and thickness suitable for your product? Have you done a wash test, as directed on the care label, to ensure there are no issues?

4 When the pre-production sample comes in, ensure the placement of the embroidery or print is correct.

Let's Spend Some Quality Time

By definition, "quality" refers to a perceived high level of value or excellence. However, in the apparel industry, its meaning differs from brand to brand. From a designer's perspective, the physical quality characteristics that should be incorporated into a product are those that customers desire and are willing to buy. The consumers dictate their desired standards, and the brand creates the product to convey these standards to the factory.

As you are learning about the factory and its processes, the factory is also learning about your products and quality standards. What one company deems an acceptable end product, another may not. Therefore, it is up to the brand to dictate expectations concerning the quality of the end product.

To some brands, quality is premium luxury cashmere; to others, it's the imperfections in a handmade block printing. While some brands purposely create rips and holes in jeans, others want a more finished, polished look. It's evident that different brands use a variety of cues to determine their standards of quality through the product development process. The best way to communicate quality is through reference samples. You will communicate standards in fibers, yarns, fabrics, finishes, garment assembly processes, and so on. Factories understand and establish these standards over time. As you build your relationship with the factory, they will begin to learn your standards, and processes will be streamlined.

Offshore manufacturers have access to a wide range of resources that enable them to produce goods both economically and efficiently, especially in a higher volume. These factories have access to mills, materials, fibers, equipment, factories, dyers, printers, notions and, most notably perhaps, skilled workers. Although significant changes have been made in manufacturing tools and equipment, jobs in manufacturing production still require considerable hands-on labor. Skilled workers are trained and require a high degree of concentration and efficiency. No matter how efficiently processes are streamlined and better machinery is created, at the end of the day making garments at scale requires a high amount of hands-on work, and there will be variations from one piece to another. Take minor discrepancies into consideration when examining quality.

"Honey, I Shrunk the Fabric!"- Ways to Control Fabric Shrinkage

Shrinkage is a process in which a piece of fabric becomes smaller than its original size. It can occur in any type of cloth shrinking in length and/or width. This can be caused by various factors, including the application of water, heat and steam during the pressing, washing and drying, and cleaning. Fabric can also shrink after it is cut because the yarns may constrict when it is relaxed. It is extremely difficult to predict the amount a fabric may shrink. It also varies from one roll to the next, in the same fabric. Woven fabric shrinks an average of 2-4% while knits shrink an average of 3-8%. Depending on the fiber, shrinkage can go as high as 18%.

The Importance Of Understanding Shrinkage

For starters, shrinkage is a "loss" of material to the factory, and they must account for this in the prices they provide. Remember once again that fabric is the most significant cost in manufacturing a garment, and it's critical that the factory accounts for the shrinkage before ordering the material. Comprehensive shrinkage controls are used on fabrics such as cotton, rayon, and linen.

More than 3% shrinkage will alter the fit of most garments, especially if they are tight and form-fitting. It's important that the garment fits right, and that you manage customer expectations. Up to 3% is a standard shrinkage allowance that can be passed onto the customer, especially since they will repeatedly be washing, pressing, drying and/or cleaning. Progressive shrinkage can occur after subsequent washes: this is merely the nature of the fabric and must be taken into consideration.

The instructions on the size chart and care label also help manage consumer expectations. The care label should specify the best way to care for the fabric. If the consumer is not following the care instructions correctly, or if the brand is not supplying the correct information, it will cause unexpected fit issues.

You must address shrinkage through the production process, either by preshrinking fabric or enlarging patterns to account for shrinkage after wash. Every brand has different sizing standards. Some size the garment a bit larger so that when the customer takes it home, the product still fits after washing. Some consumers instinctively buy a size up if they know they are not the best at following care instructions. Most of the higher-rated brands pay a bit more to take care of shrinkage in production.

Let's take Old Navy, for example. Their products will shrink a significant percentage. They save on costs by not washing and preshrinking the fabric. By contrast, a higher-quality brand such as GAP will control shrinkage as much as possible during production. Two different brands, but the customer knows what to expect from each.

6 Ways To Control Shrinkage:

1 **Accounting for shrinkage in the pattern** The percentage of the width or length of the fabric that shrinks is incorporated into production patterns.

2 **Compacting during fabric process** Shrinkage of knits can be controlled with a compacting machine. After the fabric is dyed, it goes on heated rollers with steam at high temperatures. The only way to really know it has gone through this process is if your factory is manufacturing the material. The primary benefit of having the factory source and produce the fabric is owning the exact recipe and method that went into making it. The bonus? Shrinkage issues will be dealt with by the factory. The entire supply chain is transparent, and the factory is responsible for taking care of shrinkage.

3 **Relaxing fabric prior to cutting (knit fabric only)** After the mechanical process of knitting, the structure may constrict. After the material is laid out and relaxed, it may go back to its original shape. Factories should roll out the fabric in layers on the cutting table and relax it overnight before cutting. Fabrics are typically relaxed for at least 12 hours. After the relaxation process, it can be cut.

4 **Cut Panel Laundry (CPL)** To preshrink the fabric and to improve the dimensional stability, it is cut at specific lengths and washed. The material does not need to be relaxed, and the pattern does not need to be cut bigger.

5 **Heat stabilizing treatments** A resin or coating is applied to the yarn or fabric.

6 **Garment wash** Garments are washed after they have been stitched.

Some designer entrepreneurs may opt to supply the fabric to the factory. In this case, you are entirely responsible for controlling the shrinkage. Do a wash test to get a baseline of how much needs to be added to your pattern. It's critical to gauge how much the fabric will shrink, if possible, before ordering it. Another test can also be done once you receive the order. If you can, select the material with the smallest shrinkage to save you money. Keep in mind that the factory will also be applying heat when pressing the garments. You can also have all the garments washed after they are stitched to control shrinkage, but this is an added cost.

Sample Approvals Gone Wild

Sometimes, seeing eye-to-eye with your manufacturing partner can prove to be very challenging, especially when an ocean separates you. Here's a typical scenario: You spend endless hours envisioning what your designs will look like. Excitement takes over and then, one day soon, a courier arrives containing a set of samples to approve! You open the package, only to be horrified to discover that it's simply "not right."

First, you panic. Then the anger trickles in. Why didn't the factory get it "right"? What are they smoking? This isn't rocket science, people!

Before you decide to shoot off an email telling them how wrong they are...

Take a deep breath.

Designers almost always react emotionally. I get it. I've been there. You're in a state that prevents you from thinking rationally, and rightfully so! You've got your heart invested in this process (not to mention your wallet, and possibly other people's wallets, too)!

Unfortunately for anyone who is new to the industry or who has never worked in a factory, there is a lack of understanding of the manufacturing process. Sure, you've worked through the sampling process, but scaling a product for mass production while working with multiple suppliers and people is an art and skill in itself. It's very rare to find a designer who has actually run or worked in a garment factory.

Here are some typical scenarios:

Q. The designer freaked out because the print strike-offs came back on undyed fabric, which could change the overall look of inks if printed on off-white. How are you supposed to approve anything like this?

A. The factory sent the fabric dyed, so the off-white color appeared white. All the designer had to do was place a white piece of paper or change the light setting to see if, in fact, the fabric was indeed dyed.

Q. The designer was incredibly annoyed. How could they send all the lab dip options in the exact same color?

A. The fabric color standards were submitted without specifying a light source. If the colors were checked under indoor lighting, the small color variances would be more visible.

Q. The designer had a panic attack and flipped out. The lab dips were all wrong! They just didn't match the color in the Pantone book! How did this happen?

A. The dyeing mill spent numerous hours working on the recipe to match the Pantone to the selected fiber. Again, no light source was provided. Every fiber reacts differently to dyes. Matching a paper quality to a fabric quality is much more difficult than having a factory match a fabric color standard to similar material.

Q. The designer is very worried. Days have gone by and still no fit sample. Why?

A. The factory received the CADS in a version that the factory just does not support. Instead of asking the buyer for another format, they ended up looking for another supplier to open the files. Hence, the delay.

Q. The designer is uber-frustrated. The samples do not fit right. Why?

A. The designer took a risk and got the factory to make the patterns. The tech packs the factory received were missing measurements, and the point of measures (how to measure) was not clear. For example, the length 42" was given, but she didn't state the location from where it was measured, such as the back neck or high point shoulder.

Q. The designer is disappointed – why does the quality of the embroidery look so wimpy?

A. The factory is working within the target prices given, so they used fewer stitches to work within the budget. There was no thread quality specified, so they used what was available.

Q. The designer is angry. Why is the pre-production sampling taking so long? Everything has been approved! I need these samples for my photo shoot!

A. The printing mill is stuck. July is monsoon season, forcing the inks to bleed and not dry, hence the delay.

Q. The designer is upset. The print strike-off that came back looks terrible, and the inks are not registering correctly. In fact, the inks are going outside the lines. What's happening?

A. The factory is not sending the samples to approve registration. It is a manual process, and variances happen before the rotary screen is made and calibrated. The samples were only sent for ink color approvals. Registration corrected in bulk.

Q. The designer is about to lose it. The samples do not fit right. Why do they fit bigger? What's going on?

A. The CAD printer was not calibrated correctly. The printer on their end is printing ¼" bigger all the way around each pattern piece. (This one is a hard one to catch, but this has happened to local printers as well. Sending a hardcopy helped solve the problem.)

Q. The designer is scared. How can they not get this right? What will happen in production? The length is way too short!

A. Sure, the prototype and the CAD are correct. After the sample maker cut and stitched the counter sample, the sampling manager reviewed the counter sample against the tech pack. He noticed the length was 4" too long, so he had it trimmed and hemmed to the correct length stated on the tech pack.

Oops! Someone forgot to update the tech pack after asking the pattern maker to change the length. The corrected length was also not marked on the prototype.

You get the idea. There is usually a good reason why things aren't working out the way you'd hoped.

Sew...

After you've received the samples and looked at them, here's what you're going to do. Go for a walk, sit on it and then come back to it. Breathe. Turn on your empathy, put on your patience pants, and pull those rationalizing skills out of your pocket. Contrary to what many designers would like to think, your partner - the factory - does not have telepathic powers. They cannot read minds. For this very reason, from the get-go, the pre-production package must be crystal clear. The factory's job is to decipher what you are trying to communicate, typically without talking face to face. I know it's difficult to put yourself in their shoes because you have no idea what they do on their end. That's the reality, but I'm also sure you can appreciate that they have a tough job.

So, who's at fault here? Most likely neither of you. No one is trying to mess the other up. If that was the case, well, I'm not sure how anyone would stay in business. The point of doing the sampling is to get approvals and comments from you. This is a learning process for everyone. The key thing to remember is that the factory is working to get a better understanding of what you want while maintaining costs and capabilities to scale. What motivation does anyone have to make an effort in creating samples that are going to be rejected? What if they went straight to production based on your prototypes? Just imagine.

Now... aren't you glad you got these counter samples?

Remember that the counter sampling process is similar to the prototyping process, except it takes more time with less face-to-face communication. Don't give up that easily. You chose your partner for a reason, and as you move forward, you will learn more. In most cases, the factory does not have time to tell you they are missing information. Over time, you will get the hang of things, your visits will clarify issues, and you will become stronger.

Merchandisers are running around meeting suppliers and different departments, meaning getting to a computer can be challenging. In a perfect world, they will stop what they are doing to tell you what they need. Unfortunately, the apparel world doesn't always work this way. The only thing we can control is ourselves. Ask them, "Is everything okay with what I sent?" Pick up the phone or message them via Whatsapp. After the order is complete, hand-deliver the next pre-production package. Talk face to face about issues. Take your merchandiser out for dinner.

And sometimes, unfortunately, partnerships simply fail. If you really feel they cannot meet your standards and you cannot communicate with each other effectively, pay them for their time and go find the right partner. Take it as a learning experience. Maybe you need to investigate samples more closely to ensure the factory meets the required skill sets. Perhaps your designs are relatively intricate, and you need to stay close to the factory for a few weeks to make communication easier.

Question yourself. You get me? There is always something that YOU can do better to make things go more smoothly. We cannot control others, but what we can do is better ourselves.

Part 6, is all about the *Benjamins*, baby! The least favorite yet most important part about being a designer entrepreneur is knowing how to manage and make money. You love what you do, right? Well, let's get the numbers right so the brand can support your design ambitions.

BUDGETING, PRICING & TARGET COSTS

OVERVIEW

You should know upfront, this chapter's gonna be about numbers, but don't let that scare you. If you're anything like me, your first experience with numbers was on *Sesame Street*. Remember The Count, the charming, loveable vampire who spent his time teaching math to kids, rather than flying around scaring people at night? I don't know about you, but I certainly looked forward to hearing him say things like "TWO! TWO more cookies! AH AH AH!" Numbers were once our friends, and by the time you finish this chapter, I hope they will be again!

Whenever I meet a designer entrepreneur, I get asked one question more than most: "Dee, how much will it cost me to get my stuff made?" The truth - which I hate to tell them because they're so hopeful for a simple answer - is that there's no universal formula to accurately calculate an estimated cost, especially for a customized product that you've designed that hasn't been made (yet). In reality, your customer sets your prices, not your manufacturers or suppliers. A better approach to figuring out your costs is to work backwards, starting with what the market will pay, to find your prices, and go from there.

Did you know that cotton fiber is a commodity, just like crude oil, and that prices change daily? Numerous variables affect the cost of a product, and values can fluctuate. Vendors' supplies and materials' cost change; fuel and energy prices also affect costs. A quote for a product price can change between the time a cost is given, (after counter sampling) to the time you actually place an order.

Even a simple T-shirt has numerous variables that affect cost: fabric quality, fiber, quantity, colors, styles, duty rate, the speed of delivery, supply and demand, sewing efficiencies, embellishments, trims...and the list goes on. Asking about the cost of a T-shirt is like asking for the price of a car. The make, quality, date, upgrades, delivery, the location of purchase, supply and demand, and other features all affect the price. There are so many variables. Just like buying a car, you have to work within your budget to determine what features you can afford (I mean, do you really need those fancy rims?).

When you contact the factory, they will ask, point blank, "What are your target costs?" *Sew,* you'd better be able to give them the numbers right away. If you don't provide them with these numbers, the factory has no idea what budget or quality standard to work within. It may seem a little backward, but the only way to ensure profitability is by knowing the retail price and target costs up front. Specific information must be provided to the factory to get initial estimates. After the samples are sewn, and fabric approvals are completed, the factory is able to give a more realistic quote.

Over the past ten years, I've found that there is no magic number for opening orders (that is, starting budgets), but a majority of my clients have allocated around $20,000 to $70,000 USD to cover all manufacturing expenses to start. Before you pack your bags and leave, remember that you'll need to invest in your inventory. It's pretty hard to operate a business if you don't actually have the products. A quality team that produces a quality product will need compensation, including yourself, which requires a specific minimum volume.

While an order like the one mentioned above, may seem high to you, it is definitely not high for an already established factory. Remember, they are also making an investment in your business too, in hopes that it will grow. Working on minimum orders do not provide much of a profit for factories. For example, a small order of 1,000 units at $1.00 profit per unit is not sustainable in the long run for a factory.They would rather be selling 100,000 units - which would return a $100,000 dollar profit - compared to the $1000 profit. Or as our friend The Count would say, *100 thousand ah ah ah!*

This part begins by discussing how to uniquely position products in the marketplace and determine prices. It will also help you to walk backward through the process, to better understand pricing, target costs, minimum purchase orders, economies of scale, and budgeting, and to recognize often forgotten or invisible costs of shipping the products. We're going to start by talking about research on retail prices that will help you stay within your budget.

The Real Cost of Fabric

Photo | *Fabric Costs*

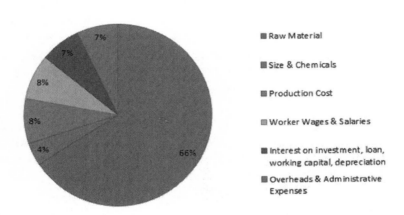

The textile industry is a global commodity chain, with the fabric being one of the most critical pieces that determines how much the final product will cost. Textile manufacturing involves several steps, from cotton picking and spinning to weaving and finishing. The industry provides a livelihood for over 45 million people in India alone. To fully understand the creation of fabric and its costs, you may want to know there are different parameters involved. These can be understood as *direct* and *indirect costs*.

Direct costs would include:

1 **The cost of the raw materials** (fabric or yarn) – makes up 66% of the total cost.

GSM (gram per square meter) The amount of raw material used to make a piece of fabric is reflected by the weight of fabric in grams per one square meter - the GSM of the fabric. A **GSM cutter** is used to cut the material, and the weight is taken with a scale. For the same variety of fabric, as the GSM increases, the cost increases.

Yarn count Yarn count refers to the thickness of the yarn and is determined by its mass per unit length. The yarn count is a numerical value which defines its fineness or coarseness. It also expresses whether the yarn is thick or thin. The cost will depend on the yarn count: the finer the yarn, the more expensive it can get. Combed yarns undergo a time consuming **combing** process and are more costly than carded yarns because of the removal of the short fibers. Combing creates a smoother yarn as the fibers are more aligned. All finer counts above 40 are generally combed yarns. The higher the number, the finer the yarn.

Every fiber is measured differently. Cotton count measures are based on a count of 840 yards of yarn that add up to a weight of one pound. For example, if anyone in the production process talks about a "30 count yarn," it means you need 30 yarns of 840-yard length to make it one pound of weight. In cotton count, the higher the count, the finer the yarn. For example, a 40s yarn is two times finer than a 20's yarn. The yarn count of a regular T-shirt made of single jersey falls in between a 20s to 40s count. Higher yarn count fabric will be thinner and finer. In a synthetic material, it's reversed: higher yarn count fabric is thicker.

For man-made or synthetic fibers, yarns are measured in *tex* and *denier*.

Thread Count is only measured with woven fabrics. It is the number of threads in the weft and warp per square inch of fabric (*warp* and *weft* are horizontal and vertical threads running that make a cloth). These two are related to each other directly, as the finer the yarn, the higher the thread count will be. Thread count is the number of ends per inch or picks per inch. Along with the yarn count, they will both determine the weight of the fabric.

Type of Fiber The cost will depend on the type and the quality of fiber. Fiber is a single filament of natural material - such as cotton, linen or wool - or man-made -like nylon, polyester, viscose or rayon fiber. It is measured by linear mass density, the weight of a given length of a fiber. Prices fluctuate on a daily basis for commodities, such as cotton. Choosing certified materials such as Certified Organic further increases costs.

2 **The cost of chemicals and water** – this makes up 4% of the total cost.

Weight Dyeing lighter-weight fabric reduces the cost of dyeing. This is because the capacity of the machine is expressed in weight of the material, so when dyeing lighter weight fabric, more length of the material can be processed at the same time, reducing the dyeing cost.

Shade When considering the color, the lighter the tone, the lower the cost. This is because the amount of dye and time required for processing are less than what's needed for darker shades. For example, dyeing pastel shades takes one and a half times the amount it will take to dye black and burgundy tones. The cost of dyeing also depends upon the class and quality of the dyes used.

Vat dyes are more expensive than reactive dyes, and better expertise is required for dyeing. Vat dyes are insoluble in water and cannot dye fibers directly, whereas reactive dyes react directly with the fiber. So, for the same shade, the cost of dyeing fabric with vat dyes is higher than dyeing it with reactive dyes. Also, within the same dye class, some colors are more expensive than others. For example, turquoise and reds are more expensive.

Length and Width For industrial dyeing, a minimum of 2,000 meters of fabric and specific weight is required to have it dyed. It's beneficial to go for larger widths instead of longer fabrics: costs related to running the material are based on length, so if you double the width, it won't incur additional processing costs. The factory will work with the mill to determine suitable dimensions.

Water Lastly, you can't overlook water, as the textile industry is dependent on it in virtually all steps of manufacturing. Most importantly, it uses a lot! Dyes, specialty chemicals and finishing chemicals used to produce the fabric, are all applied in water baths. These finishing chemicals or washes, such as softeners, are added to enhance the material. After it is dyed, it undergoes a process called compacting where extreme heat and steam are applied to help control shrinkage.

3 **The production costs** – these make up another 8% and comprise the expenses incurred in running the machinery, maintenance, fuel for power, humidification and other utilities.

Spinning Open-end spun yarns are cheaper than ring spun yarns because the cost of manufacturing is less. The number of fine filaments used to make the yarn will also affect the price. Bright yarns are more expensive than dull yarns, and textured yarns are more expensive than flat yarns because of the additional process cost.

Weaving The weaving cost is affected by the beam size. If the beam is small in length, the cost will be more, as beam gaiting and knotting will add to the total. The quality of mill-made fabrics is better than power loom-made fabrics concerning yarn quality; hence, the cost is higher, sometimes by as much as 25 percent. Wastage of 2-3% in warping and weaving and shrinkage of 1-1.5% from loom to the greige folding stage are included in the weaving cost.

4 **The worker wages and salaries** – these make up another 8%. Fabric manufacturing is a labor-intensive process. Many factories train unemployed or unskilled labor and recruit them into the various stages of production. While this sources the factory's much-needed labor, it also serves as an additional source of income to the families of the workers.

Indirect costs include:

1 *Interest on investment, loan, working capital, and depreciation* that comprise 7%.

2 *Overheads and administrative expenses* like traveling, telephone, couriers, legal issues, and taxes, making up another 7%.

The big picture is that direct and indirect costs can influence the production of fabric. The different parameters that make up the costs of the fabric can be grouped in two different ways. That is, raw material, size and chemicals, production cost, worker wages and salaries make up the direct costs. On the other hand, interest on investment, loan, working capital, depreciation and overheads, and administrative expenses make up the indirect costs. Amidst these costs, a 10-20% profit margin is achieved, making fabric production a worthy but intensive process.

Sew, as you can see, there is a *lot* that goes into the cost of your fabric.

Value & Pricing

From my experience with startups, I've learned that, more than the uniqueness of a product, it's quality that sells. A new brand should always add value and quality before competing on price. Surveys by Cotton Incorporated revealed that a majority of consumers will pay more for "higher quality" clothes[1]. More than half (52%) say the clothes they've purchased lately don't seem to last as long as they used to, consistent with October 2011 responses (50%). Meanwhile, 44% of consumers say they would pay more for better quality apparel, up from 41% in 2011, according to the *Monitor*.

Journalist Elizabeth Cline, author of *Overdressed: The Shockingly High Cost of Cheap Fashion*, sees the shift in the way consumers shop. "When people reconnect with the feel of good materials," Cline says, "and the way something fits and is sewn really well, it adds to the experience of wearing the garment. It makes you want to wear it over and over again, and that's different than your relationship with a fast fashion garment that doesn't feel good and loses shape."

This is especially true when ordering lower quantities, as compared with many mass-produced brands, which typically order thousands of pieces in one style. Their prices may be low, but their product quality is also low. Furthermore, increasing retail prices over time is a lot harder than discounting them.

Never undervalue your product. It has taken you and your team a considerable amount of time and energy to design, develop and manufacture. Many people have worked hard to produce your product. Keep in mind: minimum quantity orders do not allow much profit for the factory. As we've been saying throughout this book so far, keeping partners happy leads to smoother manufacturing.

Sew, where to begin?

First, estimate how many products you plan to retail. Then, backed by your research, determine how much the customer will pay for each product. **Be sure to select and design products that can be sold at higher price points.** This will allow more room for profit per piece.

Never sell yourself short by pricing low (and never sell your shorts for too low a price either - hehehe!).

Pricing your products is one of the most essential components in business planning. To run a successful business, customers must be willing to purchase products at the prices you set. The retail price must be high enough to cover the cost of goods (materials, labor, and expenses from the manufacturer), transportation costs, your own operational costs, and any marketing and administrative expenses you would incur to promote the product. Not only must the price of the product exceed your operating costs, but it should also generate suitable profits to drive business growth. Factor in discounts as well. Profit margins vary from company to company.

The fashion industry uses the following method to set prices: *double the cost for the wholesale price,* and then *multiply the wholesale price by two for the retail price.* For new brands this can be very frustrating because it's challenging to calculate estimates early in the process. For this reason, I recommend working *backward*. Instead of starting with a target cost or asking for a quote, **start with the target retail price**. It's much easier, faster, and will help you make better decisions. With the target retail price, you can estimate how much you are able to spend on each selected style. Please see the pricing success strategy below to help you.

Target Costs

You determine how much you want to pay for products. The target cost is the amount you aim to give the manufacturer to produce the garment. The price typically includes everything from the fabric, materials, and embellishments to trims, labels, packaging, and production.

Use the diagram below as a formula and pricing success strategy to help you estimate the target prices to give the factory.

Photo | *How to determine a target cost*

4 STEPS TO CALCULATING YOUR TARGET COSTS

A general rule of thumb

STEP **1** DO YOUR HOMEWORK

Decide the ideal retail price for your products

STEP **2** WORK BACKWARDS

We can reach your ideal target cost by working from your retail price.

Let's say your retail price is $100.

$100
RETAIL PRICE

STEP **3** FIND YOUR WHOLESALE PRICE

Your buyers love a good margin. The industry standard is 2.

To know your Wholesale Price we will divide the retail price by your selected margin.

$100 ÷ 2 = $50
WHOLESALE PRICE

STEP **4** ARRIVE AT YOUR TARGET COST

Repeat the previous step by dividing your wholesale price by 2 or 2.5.

Minimums ÷ 2
Regular (qty above minimums) ÷ 2.5

$50 ÷ 2 = $25
TARGET COST

A total product cost refers to more than the cost of the product. Duties (16-18% on average) on apparel, from India into North America, should not be included in your target cost to the factory. Delivery charges also vary and are not included. Both duties and delivery charges should be separate line items in your budget. The landed product cost includes delivery and duties.

Let's say you start developing a product without a target retail price and you don't give the factory any target costs... Without any specific direction, the factory will work with the easiest, cheapest and closest available fabric and suppliers to make the product. As a result, your final quote from the factory could have a low cost, but also inferior quality. Without a target price, the factory has no guide to help them source.

As mentioned earlier, without target costs, it's impossible for the factory to achieve your goals. It is also impossible to estimate profit. Bottom line: you set the parameters, and the factory will give you feedback on what is possible.

Fabric and materials make up a substantial portion of a product's total cost. Giving the factory a target cost will help them gauge which materials and suppliers to procure within your price range. Negotiating a lower a price will only give the factory a small budget to work with, sacrificing speed of delivery, quality materials, and craftsmanship. Remember, as with almost everything else in life, you get what you pay for, especially working on minimum orders.

Pricing Success Strategy

Example 1: Let's say you want to start a line of unique cut T-shirts, similar to a $150 jersey top from clothing chain Anthropologie. To estimate the wholesale cost, divide $150 by two (retail markup, ranging from a minimum of 2 to 2.5) for an estimated wholesale price of $75, and then divide that $75 by two (wholesale markup) to arrive at the estimated target cost of $37.50, inclusive of import duties. Another formula to estimate target cost is by taking 25 percent of your retail price of $150.

Example 2: Now, take the case of a basic, eco-friendly T-shirt line for adults, similar to a $30 T-shirt sold at American Apparel. You divide the $30 by two (retail markup) for the estimated wholesale price of $15, and then you divide the $15 by two (wholesale mark-up) to arrive at the estimated target cost of $7.50, inclusive of import duties. Can you manufacture and pay duties on an ethically-made quality product for $7.50, with low order quantities? Not likely.

Please note target costs vary depending on many variables, this formulas can can used as a starting point.

Photo | *Pricing comparisons at different retail prices*

PRICING COMPARISONS

EXAMPLE 1: High Retail Price	COST
Retail Price	$150.00
Estimated Wholesale Price	$75.00
Estimated Target Cost	$37.50
Your Profit	$112.50

☺

EXAMPLE 2: Low Retail Price	COST
Retail Price	$30.00
Estimated Wholesale Price	$15.00
Estimated Target Cost	$7.50
Your Profit	$22.50

😐

Photo | *Product cost comparison at different quantities*

QUANTITY COMPARISONS

REGULAR (approx. orders above minimum qty)	
Wholesale Price	$100.00
Divide Wholesale price by 2	$50.00
Target Price Divide by 2.5	$20.00

☺

MINIMUM	
Retail Price	$100.00
Divide Wholesale price by 2	$50.00
Target Price Divide by 2	$25.00

😐

The profit margin is the difference between a product's selling price and the cost of producing it. Selling your product at a higher retail price yields a better profit. For example, selling one item for a retail price of $150 will earn you $112.50 profit, versus a profit of $22.50 on a product sold at $30. It's crucial that you make enough profit to account for all the hard work and countless hours that have gone into your design. Example 1 is more ideal for businesses that want to grow while ordering minimum quantities.

In addition to selecting your ideal retail price, it is crucial to compare advantages when buying in bulk. In the example above, you will see that regular orders above the minimum will get you a better target price from the manufacturer. For minimum orders, target prices are usually divided by 2, while orders above the minimum quantity are generally divided by 2.5. In this example, we have a $5.00 saving per item. On orders of 1,000 pieces, that is a saving of $5,000. Who doesn't want some extra dough in their pocket? I know I do.

See? I told you we'd make the numbers work for you!

Order Complexity

Use this pricing formula as a gauge to estimate the target cost of a more complicated product order. Working on minimum orders further complicates the formula. Generally, an order of 1,000 pieces per style on one fabric structure/color is considered a "minimum order." When you place a minimum order that is considered "complicated" your target cost can increase and the factory will provide a higher quote. For example a lined technical jacket may have three fabrics, six trims, four embellishments, five sizes and 20 seams. Compare the jacket with a basic t-shirt that has one fabric, two colorways, a few seams and sizes,and the jacket target will likely be higher than what you came up with as your target cost.

Total Order Complexity: Factory's Point of View
The higher the # in each column
the more complex the order

#Styles	#Fabrics (includes contrast parts)	#Colorways	#Trims (notions, labels, packaging etc.)	#Embellishments (prints, embroideries, beading etc.)	#Seams (Sewing ease)	#Sizes (consider fabric consumption per piece)
1	1	1	1	1	1	1
2	2	2	2	2	2	2
3	3	3	3	3	3	3
4	4	4	4	4	4	4
5	5	5	5	5	5	5
6	6	6	6	6	6	6
7	7	7	7	7	7	7
8	8	8	8	8	8	8
9	9	9	9	9	9	9

Photo: *Costing comparison based on order complexity*

Instructions: Circle each number that applies to each column to give you an idea of how complex an order is to process. The higher the number, the more complex the order. If an order is more complex, its an indication that you may need to allow a higher target cost.

Total Product Costs

Once you calculate the product production costs, you must include all other expenses related to running your operations, such as marketing and administrative expenses. In most cases, the factory will not be including the duties, taxes, and shipping, so you've got to add these as well. That cost will become your total product cost.

So now, the million dollar question: why are higher-priced products critical to your success?

1 **Bigger Profits**: In the first example, the higher-priced T-shirt will earn you $112.50 per item, compared to $22.50 for the lower-priced product, when selling retail. The higher-priced product gives more margin to cover other costs, which will mean more profit for you. You will be more profitable and have a better gross margin. A gross margin is merely a measure of profitability: it quantifies the earnings or profit that's left over after you subtract total product costs.

2 **Better Quality and Service:** The higher-priced product allows the factory to have a bigger budget to source higher-quality materials and suppliers, which will ultimately yield a better product. You're giving the factory more room to source higher-quality fabrics and the ability to get quicker service from partnering vendors.

3 **Ethical Manufacturing:** Ethical manufacturing is a significant concern for consumers. Lower, unreasonable prices often indicate that someone in the supply chain or the workers are not being treated fairly. In my opinion, the bad karma that comes from hurting overseas workers is never worth the few cents of savings per unit that you get from partnering with unethical partners.

Economies of Scale & Minimum Order Quantities (MOQ)

Most companies seek to grow and increase profits. Increasing the overall volume of a business can lead to significant reductions in costs. When more units of a good or a service can be produced on a larger scale, yet with (on average) fewer input costs, economies of scale are said to be achieved.

According to this theory, economic growth may be achieved when economies of scale are realized. It's kind of like shopping at Costco: the more you buy of the same product, the less it costs. Economies of scale mean that as you increase in size, you can become more efficient. For example, as your business grows, it will require a larger warehouse and distribution operation. As you handle more sales transactions, you will be able to move a product faster and get better deals from suppliers in more significant quantities.

BENEFITS OF
ECONOMIES OF SCALE

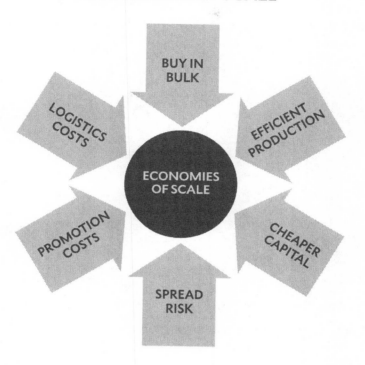

There are numerous benefits to achieving economies of scale. The most significant advantage is a reduced cost per unit of production. An efficient factory can often purchase supplies in bulk, which leads to lower costs of goods sold and lower supply expenses. Buying in bulk, lowering risk, streamlining manufacturing processes as well as cheaper capital investments, and saving money in advertising and logistics, are other benefits. Economies of scale even help you save money on advertising because you're spreading costs out. For example, if your total advertising spend is $5,000, and you only produce ten pieces, you'd be paying $500 on advertising on each unit. Produce 1,000 pieces, however, and you're just spending $5 per unit.

Finally, achieving economies of scale also leads to quicker turnaround or manufacturing production times, saving you time as well as money. Now that's something we could all get used to.

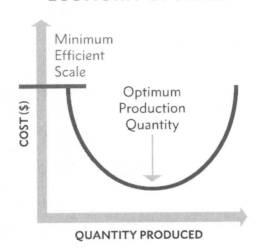

Photo | *Economies of scale: production quantity*

ECONOMY OF SCALE

A minimum efficient scale is the smallest amount of production a firm can achieve while still taking full advantage of economies of scale. When you order a product in minimum quantities (MOQ), you force the factory to operate at minimum efficiency or low margins.

When you achieve optimum production and economies of scale, making more money is inevitable. For example, if you are selling 1,000 units at $150 each ($150,000), you make twice as much, as if you were to sell 100 units at the same price ($15,000). It's a constant balancing act of minimizing substantial investments in the product while getting a price that your customer will ultimately pay.

After the optimal point, costs will eventually increase. As the demand for your products increases, you'll need to source more materials and use more resources. For example, the raw materials may have to be sourced farther away, possibly with lower-quality suppliers, thereby increasing costs.

It's also possible to get too big and expand too quickly, as the Canadian coffee chain Tim Hortons learned the hard way with their initiative to expand their stores in the U.S. Organizations must be careful not to outgrow their economies of scale. In the case of Tim Hortons, average unit costs were low, but they began to rise as the company created unwanted inefficiencies, alongside other increasing costs in areas such as technology. As a result, many of the coffee shop's new locations across the U.S. lost a lot of money and had to close.

Factory Order Minimums

When sourcing the right factory, it's not only important to ask the factory if they manufacture products similar to yours, it's also crucial to understand the minimum they require in order to work with them. **Minimum order quantity,** or **MOQ,** refers to the lowest number of items that the manufacturer needs to accept an order.

The MOQ varies, depending on the product and its specifications. To start, they would give rough numbers, because not all the information on the order may be available. Keep in mind that as you begin to work with the factory and they learn more about the order, numbers can change. Although factories don't like to push more quantity on you, remember that they have many partners and departments within the factory and need to work with everyone to execute the order quickly and at the best quality.

An MOQ is the minimum quantity of pieces a factory is set up to work with. Factories vary in the number of units they produce per style: small batch manufacturers can produce between 200 to 250 units per style if a few styles are spread over a minimum of 1,000 pieces of one fabric. A factory prefers to do 1,000 pieces in one style. Typically, an MOQ in a larger factory is in the thousands, with large batch manufacturers producing around 10,000 units per style. This is when you will see better price breaks. Not only do workers on the production floor need to be efficient to make a garment at your cost, they also need to meet minimum requirements from other suppliers.

The MOQ can also be set by the suppliers and mills. As mentioned in Part 1, factories that take orders with minimum quantities have a 30 percent efficiency rate, which means they are not making as much as they need to operate efficiently. Often, larger orders that can be processed in big batches drive their unit costs down, making orders more lucrative, so manufacturers prefer to process larger orders. At the same time, larger orders mean lower costs for you as well.

The diagram below illustrates how factories are efficient at different quantities.

Table-1 | Line efficiency at different order quantity

Order Qty.	Average Style Efficiency
100-500	30%
501-1000	35%
1001-3000	40%
3001-8000	50%
8001-10000	55%
10000 plus	60%

Photo credit: *Online Clothing Study*

Rough MOQs are given based on factory size and vary from order to order. For the factory to cost out and ensure that they are meeting the MOQ is no easy task. To truly establish an MOQ, the factory needs to analyze your tech pack(s), mock purchase order, fabric and, if possible, the prototype sample(s).

As a designer entrepreneur, understanding MOQ is essential. Your first set of goals is to get the order right, build your factory relationship, and understand your product. You must master the entire process from idea to delivery and do it all over again. Over time, as you build your sales and increase your order volume, the factory can move faster and you're in a position to negotiate a lower cost.

Materials and Supplies MOQ

From trims and embellishments, such as embroideries and screen printing, to ordering buttons and zippers, every supplier has set minimums. Unless these minimums are met, they won't give anyone the time of day.

Fabric and Dyeing Minimums

Fabric processing and dyeing are two critical components of forming an MOQ. Not only is fabric costly to store, but quality standards are difficult to manage once the fabric is stored. Factories simply don't store fabric; it comes at a cost to them.

It is critical that the factory clearly understands the measurements of each product and how they are measured at each size. Any error on their end can amount to massive losses. Providing accurate technical packages and information on samples is equally as critical.

The factors below are just a few areas that affect fabric consumption:

1. **Markers**: Are a guide or template, often made by computer and printed out with a plotter and used in the cutting process. All pattern pieces for a given style, including all sizes - used to make a style are laid out in a formation intended to reduce fabric waste. After the marker is made, the fabric is laid out in layers, and it is laid on top of the fabric layers. With a cutter machine the pieces are cut all at once. Marker making can effectively alter fabric utilization. Typically, a marker containing a higher number of garments will be more efficient and consume (hence, waste) less fabric making it more cost efficient.

PATTERN MARKER

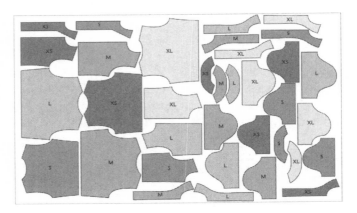

2 **Fabric width and shrinkage** The width of the fabric determines the area available for making a marker and, therefore, greater fabric width will give more efficient markers. If the shrinkage is greater, fabric consumption will be higher, and if it is lower, fabric consumption will be lower as well.

3 **Fabric repeat size or prints** Solid color fabrics will be easier to deal with while making markers and laying fabric. Prints such as checks or stripes take much more fabric, as pattern pieces need to be placed in certain positions. The repeat size also directly affects the fabric consumption. If the repeat size is bigger, consumption will be higher.

4 **Center-selvage variation and other fabric defects** Fabric must be checked before cutting, and any flaws will need to be avoided when cutting. Defects like these cause the marker to be inefficient and can substantially increase the fabric consumption. These defects are mostly unavoidable and can be resolved, to an extent, through effective marker making.

5 **Grain** In the case of specific style requirements or garment parts like the waistband, fabric needs to be cut on the bias (diagonal). The fabric consumption for these styles is higher than the ones cut straight on grain.

Dyeing and color minimums make up another aspect of MOQs. The first thing that factories look at are the number of colors in an order. Dyeing plants, no matter how large, have a limited number of dyeing vessels that accommodate MOQs. These vessels can only process a few colors per day. If you are working on an MOQ, the average time it takes to get your clothing dyed is approximately 30-45 days.

Offshore Sourcing Cost Considerations

Photo | *Manufacturer service types*

If your plan includes working with garment factory minimums to source cheap overseas prices, think again. I know I sound like a broken record but, *factories working on minimums are only 30 percent efficient*. Factories take minimum orders as an investment and work to grow with you. There is a common misconception that working offshore means lower costs no matter what. To get lower prices, though, you need to purchase a very high volume. Cost savings happen with larger quantities. The higher the quantity, the lower your prices, and the better the margins.

Offshore may have lower employee wages and access to a wider assortment of cheaper materials, but again, this happens when the economies of scale are reached. Gone are the days when sourcing decisions were based solely on the country with the lowest wages or costs. Environmental impact and the ethical treatment of people are global issues, and cost all of us. Fast fashion needs to slow down, and as designers we need to understand that quality clothing made in fair working environments comes at a price. The key to addressing these concerns is by paying factories fairly and following fair trade principles. The goal is to grow with the factory by increasing your order quantities over time, at a sustainable pace, which will then lead to more sustainable profitability as well.

Budgeting

A budget estimates revenue and expenses for a specific period of time – companies periodically compile and re-evaluate these budgets. Creating a budget is the most effective way to keep your business, and its finances, on track. Structured planning can make all the difference to the growth of your brand. Beyond your manufacturing costs that you have planned for the year, there are other expenses and costs that you need to take into account.

Photo | *Steps to establish a manufacturing budget*

STEPS TO ESTABLISH YOUR MANUFACTURING COSTS

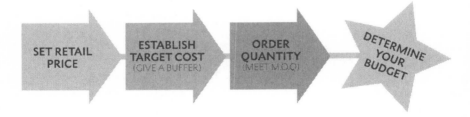

By creating a mock purchase order, you can estimate your budget for manufacturing expenses using projected quantities and target costs. The mock purchase order should outline all styles with target costs, colors, and quantities in each size.

Starting a fashion brand doesn't come cheap. As we previously discussed, average opening orders can range anywhere from

$20,000 USD to $70,000 USD. Opening orders can seem tricky. To make a profit, a higher investment always yields a higher return. The trick is being able to invest as little as possible to mitigate risk while keeping the factories efficient and profitable. If your factory is making a profit from your orders, then you will also reap the benefits. Over time, as your orders and business grow, product costs will begin to decrease.

Most clothing companies ship products twice a year to keep inventory fresh for customers. If you plan on shipping more than once a year, it's imperative that you budget for the entire year. Before your first order is sold or received, the next order will need to be placed, which will tie up some of your cash flow. As a best practice, startup companies should budget for at least two shipments. Keeping your orders to six styles or less will also help manage your budget and cash flow.

Purchase Orders

When placing a purchase order, keep in mind that you'll need to pay a deposit up front to help procure fabrics and pay for labor. A typical and fair deposit is 50%. This may seem like a lot if you're doing this for the first time, but you know how they say "you have to spend money to make money"? This principle very much applies here.

The factory also cuts extra pieces of the garments. Factory efficiency is vital to their success and laying out patterns is a major focus. Pattern pieces must be cut in bulk according to size, consumption, quantities, etc. As a result of how the pattern was laid out for cutting, extra pieces are cut, and any surpluses are shipped.

On the flip side, shortages may happen due to rejections in quality standards that you set. Instead of sending garments with errors, they just pull them from your shipment. Prepare to receive products of plus or minus 5%.

Letter of Credit (L/C or LOC)

Ever had someone say to you, "Oh, come on, give me a little credit...."? Well, now's your chance. We're on the homestretch of this process and are going global!

Importers and exporters regularly use letters of credit to protect themselves. Letters of credit are used to minimize risk in international trade transactions where the buyer and the seller may not know each other. As an importer of products, using a letter of credit can ensure that your company only pays for goods after the factory has provided evidence that they have been shipped. It also allows you to conserve your cash flow because you won't have to make any advance payments or deposits to the exporter or factory. The factory will take the letter of credit to the bank and request an advance from their bank to help procure materials. Also, the letter of credit gives you instant credibility with an exporter by demonstrating your credit-worthiness.

The International Chamber of Commerce (ICC) in the Uniform Custom and Practice for Documentary Credit (UCPDC) defines L/C as:

"A letter of credit is a promise by a bank on behalf of the buyer (customer/ importer) to pay the seller (beneficiary/exporter) a specified sum in the agreed currency, provided that the seller submits the required documents by a predetermined deadline."

The letter of credit outlines the conditions under which payment will be made to an exporter. As a buyer, you set a list of terms and conditions under which he or she would like to buy and ship the cargo from the exporter. This is typically done *by providing documents* that show what was delivered and where. This list generally has the following:

> **Commercial invoice:** The commercial invoice is more like an invoice and the legal document of the actual sale when ready to ship.

- > **Proforma Invoice (PI):** The PI document that shows a commitment on the part of the seller to sell the goods according to the pre-decided terms, prices, and conditions.
- > **Purchase Order:** Once you send a purchase order, a PI is sent back to you, and you can open an L/C.
- > **Packing List:** Outlines the details of the shipment regarding packaging, weight, box dimensions, quantity, and units.

Determine what documents are required to export your garments. Speak with your customs broker and ensure they are on the L/C.

- > **Bill of Lading:** The bill of lading (BOL) is a required document to move a freight shipment by sea. The BOL works as a receipt of freight services, a contract between a freight carrier and shipper, and a document of title.
- > **Airway Bill/Railway receipt:** Same as above, but for air or railway freight transport.
- > **Insurance Policy:** Questions regarding types of coverage during shipment should be referred to a freight forwarder or a customs broker. Issued by an underwriting institution, the Insurance Policy states that a specified party will be reimbursed an amount in the event merchandise is damaged or destroyed.
- > **Certificate of Origin:** This is a document that identifies the origin of goods being exported and required by almost all of the export and import shipments in international trade transactions.
- > **Bill of Entry:** The Bill of Entry is a legal document filed with the Customs department by an importer or his/her customs broker to undergo necessary import customs clearance formalities to take the goods out of customs.

The issuing bank generally acts on behalf of its client (you, the buyer) to ensure that all conditions have been met before the funds of the L/C are released. The finished garments' quality does not apply to an L/C.

How The Letter Of Credit Works (A General Guide)

1 You, the buyer/importer, create a purchase order and open an L/C with a bank in favor of the supplier.

2 The opening bank issues a letter of credit with your terms.

3 The opening bank forwards the L/C to the advising bank who verifies and contacts the factory (exporter/supplier).

4 The factory reviews Terms and Conditions and confirms. They request a deposit or advance from the bank to procure materials and proceed with production.

5 Upon completion of production, the factory/supplier provides necessary documents to their advising bank and verifies them.

6 The opening bank (your bank) receives the bill and documents from the exporter/supplier's bank. The opening/issuing bank reimburses the advising bank the amount of the bill if all the documents are in order.

7 Upon receipt of these funds, the issuing bank then endorses the bill of lading (or at whichever point terms were) so that the cargo can be released to the buyer.

How To Open A Letter of Credit

To get a letter of credit, contact your bank directly. You'll most likely need to work with the international trade department or commercial division. Not every institution offers letters of credit, but small banks and credit unions can often refer you to somebody who is able to accommodate your needs. Generally, the buyer absorbs most of the costs incurred in setting up the L/C. The banks naturally charge interest for this service, typically 0.25% to 2% depending on the LC margin, tenor, customer credit rating, etc.

Qualifications for a Letter of Credit are based on many factors, but the principal ones are the individual's or business' credit-worthiness, as well as their liabilities and assets, the legitimacy of the product/ goods and seller, and the ability to deliver said goods in a timely manner and in excellent condition for the purpose for which they are intended. As the buyer, you may need to have funds on hand at that bank or get approval for financing from the bank. When arranging for an L/C, carefully review all terms and conditions.

Freight Expenses

In the budget, include a category that accounts for delivering the finished products to the warehouse, where the inventory will be stored. Factories can provide for all-inclusive costs, but those are difficult to determine 75+ days in advance. Estimates can be provided upon placing an order. Once the product is packed, the weight, dimensions, and the number of boxes will determine an accurate shipping cost. Costs differ according to the chosen service provider, as well as speed and mode of delivery (sea or air). Freight should include insurance, brokerage (person to clear goods), residential/commercial delivery fees and air or sea costs.

Remember: Bigger profit margins give you the flexibility to save on time by shipping via air. Exam fees and warehouse storage could be additional fees.

Generally, air freight costs twice as much or more than ocean freight. The greater the quantity that you ship, the better the per-unit shipping cost you get.

Taxes

All products that are imported into any country are subject to provincial or state taxes. If the products are bought for business purposes, the taxes can be collected back from the consumers. The difference is always paid or owed by the government. Regardless, taxes should be set aside in the budget.

Duties

All products imported into any country must pay duties. Duties are fees imposed by the government on goods brought into the country. Duty rates vary greatly depending on the product and the country in which it was manufactured. Every product is classified with a code, and the duty rate is given as a percentage of each product.

International Commercial Shipping Terms

Trade terms are crucial elements of international contracts of sale, as they explain to the buyer, seller, and other parties what to do concerning:

> Shipment of the goods from the seller to the buyer.

> Customs clearance (duties, brokers, etc.).

They also explain the division of costs and risks between the parties such as:

> Who should pay the costs of loading and unloading the goods.

> Who is responsible for the risk of loss or damage to the goods, and who should take out insurance to protect against these risks.

Below are the most common terms for delivery:

FOB (Free On Board): FOB value includes all the costs related to materials, production, and transportation to the closest loading point to the factory. The seller owns goods until they are delivered to the air or seaport in question. The seller or shipper arranges for goods to be moved to a designated loading point. The buyer assumes responsibility of insurance, freight and all other costs from that point on. The factory quotes product cost and delivery to port of export.

CIF (Cost Insurance Freight): The price includes sea freight charges and insurance to deliver the goods to the port nearest port to the final destination. But only to the port – from that point onwards, you take the shipment into your hands. You are responsible for insurance, freight and all other costs from that point forward. The factory (seller) provides you, the buyer with the documents necessary to obtain the goods from the carrier. The responsibility of the seller ends once the goods reach the buyer's port of choice.

EX-FACTORY: The seller owns goods until they are picked up from their factory where is was manufactured. The selling price is the cost of the goods. The factory only quotes the product cost.

DDP Delivered Duty Paid (named place of destination). The factory (seller) takes responsibility until an agreed-upon point at the named place in the country of importation, often the buyer's premises. The factory has to bear the risks and all costs, including duties, taxes and other charges of delivering the goods to importation clearance. The buyer must have an import license and/or any other authorization forms. The factory gives the price of product(s) including taxes, insurance, duties and delivery charges.

Partner with a Freight Forwarding Agent These companies will take care of *everything* mentioned above and will deliver the goods to your door without you having to mess around with the customs clearance procedure. It can be easy to misclassify goods unless you understand the essential characteristics of the garments and specific definitions. Importing can be incredibly daunting, particularly to those who may be new to the business. There are so many regulations and responsibilities to adhere to that anyone attempting to navigate through the process with little knowledge can be left with a mess of penalties and one giant headache. The good news is you don't have to figure all of this out on your own – there are licensed freight forwarding agents who can assist with the importing and delivery process.

Customs broker's are great. Here's why:

1 You have a go-to person for up-to-date information on what's going on in the world of importing.

2 You have a go-to person for duty rates on products, which is especially helpful for costing products when establishing budgets.

3 You have a go-to person regarding labeling of products before products are manufactured.

4 You have a go-to person for tracking deliveries and managing any delivery or importing issues.

(Notice a trend here?)

5 And finally, freight forwarding companies are very affordable and can actually work out to be cheaper than if you try to do it all on your own.

Courier Expenses

You pay for counter samples and sample approvals sent to and from the factory. Set aside some cash flow for couriers. Typically, an average order of four to six styles will have approximately five to six packages sent back and forth. The most reputable and commonly used couriers are DHL and FedEx. Shipping offshore starts from $75 and above depending on the weight and size of the package.

Product Development Costs

Many fashion professionals are involved in the design and development of your product. Taking your concepts from drawing to prototype requires collaboration among many fashion experts, including the tech pack and graphic designers, sample sewers, pattern makers, and fit models. You should work through prototyping locally. The factory will counter sample to get your garment production ready.

Average costs for a single prototype range from $1,000 to $2,000. Costs include making the tech packs and patterns, and creating prototypes, as well as purchasing materials/trims and store-bought samples used for references. You will also need to set aside a budget for the factory to make a production-ready sample. It is vital that you understand your budget and how much you have to spend because that will ultimately be the guide in determining how many samples you can afford to make locally and counter sample offshore.

Shopping The Market

In the early stages of the production process and throughout the year, designers study the market and gather images and purchase samples to reference. Designers travel near and far to collect samples, looking for inspiration everywhere, from vintage stores to high-end boutiques. The physical samples aid in product development and communicating quality standards to everyone in the process. A budget is set aside for samples and, in some cases, travel.

Counter Sampling Costs

The factory makes a counter sample using a similar and available fabric before production. The counter sample helps to achieve sewing efficiencies, establish costs, and source all other materials in the product for your approval. The designer makes comments or gives approvals on product trims, quality standard selection, and other items that impact price. Once all items and details, such as materials, fit, stitching, prints, color, lab-dips, and tags are approved, a final cost can be calculated. Just like any other company you work with locally, the offshore manufacturers also have a cost to produce these samples. Costs vary according to product complexity, manpower and materials required.

The Misconception of Low-Cost Garment Sampling

It's a huge misconception that it is cheaper for a factory to produce samples at a fraction of the cost you pay locally. The majority of apparel factories charge approximately three times the cost of a garment in bulk production. For example, if the order is for 1,000 basic T-shirts and the cost is $10.00, typically they will charge $30 for each sample. The total number of samples must also be factored in.

Sampling charges are actually a formality. Due to heavy competition and fear of losing you as a potential client, they feel pressured to absorb the cost in hopes of getting an order. Sample runs are expensive as they aren't spreading the setup time across very many garments. Once an order is placed, the costs are added back into the cost of bulk orders.

Requesting sales samples to be received once orders are placed, substantially lowers sampling costs because the fabric and materials are ordered at the same time of production and sewn when in house. If fabric or materials need to be ordered before bulk production, costs are substantially higher.

Please consider that all counter samples or approvals will be made *twice*. Offshore factories keep one copy to reference and send the other one to you for commenting. The factory needs a reference for corrections that may be requested or as a guide for production.

Who Gets Paid for Samples?

1 **The Apparel Production Merchandiser**: The person who orchestrates the entire sampling process and communicates with the sampling department.

2 **The Fabric Weaver**: May be involved in the purchasing and sourcing of yarn. Produces a small batch of fabric or sample swatch based on your requirements. They are extremely busy, and this takes time.

3 **The Fabric Dyer**: Produces lab dips for color approvals (which may be developed a few times until they get it right). Production fabric is dyed only once the lab dip is approved.

4 **The Garment Washer**: In most cases, this is also the dyeing unit. After dyeing, the fabric is washed to control shrinkage, known as *compacting*. Finishes, for hand feel or aesthetic, may also be applied (for example, fabric softener, enzyme wash or bio wash). Sometimes, garments are also washed once they are assembled.

5 **The Hang Tag Maker**: The hang tag screen and sample is created for you to approve. Unique paper qualities may need to be sourced.

6 **The Care Label Maker**: Screens must be set up and samples sent before production. Material for labels must be purchased and sourced.

7 **The Screen Printer**: If a screen print is required, inks/color/quality must be sourced and sampled, and the screens need to be set up.

8 **The Pattern Maker**: In cases where the patterns are made offshore, the pattern maker follows the sample and tech packs to create patterns. Revisions and changes to patterns add to the costs.

9 **The Sample Sewer (sewing department)**: The prototypes may be sewn several times until a final one is achieved. Machinery must be set up accordingly for each sample order. If machinery needs to be outsourced, that incurs additional cost.

10 **The Trims/Thread Coordinator**: Trims may need to be customized. For example, zippers are generally customized and need to be made according to color and length.

As you can see, there are many people involved, and without even going into much detail, it takes everyone a lot of time, money and resources.

❋ GOLDEN NUGGET

Working with the factory to procure fabric allows for better price breaks. Manufacturing fabric from scratch involves working directly with the mills. Generally, factories require a large order volume to work directly with mills. The cut-and-sew factory works with many clients who require fabric to be manufactured and who work with mills. Thus, having greater buying power, mills are more open to manufacturing orders with a lower quantity.

The Number of Styles Directly Impact Your Budget

Ever notice how many dishes are on a typical Chinese restaurant menu? Next time you're placing an order, take a look. It's quite a lot. The restaurant is buying a lot of different ingredients because there are so many recipes and it takes much more time to make each one. Still, what do you think typical Western customers tend to order? General Tso Chicken, ginger beef, chow mein, etc. The menu may have literally dozens of options, but by and large, the customers are going to buy some things more than others. What do you think happens to the ingredients of all those dishes that never get ordered, the ones the chefs can't use for other dishes? Apparently, they get thrown out. Such a waste, not only of food but of money and time.

Designers often make a similar mistake when it comes to how many styles they want to offer right out of the gate. If you're wondering, as most designer entrepreneurs do, how many styles you should start with, I have a fortune cookie message for you. It says, "Before you begin the design process, plan how many products would work within your budget." The more styles you start with, the more money and time you will need, and some will always sell more than others.

Regardless of how much capital you have access to, the best strategy is to always minimize risk. As product development is complicated and time-consuming, the fewer styles you manufacture, the better. A good place to start is between one and six styles, and no more than two colors. This may seem small, but there is still a lot to juggle.

The more styles you have, the more capital you will need to invest into the business, and the more time you'll need to manufacture the product. Moving forward, if you do add more styles, try to keep your basic bodies (silhouettes/styles of pattern), or pattern blocks the same, making variations of styles that have proven to be profitable. Variations may include changes in color or fabric, or other small design changes that don't require you to start from scratch.

Think about it. If you have a proven style that works, why change it? You may be bored staring at your product, but consumers are not. Remember, customers and buyers don't look at your product every day, and they also quickly forget. Think back to earlier in the book when we talked about walking into Old Navy or other popular chains: the seasons may change, but the basic designs of the outfits themselves are the same. The way you market a product can completely change a style. Photoshoots can change the way products are seen and perceived.

Sew... basically, if it ain't broke, don't fix it. This strategy can increase company profits, introduce products to the market faster, and allow your business to grow at a steady pace.

The Number Of Colorways Directly Affects Your Budget

Styles differ from piece to piece. If you have four styles and two colors per style, you'll have a total of eight pieces, which is enough to start an online shop. Starting with too many choices can intimidate potential customers. Shoppers make decisions quickly and want things to be kept simple and precise.

The Number Of SKUs Directly Affects Your Budget

A Stock-Keeping Unit is an identification code, usually alphanumeric, of a particular product that allows it to be tracked for inventory purposes. If you are producing a garment that comes in different sizes, it will affect your budget. How many sizes do you have? SKUs refer to every size, color, and style of a product. A product with five sizes (XS, SM, MED, LG, and XL), four styles and two colors, equals 40 SKUs. *Sew*, although you may have only eight pieces with five sizes, you end up having a lot of SKUs.

The higher the number of SKUs, the more time and work it is for your company. Each SKU will entail more administrative work, photography, inventory management, back-end work, and shipping/logistics. Minimizing SKUs will give you greater control over your brand and the manufacturing process. It also helps minimize risk so the brand can grow at a steady pace. Start out small, establish the viability of your product, and streamline your process.

With that in mind, it is challenging for the factory to manage a large number of SKUs. There is a learning curve for each department in the factory, and this affects both speed and costs. Minimizing SKUs and increasing total quantities per piece also helps the factory move through production smoothly and give better product costs.

Money-Saving Tips

1 Ensure the bulk production POs have no more than two product colors in total.

2 Minimize SKUs.

3 Ensure the bulk production POs have no more than six styles.

4 Always simplify designs.

5 If possible, try to increase the MOQ suggested by the factory to help maintain better costs.

6 Have a perfect "production example" prototype and a clearly communicated pre-production package, making it more comfortable for the factory. (Less back and forth means lower courier costs.)

7 Negotiate a discount for international shipping rates. Contact a courier company and ask for a discount. Tell them you ship 10-20 packages a month with a competitor (wink-wink!). They should lock you into a good discount for a year. In my opinion, FedEx offers reliability and the best customer service.

8 Ship bulk production orders via sea. And, of course, if you can, order more than the MOQ.

9 Complete designs and tech packs for a minimum of three seasons (or orders) before you start working with the factory.

10 Create prototypes and do pattern making locally. Close communication is crucial to prevent costly mistakes.

11 Be flexible with the sample approval process because it will save both time and money.

Asking For Prices

Everyone is trying to save money, and I hate to say it, but more often than not, they're just cheap. We all have that one friend. You know, the one that finds a way to get in on every round of drinks with the squad then pulls out nothing but pocket lint when it comes their time to buy. In garment manufacturing, cheapness shows up in the attitudes that many first-time designers have towards the process. "Let's work offshore!" they declare. "Cheap prices!" This is the first thing that *everyone* assumes. Sure, that assumption would be true, but are you ordering a large enough quantity to justify a significant price break? A factory makes very little per piece on an order of 200 pieces in comparison to 2000 pieces. How much do you think the factory can make and survive off of 200 units with a really low price? How can they stay in business with all of their overhead expenses? Just like you, they have a business to run too.

Costing is no walk in the park for a factory; it takes a substantial amount of effort and time to calculate costs, especially given the number of people involved. Let's take a simple T-shirt as an example. It can involve at least ten different suppliers: the yarn supplier, dyer, knitter, hang tag supplier, label supplier, screen printer, button supplier, elastic supplier, the various departments within the factory, and so on. Imagine having to get costings from everyone and having to meet their requirements. Everyone is busy.

The factory requires detailed information from you to calculate fabric consumption so they can provide you with costs and estimate minimums. Beyond fabric and materials, technical details matter. Let's say your product requires a specific seam. If they don't have the machine on site, they will have to outsource, thus increasing costs. These realizations often happen after the fact, especially with inadequate tech packs. For something that may seem minor, it can be a massive cost to the factory.

Let's take one of my clients as an example, a reputable company that manufactures designer wallpaper. After many successes, the company moved into offering home furnishing products. After the product cost was given, the company decided to place the order, but this was two weeks later, and the deposit was not received until a week after that. When it came time to purchase the yarn, the price of cotton went up. It's difficult to control every cost that goes into a product. The factory again hit a loss.

Pantone colors were listed on the purchase order, but it wasn't until after the order was placed that the factory was told to match the fabric exactly to the wallpaper. Matching paper to fabric is tough.

The factory provided several rounds – more than the norm – of sample approvals, which brought up the costs for the factory and the printing unit. Also, it wasn't until the fabric was printed that the company told the factory that the repeat prints of the curtains could not be randomly cut off at any point. Each print had to be identical and cut at specific points, increasing fabric wastage. The costs went up *again*.

More often than not, the initial prices given to you will be a lot lower when you first do business. They are working with you as an investment to not only prove that they can do the job, but to grow with you. If you don't increase the quantity or pieces in the next order, the prices will likely increase. It takes time for the factory to understand your product and quality standards. It takes time for the factories to understand your process.

Often, there are more losses as they start working with new clients. As you grow with the factory, they make investments to help control costs. If, for example, they know you need a particular machine, they may opt to purchase it in the long run because they're confident you'll stick around. Costings are so tight for small orders, yet we all expect low prices. Everyone is working hard.

The ultimate goal is to understand one another's needs and grow together over time. Over time, things get easier for everyone to manage, including for you. The factories are under a lot of pressure to give a competitive price. They need consistent orders to survive. After quoting a price and during an order, they try their best to not increase a price.

And what about those cheap prices? Again, generally, we live in a reasonably frugal culture right now, but although people had been "poppin' tags" long before Macklemore wrote a song about it, as things get more expensive, more and more people want to spend less. It's only natural. This applies doubly so to business owners operating on small margins.

I get it: you don't want to spend more money than you need to on production. What you may not realize (or want to think about) is that there is always a cost to your savings.

Doesn't anyone stop to think about the energy and people that go into the product? Sure, the labor may be cheaper, but cheap prices also come when you buy more. Sure, you can say to yourself, "I'm a business person, I need low costs," but a successful businessperson also considers growing long-term relationships. Is a cheaper cost more important than getting your product produced consistently and in a timely manner? Is it more important to you to squeeze your partner, or are your margins too low and you're not asking your customer to fork out the dough for a niche product?

Negotiating Prices

Price breaks are fantastic, but isn't selling all your inventory way more important? Friendly reminder once again: if you've placed an order with minimum quantities, the factory is only 30% efficient! *Sew*, what does that mean for them? Well, they have little to no room to profit. They are working in hopes that the re-order will increase in volume. Always remember that you and your factory are a team, and a successful partnership only grows if both parties are making profits. In the beginning, it may seem that you are forking out so much dough, but really, most factories are working with much larger orders, typically more than $500,000 for a mid-sized factory. To the factory, that's a proper order.

As we've discussed, factories will give you price breaks when ordering higher quantities. This is because each machine needs to be set up for the run, including adjusting the machines, re-threading with your threads, cutting, etc. The higher quantity ordered, the more you are able to stretch that time across your run. The manufacturing process becomes much easier to streamline.

But, that being said, it may not make sense to start a business with so much inventory that it is impossible to sell it all in one season. Fashion moves quickly. You have to be able to refresh your stock with new items or colorways on a regular basis. If you've followed my formula, but are selling higher-priced products, you will have higher margins and profits. And negotiating with the factory won't be as much of an issue.

Ordering smaller quantities to start may be a safer bet. It's always better than sitting on a multitude of pieces of dead inventory, which makes you no money at all (and is, in fact, a loss). Although producing lower quantities increases the per-piece cost, it ultimately keeps your total purchase order or budget down. As your company grows and the purchase order dollar amount increases, costs per piece will go down.

Fashion startups may not be in the best position to negotiate prices, but you can always ask a factory for tips on how to lower costs. Remember that they are a part of your tribe and the more you communicate with them and learn their process, the more you will learn about costs.

Golden Nuggets I've picked up along the way:

1 Factories can suggest alternatives in the fabrics' qualities, the most significant cost in production. Could you save a bit by doing the markers and grading locally?

2 Maybe instead of using five different screens for each back neck size label, you can use one print for the label and use a size flag for each size.

3 Can you buy a larger amount of fabric and set aside the greige (undyed) fabric for the next order? There are tons of ways to save, so both you and the factory are happy.

Part 7 is all about finding your new best friend that we've spent so much time hyping: the factory. I know you might be thinking to yourself, "Never mix business with pleasure," but anyone who has watched Jay and Beyoncé over the years knows there are exceptions to the rule. And if part 6 has got you lookin' so crazy right now, Part 7 will help you cultivate a friendship with your factory that is irreplaceable.

NOTES

1. Salfino, C. Quality Over Quantity. http://lifestylemonitor.cottoninc. com/quality-over-quantity/. December 20, 2012.

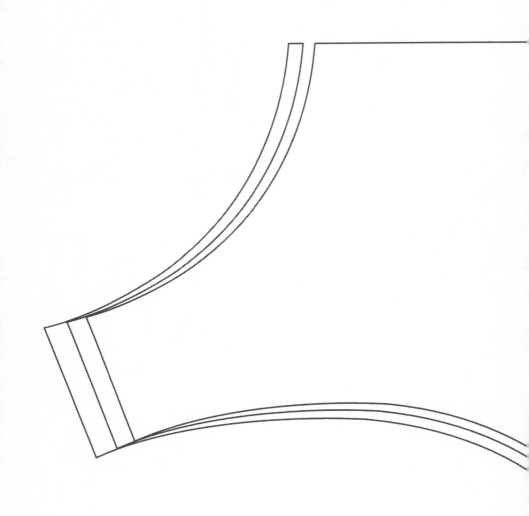

FACTORY SOURCING

CHAPTER 7

OVERVIEW

Long distance relationships are hard. You wonder what they are doing. You lie awake at night wondering if they understand you and are interested in your needs and desires. Sometimes, you even wonder if they are cheating...

Okay, before you start getting the wrong impression here, I am actually talking about your relationship with your offshore manufacturer. Designer entrepreneurs generally view offshore manufacturing relationships as problematic and tense. You've heard the horror stories - extremely late deliveries, defective shipments and much more.

What you don't know is this: way across the ocean, they too have their share of horror stories working with brands. But, as the saying goes, there are two sides to every coin. Factories and designers are critical of each other. There is always a mismatch in expectations, a lack of understanding of each other's business operations, or workflow, or financial restrictions... the list goes on.

Relationships between designer entrepreneurs and factories can be problematic, especially for those who fail to remember that products go through many iterations and touch many hands. It's complex and hard to control. Clothes are not made by machines. Working with any partner, both locally or offshore requires a little give and take. Issues will always come up. There is no way to sugar coat it.

After all, every couple has their bad days...

Here's what I've learned.

One of the most important things I've come to realize is how we all perceive the word *"factory"*- it's a very misleading term. The Oxford dictionary defines a factory as "a building or group of buildings where goods are manufactured or assembled chiefly by machine." Now, call me crazy, but reading that definition, it sounds like products are made by machines all on their own. The truth is that garment factories are not run by machines; they are run by people, no matter how many units are produced. Yes, machines are used, but I've seen how labor-intensive the work is, requiring an almost insurmountable amount of skill. The fact is, everything we wear is made with hands. I challenge everyone to shift their perceptions around how our clothes are made.

When you're ready to take the leap into offshore manufacturing remember to develop a long distance relationship like you would a personal one. If you're new to the industry, you may not realize how important building relationships is to building a successful brand. These are relationships that you need to foster and nurture, so they grow in the long-term. It is, therefore, essential to build up a good working relationship with factories. Without them you have no product. What keeps them happy is smooth and constant production. Happy factory, happy life, remember?

Sew, how do we develop a good customer-supplier relationship? A good relationship starts with excellent communication. This can take many forms, including just being kind when writing emails. Sharing is important. It may also involve sharing a meal with them over dinner, or even sharing your lookbook (your product catalogue of photos showcasing you styles for marketing purposes) or press achievements. Get to know each other. Factories love to see what becomes of the products they make because lots of love and care goes into the manufacturing process. If the order starts small, consider showing them how much effort you are putting into your work and that the intention is to grow. It's easy for the factories to lose interest in your brand. Factories see a lot of buyers, so you want to stand out to them just as much as you want your consumers to notice you. Get them excited!

The truth is, no one is ever going to care as much about your product as you do, but if you build a relationship and get them just as excited as you are, you'll have an ally who will have greater care for your production.

The Boy/Girl Next Door or Long Distance?
Offshore vs Domestic Manufacturer?

Ready to start dating?

One of the first of many important choices you will have to make is who manufactures your products. What are your needs in this relationship? Do you want to start small and modestly, or do you want to dive right into a sizeable offshore run? Each of them has their benefits, but which one is right for your brand? Regardless of where the garment factory is located, it's crucial to be confident about your strategy and know who you're giving your money to. Ultimately, the decision lies in your manufacturing needs and budget. There is no one right answer for all companies. There is no single factory-soulmate for you waiting out there.

What makes the most business sense depends on your unique needs and business goals. For example, do you sell a product which isn't time-sensitive and can ship anytime? Or, do you sell a highly-specialized product that requires quality machinery and skilled workers? There are so many factors to consider.

One suggestion though, if you can help it, try to avoid going with the cheapest option. Instead, choose the factory which will deliver the most value in the long-term. What good is a "cheap" product if it doesn't sell? Right?

Domestic or offshore manufacturing? Which one best fits your needs?

Below are some pointers to help you choose:

Domestic Manufacturing - PROS

> The convenience of working closely with people, monitoring quality and visiting the factory.
> Savings from not getting international courier charges and shipping costs.
> The elimination of import customs duties.

> Faster turnaround times thanks to fabric suppliers carrying in-stock materials.
> The ability to produce lower quantities.
> Attracting patriotic customers who prefer garments made at home.
> Eliminating language and cultural barriers, as well as time differences.
> Quick order-to-delivery times.
> The support of local labor & economy.

Domestic Manufacturing - CONS

> Lack of sophisticated machinery drives quality down.
> Lack of skilled labor drives quality down.
> Higher labor costs.
> Purchases from fabric suppliers and trims can be out of stock (with no notice) and no ability to reorder.
> Purchases from fabric suppliers and raw materials give you less control over quality.
> You are responsible for procuring and sourcing all the raw materials and delivery to the manufacturer. Therefore, you must deal with all the issues.
> You are responsible for storing or disposing of any leftover raw materials.
> Most raw materials are sourced and manufactured offshore.
> Lack the ability to meet production needs as a company grows.
> Special Consideration for Domestic Sourcing
> Domestic sourcing is not a guarantee of social responsibility. We'll explore this issue in greater detail in Part 8.

Overseas Manufacturing - PROS

> The convenience of communicating with factories from the comfort of your own home.
> The convenience of full package contracting: you can coordinate with a merchandiser who can orchestrate the entire manufacturing process and sometimes delivery.

> Cost benefits: costs drop with subsequent orders and larger orders.
> The capability of manufacturing larger orders in the future.
> The convenience of having the factory source, procure, manufacture, and warehouse raw materials including the labels, hang tags, and packaging (which also eliminates your warehousing expenses for raw materials).
> The factory is responsible for all issues on raw materials and fabric.
> Access to higher quality machinery, yielding a better quality product.
> Access to a specialized machinery that may not be available locally.
> Supporting underprivileged and skilled labor.
> Access to a large pool of skilled workers and lower labor costs.
> Close to a more extensive selection of raw materials and subcontractors.
> Someone else (like your agent) is monitoring and managing production.

Overseas Manufacturing - CONS

> Minimum order quantities are much higher.
> Requires up to 50% deposit up-front for production.
> Must pay in full before shipment leaves port in most cases.
> Longer lead times: transit times for delivery influence a longer lead time.
> Communication barriers (time differences, language).
> An increase in costs with the courier, shipping, insurance, and duties.
> Difficult to identify and correct social compliance issues.
> Fluctuations in traded commodity prices of raw materials such as cotton and wool.

Special Considerations for Offshore Sourcing

Political Stability and Economic Climate

A country that is stable welcomes foreign investment and tends to favor fair labor wage practices. It's also important that the currency is stable so that the agreed-upon prices do not negatively impact either party. Countries like China and India would be considered stable nations. Most offshore factories prefer to sell products and invoice in U.S. currency.

Infrastructure
Consider a country's infrastructure, which includes its transportation and communication systems, telephone, electricity, and water utilities, as well as resources for both labor and management.

Sourcing

In the business world, the term sourcing refers to many procurement practices, aimed at finding, evaluating, and engaging suppliers in acquiring products and services. Sourcing may include finding out where materials come from, where product development happens, or where it's made.

A factory can source materials from anywhere in the world or right at home. They even work with manufacturing subcontractors and they, too, can outsource and also be found anywhere in the world. It's rare for the entire production to be completed entirely in their own manufacturing facility: subcontractors are often better equipped to take care of specific steps of the process. For this very reason, the final outcome of the products and manufacturing process is not in the factories' complete control. Subcontractors such as screen printers, embroiderers, dyers, fabric suppliers, washers, packaging suppliers and many more, all work with the factories to manufacture a garment. It's a genuinely collaborative effort.

Sourcing Costs

Source like a boss (but don't get too bossy). Sourcing decisions should never be based solely on costs. What good is a product if the transactions cause you stress by not meeting quality expectations? When comparing the prices of manufacturing domestically versus offshore, remember to include all the hidden costs that go with both options. For example, if you decide to work with a local manufacturer, your time will be spent running around - sourcing and procuring raw materials, finding storage, delivering them and managing quality control. It may leave you little to no time to run the business. Often, overseas garment factories are a complete package where a merchandiser is orchestrating the entire manufacturing process.

As I said before, most entrepreneurs believe that offshore manufacturing means lower costs. This is only true if the quantities are high enough that the factory can manufacture efficiently. However, if the plan is to grow the brand and business, developing a relationship and understanding of the product, it makes sense to go offshore.

Remember, offshore garment factories only work with small-to-medium sized brands in the hopes that they will be repeat customers who return with consistent and ever-increasing orders. The significance of this is that consistent purchase orders help factories to better plan their manufacturing schedules, which help to keep business operations running smoothly, while large volumes help to drive down costs and yield a better return for both parties.

When To Seek Out A Factory

Are you truly ready to date? Do you design first and then seek out factories, or do you seek out a factory and then design? This is the classic "chicken and egg" question: which comes first? Some companies seek out a factory first to learn about its capabilities and specialties before designing. Others create a product and find the perfect match.

Factories are full of unique construction and design ideas. Let's say you visit the factory's showroom. After checking out showroom samples, you've seen that they have mastered several creative pintuck techniques. This draws inspiration for new designs featuring pintucks, *sew* you play off their skills. The process will move faster as the sewers have already mastered the skill.

On the flip side, the majority of designers will design first, then seek out a factory.

Before you take the leap into offshore manufacturing, consider the following:

1. Do you have a production package? Refer back to the Pre-Production Checklist. At the very least, you'll need a tech pack, sample, and fabric standard to get a quote.

2. Is your fabric structure a knit or woven? Factories are set up according to fabric structure: most either specialize in one or the other. Consider creating products with either knits or wovens for the first production run.

3. Do you have a budget for production? The factory will ask you for target prices for every style. Refer back to Part 6.

4. How well do you know your target market? Likely, you have a good idea of who your target market is, but do you really understand them the way you should? Have you analyzed them thoroughly with both secondary and primary research? Understanding the data helps establish everything from design features and price points to quality standards and more. While some consumers like the worn-out, ripped look, other consumers' standards will be crisp and clean. This information will need to be conveyed to the factory. Every brand has its own quality standards.

5. Have you established your sales channels? Will you be selling wholesale, retail or online? Where will you be selling? Have you considered home parties, crowdfunding, fairs or pop-ups? You can use a showroom, sales reps, distributors, trade shows, and the list goes on. Better yet, have you lined up potential buyers or pre-sold designs? Never assume that buyers will flock to you.

6. What is your goal for the first production run? Are you testing out styles to see how well they sell, or testing to see how well the manufacturing process goes before you invest in a larger order? Are you trying to establish which styles will be repeat orders or sell through the quickest?

Dedication To Relationships Creates Opportunities

Gone are the days where sourcing decisions are based solely on product costs. As I've been saying throughout this chapter, the best way to approach and source a factory is just like dating. They're your partners, so, why not? Size them up, assess whether you both communicate well and if your values line up. Relationships are a two-way street and they are built on trust. Your partner is as human as you are, with feelings, hopes, and needs, the same as you.

The beginning stages of any relationship involve a lot of vulnerability and can be overwhelming, yet exciting. You might even get butterflies in your stomach! You are investing time to build a relationship with someone, trusting that they are doing the same. Being open and honest with each other is critical to having transparent communication. Most importantly, you need to be sure that you both have similar values. And just like any "new relationship," both parties must put their best foot forward.

Below are my five tips to help you establish a successful and long-lasting relationship with your offshore manufacturer:

1 The Vetting Process

You vet a potential love interest to make sure that they are credible and trustworthy. You do the same thing when you are looking to partner with a factory: do your homework and make sure they have the same values. A mutually-respectful working relationship involves building trust on both ends to reduce risk and uncertainty for both parties.

2 Stay Connected

Dating is exciting and generally means being in regular contact. You need to call and text this fantastic person to get to know them. You're engaging in conversation. The same thing applies to factories: you need to be in regular communication, whether that be via Skype, email, text, or phone. Above all, visit them in person! Getting to know each other on a regular basis builds understanding and trust.

3 Put Your Best Foot Forward

Romeo wasn't romantic for no reason. He was memorable! Take the factory owner out to dinner and share a meal. Get to know them on a personal level. What are their values? Do you connect? Open up and tell them about your vision. "Sell them your company" and get them motivated to want to work with you. You need them as much as they need you. They have a lot of other brands working with them, so make a good impression.

4 Show Appreciation & Gratitude

Couples who actively practice gratitude and appreciation feel a deep sense of connection with one another. It's too easy to merely focus on what bothers you about your significant other, while ignoring why you fell in love in the first place. The same holds true for your relationship with your factory. Show them appreciation and gratitude. You need to be sensitive to both you and the factory's feelings because this is a partnership. The key takeaway is that you learn from each other.

5 Manage Expectations

When it comes to love, most of us bought the fairy tale. Just like true love, you can't expect your relationship with a manufacturer to be perfect. Let the factory know what you are looking for. This could be about deliveries, product quality, even social responsibility or how they treat their workers. Be transparent with your manufacturers by telling them what matters to you and ask if your requests are manageable. An important characteristic of a healthy relationship is being able to state your desires as preferences instead of demands. Send compassionate emails instead of harsh commands. Be cognizant of their expectations to create a lasting relationship.

A significant portion of your time spent building a fashion brand goes towards manufacturing a product. Therefore, the value of having a nurturing and evolving relationship will outweigh any cost and enable your company to grow and be profitable. At the end of the day, "dating" your factory is more than just knowing where your products are made. It is about building relationships with the people who are involved in the manufacturing process. And without it, it will be almost impossible to successfully produce the product that you envision.

Sourcing A Factory

Time to put your feelers out!

Now that you have a better idea of the pros and cons of seeking manufacturing partners domestically and abroad, and if you are ready, you can begin to start the sourcing process. Many designer entrepreneurs find themselves hitting a brick wall and losing momentum when it comes time to actually source a factory. Finding one is difficult and reviewing factories and contractors can be very exhausting. Next to selling the products, choosing a factory is the hardest decision you will make. They are, of course, a partner and are responsible for creating the product, which is obviously a huge aspect to the success of your brand.

As a newcomer to the apparel industry, sourcing a good manufacturer can be a significant obstacle. The best way to go about this? Network, network, network! Ask for referrals or recommendations from industry contacts. A good pattern maker or fabric supplier would be able to help. If you are bold enough, it's worthwhile contacting retailers who offer a product similar to yours, tell them you're new to the industry and ask for a referral. Unfortunately, the best factories are so highly prized that many designers are hesitant to share their contacts. Get what you can from them: even knowing the city or country they manufacture in can help you narrow your search, as you might find a district that specializes in what you do.

Do Incredibly Thorough Research

Ever Googled someone before a first date? You have? Great! Then this will all be familiar to you...

The first step in sourcing a factory is, yet again, research. Running a business and conducting research, no matter what stage you're at, go hand-in-hand. There's no one-size-fits-all rule, and the more you know what is going on on the manufacturing side, the better the position you will be in to make your final decision.

Let's say you want to manufacture shower curtains with unique prints. After much research, you may find that you have no choice but to go offshore. Specialized rotary printers that can handle large-scale fabric widths are just not available in North America. Your research, in this case, has led you overseas.

Below are a few key places to start that can put you on the right track to finding your perfect apparel manufacturing soulmate, I mean partner.

Where Does Your Perfect Partner Hang Out?

Now that you have a better idea of exactly what you're looking for, as well as the advantages and disadvantages of domestic vs. overseas sourcing, where do you begin your search? Naturally, the Internet is the best place to start, but there are a few places in particular that can help with your search. After all, if your dream partner likes to hang out at bookstores, then it would probably be a good idea to go pick up that new edition of Girlboss that just came out.

Trade Shows

Trade shows are a gold mine for meeting potential factories face to face. You have the opportunity to discuss both companies, products, production capacity, and other key business areas. You can see if there is a good fit before making the leap to visit the factory overseas. Direct interaction can help you evaluate and verify their abilities.

It's a little like speed dating: you meet a lot of potential suitors up front and get the basics of who they are and what they're about.

Here's a couple of popular industry trade-shows in the U.S. to get you started:

Texworld USA (texworldusa.us.messefrankfurt.com)
Sourcing at Magic (www.magiconline.com/sourcing-at-magic)

> ✳ **GOLDEN NUGGET**
>
> Trade shows take place all over the world. Search online to find trade shows located in a specific region you want to manufacture. If you are unable to attend a trade show overseas, take a look at the exhibitor listing.

Online B2B Directories

Some of the best sources can be online supplier directories. Most are free to use, though some are subscription-based. These directories contain profiles for hundreds of manufacturers, wholesalers, and suppliers. It's the easiest way to find factories.

The downside is that offshore factories do a notoriously poor job of keeping their websites updated and optimized for modern times. They don't specialize in marketing and have limited resources to invest in online marketing. That means that most of the websites for factories are very outdated, lack the aesthetics, and aren't optimized for Google searches.

Most of the online directories are focused on a core region. Some examples include IndiaMart in India, Alibaba in China and Makersrow in the USA. Remember every country has its strengths and weaknesses, so be sure to research before you make your decision.

IndiaMart (www.indiamart.com)
Alibaba (www.alibaba.com)
Makersrow (www.makersrow.com)

Agents & Consultants

Working with an agent or a consultant will take a huge load off your back, especially when working with an overseas factory. Not only will you save time, but you will also allow someone with expertise in the industry to help manage production, thus lowering your risk. Although the agent you are working with should be able to guide you along the way, it is your responsibility to be informed. You are ultimately the responsible party.

Typically agents give you an all-inclusive price per garment. They have established relationships with factories. Since they manage many clients, the factory is able to provide the agent with better pricing. The savings is where they make their money. As a newcomer with a smaller order, you have a smaller buying power, and thus will not be able to negotiate.

Regardless, if you go straight to the factory or work through an agent, you will get similar pricing. For many, the added expertise, peace of mind, and time savings are enough for them to go for an agent or consultant. A skilled expert in the field can identify and handle production problems, as well as manage communication at odd hours of the night.

Agents located offshore are called **buying agents, buying houses,** or **exporters**. They work as mediators between you, the apparel buyer, and the factories. Be sure to check profiles carefully, as some agents have their own factory. It's critical that you have excellent communication with your go-to person or buying agent. Keep in mind, they may not have the best understanding of North American products or concepts, but the good thing is they can follow up there and do quality inspections. The best buying houses are set up as foreign businesses and have an excellent command of the English language.

Social Media

Social media is an easy way to get a recommendation. Tweet your search and ask for a factory recommendation. Join LinkedIn apparel manufacturing groups or Facebook groups dedicated to fashion startups.

Short-listing Factories

After doing the research, you will inevitably end up with a list of potential factories, from around the world, to work with. This is great! But, unless you have an endless supply of cash, you won't be able to sample with all of them so you will need to cut your list down. They say that there is plenty of other fish in the sea, but in factory sourcing as in dating, you can't catch all of them!

Making a comparison is also essential to ensuring that you are getting a quality product at a fair price. Start by eliminating factories that may not be the right fit. A good three to five quality prospects will do before you settle on one factory for sampling purposes. Below are a few key things to consider:

1 Will you require CMT or Full Package Factory?

A CMT (cut, make, trim) factory will produce your product from start-to-finish. They cut the fabric, sew fabric, and attach the trimming such as hangtags, buttons, labels, etc. You source the material and components and generally supply the patterns and a cutting marker. Typically, most domestic factories are CMT factories.

An FPP (full package production) factory takes care of the entire production process, everything from fabric purchase, cutting, and sewing to trimming and packaging. You supply the designs and specifications. Some full package contractors offer additional services, sometimes including design, pattern making, grading, and marker making. Typically, these factories are found overseas If you want to focus your energies on the design, business, marketing, sales and so on, you can leave the rest to a full-package manufacturer.

2 Location, Location, Location

Every country and region has particular strengths and specialties. As I touched upon earlier, before looking for a factory, research products similar to yours and find out where they are typically made. Chances are, after researching the type of products you have designed, it will lead you to the country where the factory is located.

Let's say you sell shoes. The research will point you to big manufacturing countries such as China, Italy, Spain, or a few regions in South America. Peru is known for knit sweaters. If you are looking to manufacture socks or polyesters, China is, once again, your best bet. Bulgaria and most of South America are suitable for swimwear. Colombia: underwear and loungewear. Italy, Pakistan or Turkey for leather jackets. In India, the north specializes in woven products, while the factories found in the south region called Tirupur, specializes in knits. Large format printing mills, suitable for high-quality home furnishings, would be located only in Ahmedabad, India.

✽ GOLDEN NUGGET

Make sure that you analyze competitors thoroughly. Determine where they are manufacturing products by checking the garment labels. Look for the "country of origin." Chances are that this is the spot where you need to make your products. If your competitors are sourcing from certain places, it very likely means those countries and factories are producing high-quality garments, thus reducing your own risk.

A Special Note On India's Manufacturing Strengths

In my opinion, India is the master of manufacturing quality-driven niche products. Here, you will find a wide variety of factories catering from organic cotton kids underwear to leather bags. They also specialize in skilled artisan and handmade products. Premium quality hand beading, block printing, embroidery techniques, you name it. They have been doing this for generations, and it is a part of the Indian culture.

India remains my go-to place for reliability and quality. As a stable country, there is a lower your risk of any economic or political problems. Almost all of my clients produce in India for many good reasons. Small-to-medium-sized companies can manage average minimum orders while maintaining the ability to scale up. Most of the smaller factories ask for MOQ's of 1,000 pieces in one fabric quality and color, which can be subdivided into several styles.

Let's say you have four products, all the same fabric and color, and 250 pieces of each style; you meet the minimum of 1,000. The average minimum order in China and Bangladesh would be closer to 1,000 pieces in one style, fabric and color and it's not likely they will do just one style. The factories are massive: there is just no money in it for them.

India is the world's top cotton producer, where organic cotton is easily sourced, and the fabric is produced. From a sustainability standpoint, raw materials and resources are available in abundance. They are deeply committed to reducing their environmental footprint.

3 Size Matters

Sew.....

In dating, you may have an opinion on size (however you choose to define that term). That's entirely your call. We're not here to judge. However, when it comes to sourcing the right factory, size is undeniably a key deciding factor in who you choose to partner with, because in this game, possibly more than in dating, size matters (though not in the way you might think).

Your sourcing process may have led you to a fantastic factory that produces quality products for brands you admire. However, they may have high production minimums that don't work for your current situation. Most factories located in Bangladesh and China are massive, employing thousands of people. Small-scale designers should avoid these factories. Your order will get lost in the shuffle, while they prioritize the orders that are more efficient and turn better profit margins.

While minimum order quantities may work for you, it still may not be the best fit. The minimum order quantity can be a gauge for what is possible, but regardless, if they take the order, they may not make it a priority. They may say "yes" to the order, but culturally in many countries such as India, it's considered rude to say "no."

A better way to gauge if the factory is the right size for you is by the number of workers in the factory. Typically, orders with budgets of up to USD 100,000 should go to factories which employ no more than a total of 150 workers at peak times. Anything higher than this number and the order will not be a priority. The manufacturing industry is highly erratic, and for this reason, workers are hired based on demand. They have a minimum, as well as a peak number of workers. Ask the factory for both the minimum and a maximum number of workers.

» BEST PRACTICE

If the initial order is based on MOQ's, let them know that you intend to do a test order and based on the outcome and demand the plan is to increase quantities.

4 Fabric Structure

Ask the factory what type of fabric structure they work with. As I explained before, factories are typically set up as either "knits" or "woven" operations. The process to manufacture a product made of either structure is very different, therefore, factories choose to set up for either knits or wovens. Some work with both types, but the better ones do one or the other. Refer back to Part 2: *Designing For Production,* for more information. It's always better to stick to one fabrication type for the first order, thus lowering risks and costs. As your company grows, so can your product range.

5 Product Specialty

The type of products a factory specializes in may not be very clear-cut. No factory likes to turn away business, and for this reason, they will likely say they "do it all." Some take orders regardless of whether or not they can actually process them. They will act as agents and have the products made through their network. You want to be very sure where the goods will be produced, and if this was not clear from reviewing the factory profile and asking them, the next steps might help clarify product specialties. If they don't have the right machinery, it's likely to be outsourced.

Starting The Conversation With An Email

Think of online dating. You've identified your needs, figured out what you're looking for, and have found a few candidates that have some really lovely profiles and seem to be a match. How do you find out for sure? Time to send that first message!

Once you've found a suitable factory, how do you pre-screen them? The purpose of the vetting process is to ensure that there is a good fit and whether or not they are willing to work with you.

Initially, this should be done via email. Be prepared with your budget and target costs before you start emailing. If the email doesn't reflect business - in other words, money, they are likely not to take the email seriously. Do not ask for prices for products that are not physically made as that's a sign of an amateur. Remember: you give them the target prices.

Here are a few critical questions to consider:

How many people work at the factory? Ask them how many people work at the factory and how many can work at peak times (150 is considered a smaller factory). Don't rely on their website: it may be outdated, and the company may have grown.

What is your minimum order quantity? They can only give a rough quote with tech packs and a fabric standard. With this order information, they can provide you with a more accurate number of the minimum order quantity. Every order varies with MOQ. If they ask you for your target cost, you can provide that to them, after which they'll give you MOQ. If your target cost is too low, ask them "at what quantity do you need to get that price?". What are the minimums based on the info provided above? Tell them you are doing a test order and looking to grow orders.

What types of products do you specialize in? If this hasn't been made clear by asking the above questions, clarify. Ask what kinds of products they manufacture. Later, you can ask them what percentage of each category the distribution is (e.g., women 70%

and men 30%, etc.) to get an idea of what they are best at. You can request images of samples they have worked on. Again, ask them for more. Don't trust their website. It could be outdated.

Who are your customers? You can gauge their quality standards from the brands they work with. Ask them if they sell in North America, and if so, what brands?

The factories get bombarded with emails all the time from flaky buyers that are just 'window shopping,' so it's not uncommon for them to not reply. A lack of responsiveness is a common complaint from new entrepreneurs.

So, how do you avoid being ignored?

Avoid asking too much - Just like when messaging a potential date online, sending big, long emails right off the bat is a surefire way to be ignored. New factory requests are never easy to process, nor is onboarding new buyers. If you ask too many questions or give too much information, your efforts will likely result in no response. Stick to asking for what you absolutely need to know in order to primarily assess the fit between you and the supplier. The first email is about evaluating potential fit at a high level. It should be clear and concise.

Focus on what they care about the most: namely, the details of what you're trying to source. Keeping the emails short, concise, and well-formatted will not only help the manufacturer, but it gives you a better chance of getting replies and answers. Small but important tip: it's best to number your questions. Numbering your questions keeps your communication clean and organized. It makes it easy to reply to each point, and typically, responses are made in another font color. You can respond to their emails in the same way.

Here is an example of an email I might send out (Refer to Part 5 - Counter Sampling - The Art of Communication, as well) :

As you can see from the sample above, it's short, concise and to the point. The goal is to make sure that, at a high level, there is a fit between us. I have also set myself up immediately to send a fabric standard, thereby showing that I understand that the fabric confirmation is the biggest factor in pricing. I did not directly request costs. If they are seriously interested, they will get into more detail knowing they are not wasting their time or mine.

If, right off the bat, they give me a very high minimum order quantity that doesn't fit my needs, I move on. There are other fish in the sea. You can always keep them in mind for future orders.

If, after communicating, I feel comfortable proceeding, I will send them the fabric standard and request that they send me a few pieces of production samples from other clients, to check the stitching quality. Once the factory has received the fabric standard, they can put together a package of fabric options based on the standard and provide a few finished product samples to check quality. Once you have received the fabric options and made your selection, you can start requesting cost estimates before counter sampling.

Email Responses

When you first start emailing, watch the response time. Is it taking days to get a reply? Or are they responding within 24 hours? Based on your communications, do you feel you are a priority? Or do you feel you are at the bottom of the list? Factories that do not reply in a timely manner are a huge red flag. Anyone looking for business makes the time.

It is wise to remember that different time zones could impact your workday. When you are working, they may be sleeping, or vice versa. I always make it a habit to check the time when I send an email to someone in another country. Since I'm based on the east coast of North America and my factory is in India,that means a lot of late nights and early mornings for me. Saturday is a work day for India as well. I know when they are working and it's easier to get a response at those times. If it's urgent, I may call or send them a Whatsapp msg asking the merchandiser to reply. He's often running around so, it can get tricky for him.

❯❯ BEST PRACTICE

After emails have been exchanged, ask them for their cell phone number. Don't be shy! It's always good to call and connect via phone or Whatsapp. The ones that have the time and want the business will call or communicate via Whatsapp.

Clarify The Scope Of Your Order Upfront

Factories can't always get a lower quantity of materials in a timely and cost-effective way. The fabric dyeing plants have a limited number of vessels that can accommodate small orders. There is a long queue. Organic cotton is in high demand and is not always available. Common fabric structures that are regularly knit or woven in the mills are quicker to procure. Trims made smaller quantities or dyed to match, are also in a queue.

Once you've decided to start counter sampling with a factory, clarify the scope of the order. Make sure you are both on the same page. Give as much detail as possible so that it makes sampling process move quickly. It makes their job easier. Late changes to any purchase order can be expensive, and cause a rift in your relationship.

>> BEST PRACTICE

Order the same distribution of quantities in each size for all styles. For example, let's say you usually order 30 (s), 50 (med), 50 (large), and 30 (x-large) of any style. Instead of that, you should order all styles with the same distribution of sizes across the board. It makes cutting for the factory much faster, as well as wasting less fabric.

Once you have further shortlisted potential factories, make arrangements to meet them in person. Isn't the amount of money you plan on investing, including the partnership, worth the visit? After all, this baby belongs to both of you!

Hopefully, after you've selected a few factories, they are all close to each other. You won't get a real sense of the partnership or manufacturing process until you step through their door. The meeting request will be expected: it's standard practice for you (the buyer) to inspect and visit the factories you'll be working with. Doing so demonstrates to the manager that you are professional, experienced, and you are interested in working with a partner for the long haul.

It's time to meet the team face to face. Once the dates are confirmed with the factory, you're ready to book your flight and hotel. Ask the factory for recommendations on where to stay. Remember to check visa requirements, every country differs. Most importantly, factory visits aren't done only once. Regular visits help build the relationship resulting in improved processes.

Visiting the factory is everything. You get to learn about the manufacturer's skills and capacity first hand so you can design products that highlight their strengths. Regardless of whether or not you have had the opportunity to meet someone from the factory at a tradeshow, it is worth getting to know everyone on the team and gain a better understanding of the factory's capabilities.

In my experience, every time I went to visit a new factory, I went home with my counter samples. Things just seem to move faster. They know you have taken the time to visit and they do their best to provide you with counter samples and prices. On this visit, be sure to discuss costs for production, samples, schedules, and minimums.

Most importantly this is your opportunity to get them excited about your brand. GET PERSONAL. Your business depends on understanding your partner. Taking on new orders is no simple task, and if they don't reap the benefits of large orders, you want to give them the incentive to work with you. Not only do they want to impress you, but you also need to do the same. You want to begin to get a better understanding of their strengths and weaknesses, who the people are, and how they operate.

❊ GOLDEN NUGGET

Successful business people use a notepad. Sounds crazy, but it's true. Always, always take notes so you can refer back to them. Ask if you can take pictures and video too. Always ask questions. You won't believe how much there is to learn from the factory. Believe me, you will refer back your notepad at a later point. Pictures are always great for marketing as well.

Factory Visit Checklist:

- ❑ Get to know the merchandiser, your go-to person for day-to-day operations. What's your instinct about this person?

Have you established rapport, and are they taking the time to answer all your questions?

- Meet the general manager and the heads of each department, including Quality Control, CAD, Fabric, Trims, and Production. Determine how long the factory has been in business.
- Make notes on all the types of machinery on the premises. How many do they have? What are their capabilities?
- Check out the showroom. The showroom contains hundreds of samples that have been manufactured by the factory. What type of projects does the factory excel in producing? Check the workmanship of the samples. Take a look at the brands they have worked with. Take photos of anything that inspires you. Most importantly, the showroom provides you with an opportunity to see sewing techniques that they have mastered. Are there any techniques that the factory has done an exceptional job of that can be incorporated into your designs? Ask to see fabric selections that they may have on file.
- Ensure the size of the factory is suitable for the order. Reconfirm the number of workers.
- Find out what services the factory provides in-house and what will be subcontracted for the order. Many have screen printing tables or embroidery machines but may need to outsource to a contractor that has a buttonhole machine. In-house machines affect quicker turnaround times and better pricing.
- Meet the quality control manager and ask how they ensure that quality is met through each of the stages in the production process, from purchase and quality of materials to shipment of goods. Do they have checkpoints in each step of the process? Do they have any certifications for quality?
- Ensure there are proper working conditions (more information on this in the next chapter).
- Discuss responsibility for shipping and insurance and where the closest port is.
- Discuss payment terms. Be prepared to pay a 50% deposit. After all, you are a fair person, but be aware that factories

are also concerned with a new company's' ability to pay for the cost of production. Discuss how issues are to be handled should there be any defective products shipped. This is not common but it's worth having the discussion so both are on the same page.

❑ Ask them for a calendar of holidays, so you're prepared in advance.

❑ Find out how they deal with a situation whereby any of the styles shipped turn out defective? Most will replace any defective products when the goods are returned to them at your cost.

Photo | *The management team and Adila at Astro Apparels (2015).*

Cultural Differences

Beyond the challenge of finding the perfect manufacturers are the cultural challenges faced when doing business abroad. If you're not native to that country, you'll need to take some things into consideration. Customs and cultures affect the way in which many factories do business. Let's take the North American business mentality which is based "on honesty and transparency." It may not be quite the same in another place. If you're a woman in this industry, it, too, has its challenges. Familiarize yourself with business practices, and if possible, rely on an associate or consultant that you can trust who understands the country.

In many Asian countries, including India, getting manufacturers to say 'no' directly is a bit of a challenge. Often, even if they don't have the time or capacity to do something, they simply won't say no. Instead, answers may be a "sure" or "we will try" and come across as vague and showing lack of form commitment. This is because many cultures believe saying "no" is disrespectful and offensive.

Every country has its own unique holidays. India, especially, has numerous traditions and holidays that span throughout the year. These dates affect delivery dates. Weddings are weekly affairs, and workers travel far to attend them. Be sure to clarify holidays before starting production and add these dates to your calendar to keep you organized.

Over time, relationships will grow, thus improving processes. To learn more about the impact of cultural differences on doing business abroad, check out World Business Culture (www.worldbusinessculture.com)

>> BEST PRACTICE

Always word questions clearly and ask for precise responses. For example, instead of asking "can we get the delivery at the end of the month?" (which will probably be replied to with a yes), ask them "where are we in the production timeline?" Ask for an exact date for delivery.

Subcontractors

Sew, you've had the coffee dates, met a few excellent prospects, and found someone who seems to vibe with you.

Ask to see the subcontractors. The magic doesn't only happen at the factory, people! It's a good idea to meet with any external partners, such as the dyers, mills, or printers, etc., really, anyone they work with. It helps to put a face to your order and can help move an order along faster. It gives you a deeper understanding of the skill and complexity that goes into every product that is made.

Most importantly, it gives you a deeper understanding of your supply chain. You can confidently say, I know who made my clothes!

If you're happy with everything. That's a green light.

Street Smarts: **Finalizing The Partnership With References**

Are you ready to go steady? Go with your instincts, if you feel that you have found the right partner. To confirm your instincts, get some references.

Ask the owner or general manager for references of companies they have done business with. Many manufacturers cannot tell you all of their clients' names or disclose the brands they work for, but they ought to be able to provide a few references. A good supplier should have more than one person willing to vouch for them. If the supplier cannot provide you with one good reference... well, as the saying goes, that's a red flag!

Try not to email a reference. Rather, give them a call. Communicating over the phone can give you a better overall picture of how this person feels about the factory. Their tones, comments, and pauses can often lead you to more probing questions if need be.

It's always a good idea to prepare before you give them a call by writing down some questions, such as "How long have you worked with the factory?" "What were the major problems?" and "How do you work best with the factory?" Take their opinions into consideration. What kind of tips will help you work with the factory better? Their advice can be helpful in moving forward in the partnership and they can offer tips on how best to work together.

(If only some of our dinner dates came with references).

Remember: owning a business is always a "work in progress." There will still be issues, and relationships evolve. What you want to find out is if you feel you can effectively communicate with them and feel you can trust the factory. Ultimately, it will give you greater insight into whether or not your brand is the right fit with the factory in question.

Street Smarts: **Tips On What To Clarify Before Placing A Bulk Order**

Before placing a production order, be sure to do the following:

1 *Confirm Delivery Date(s).* Every business model is different, so be open with the factory. When do you need samples and production to be delivered and reach you? If you need sales samples for a specific trade show, or have a buyer who is expecting an order on a particular delivery date, keep the factory in the loop.

2 *Reconfirm the required samples*, especially the PP sample (sample in materials ordered and top of production TOP sample.

3 *Request a time and action calendar.*

4 Ask f*or the dates of all the holidays during the orders.*

5 Find out if the factory has any *insurance against damages or loss.*

6 Discuss any *testing reports or certification requirements.*

7 Establish *payment terms.*

8 Confirm what parts of the manufacturing process will be done by *contractors.*

Growing Pains: **View The Relationship As A Work-In-Progress**

Like any new relationship, the first time you work with them is usually the most challenging.It's a learning process. Just as you need to listen and learn from the factory, the factory should be eager to learn your needs. This requires that you both communicate with each other from a place of respect and collaboration.

Ideally, you want to do business together for a long time and grow with them. It takes two to three seasons before you and the factory really get into the groove of things. Think about the first time you used a recipe: how many times did it take to perfect it? Now put yourself in the factory's shoes. Imagine that they are learning how your brand operates, only each meal, the order or "recipe" changes. This is why repeat orders or very slight modifications in designs help you save both time and money. The more the factory works with you, the better they get, especially when things are kept relatively consistent.

Make a commitment to taking the time to get to know your partner. Have yearly face-to-face visits to trade ideas and develop a long-term understanding of the factories business, as well as your own. Both of you will profit by working together on products that meet market demands and the factory's production requirements. As processes and quality steadily improve, both businesses grow.

This might seem obvious but growing your business is important to the factory. If you are starting out, it's a good idea to reassure them that your goal is to increase the volume and frequency of your orders. If you're always ordering on minimums, the factory is not working efficiently. Just like any other business, if the factory is not making money, they will lose interest. There's no way to sugarcoat it.

It's that Slow-and-Steady Tortoise that Wins the Race

It's a widespread misconception that lower prices mean faster-selling products.

As we found out in Chapter 6, this is not true.

Sure, it's a common goal to want to get the best price, but is that all you are after to be profitable? Surely not. Beyond what is in your control, you will have expectations from your partner. You want it all: fast delivery, high quality, ethical manufacturing and the list goes on. But what are your priorities? Sure, the goal may be to have it all, but having it all also comes at a cost. If you are not willing to pay a little more, other factors will have less priority.

Be fair. It's that simple. Openly discuss what your priorities are, what you are looking for in a partnership, and what you need for the product. Understand that balancing all the variables most likely takes time. On average, it takes 2-3 orders before the factory feels comfortable, and the sewing operators genuinely understand your brand's quality standards and ways of operating. Each brand is unique.

Problems will come up. This is business. If you don't know how to run a factory personally, give a dog a bone. It's difficult, and processes may be hard to explain. Pick up the phone if there is a problem. Learn to communicate better. Sure, even after the shipment, things may not be "perfect." Likely, they won't be, especially when there are chances of human error. But at the end of the day, you should say to yourself is the product saleable? If it is, then keep marching forward. The next order will get better. And the order after that, even better. Just like in the fable, *The Tortoise and the Hare*, regardless of speed, the tortoise kept his eye kept his eye on the prize and just kept moving towards the finish line without distraction. You'll both get there in the end.

The Waiting Game: When Should You Place The Next Orders

A good business plan has a well-thought-out yearly budget. If you've created a plan, then you've put aside money to cover the orders for a year. Before you are depleted of inventory, you will need product.

Ideally, you want to give yourself a buffer of time to sell some of the inventory before you place the next order. Most of the startups I've worked with waited 4-6 weeks after selling product, before placing a new order. If all or some styles are not moving, proceed with caution. Re-evaluate the entire brand and sales strategy before you get stuck with mountains of unsold products. It's better to risk being late than being stuck with inventory you cannot sell.

On average, I'd say that new brands take a year to sell out their stock completely. As you start growing, the turnaround time becomes much faster. You will begin to learn what styles, sizes and colors sell fast and which products to focus on. The trick is to be able to sell out quickly otherwise, you are tying up your money in inventory.

My Top 4 Tips On Selecting A Factory

As I mentioned earlier, most of the factories I work with are based in India. Despite not being born in India or speaking any of the local languages, I've been fortunate to work closely and establish long-lasting relationships with manufacturers. I've spent countless hours at the factory working in every department learning about the people and the process. Kudos to all the garment manufacturers for all the hard work that goes into each and every piece of clothing! I've also met the families of the factory owners, and some have met mine.

Like many designer entrepreneurs, I too had an idea for a brand. I've been in your shoes. I get how scary it can be to give a big chunk of money to someone in another country and not feel "in control."

Located on the other side of the jungle is another person with a set of fears. Over the years, I've come to understand the countless problems they face as well, most of which go unheard.

1 TIP – The Importance of Face To Face Meetings

If you've experienced online dating then you know how very different talking on the phone or texting is from actually meeting the person face to face. It's impossible to get the full picture until you've met. The same holds true for selecting a factory to partner up with. Let's be real here: factories don't specialize in marketing, and do a poor job of creating profiles. Every factory looks the same. The truth is, just as every "potential match" has a personality, so too does a factory. You need to visit the factory to hear their story and so you can determine what skills and techniques they have mastered. Build off their personality and expertise to tell their story.

Let me explain how different each factory can be:

Assisi Garments

I found Assisi Garments through our friend Google. I scanned the profile with words like organic cotton, fair trade, Franciscan nuns and orphanage. I printed out their profile picture, printed it out and stuck it on my vision board. I knew I had to meet them. Since 2014 I've been fortunate to work with the Assisi team. It's beyond inspiring to see them in action. Just outside the factory is a mango tree. Let me tell you that the sisters make a mean mango curry! *Sew*, worth the trip.

Assisi Garments, founded in 1994, was established by Franciscan Sisters as a non-profit rehabilitation program. Initially, the factory started as a means to provide income to support a girls orphanage, an old age home, and cancer patients. The garment factory opened shortly after to support these causes.

They started with only five machines and ten girls. Today, the factory is still run by nuns and employs over 200 workers. They own spinning machines which help speed up the fabric manufacturing process. It's difficult for small factories to implement third party verification services, yet Assisi has managed to be certified by many organizations and comes equipped with ISO 9002, Global Organic Standards (GOTS), Fairtrade, and Flo-cert.

Photo | *1.Bottom Left: General Manager, Sister Vanetha speaking with a vendor 2. Bottom Right: An old age home that the factory supports. 3.Top Right: The workers are surrounded by windows, and the factory is well-lit with a lot of ventilation. 4. Top left: A worker having a drink at the water cooler station.*

UK Impex

UK Impex is the very first factory I worked with, helping me launch my first brand. I've known the owner, Shimpy, for over ten years. Over the years, our relationship has grown with understanding and trust. As with all the factories I work with, we are all on Whatsapp and in constant communication. Developing the relationship encourages Shimpy to set time aside for me and explain things in greater detail.

UK Impex was established in 1994 and has since made a name for itself as a leader in high-quality garments. They are masters in beading and embroidery and value-addition products. Many of Shimpy's clients are located in Italy. He has a strict selection of vendors and material selection. The workers are highly-skilled, and there are many quality control checkpoints throughout the manufacturing process. Shimpy is passionate about embellishments and welcomes challenges in creating new concepts in value-added products.

Photo | *1. Top left: Their showroom = my dream closet. 2. Top right: Stitching 3. Bottom left: Hand embroidery 4. Bottom right: Machine embroidery 5. Bottom centre: Hand cut-out fabric technique*

Astro Apparels

I met the owner of Astro Apparels back in 2011. He helped me get my sustainable brand Pureblankz manufactured. Over the years, our relationship has gone from business partners to more of a student/mentor. Every time I see him it's a learning experience for me. He's taught me about mirror meditation- yeah who knew that was a form of meditation? He sends me to ashrams and really taught me about staying grounded. One year, he travelled to Toronto and I asked him to come to my home where he met my dad. They instantly bonded. On his way out, he said to me, "Why are you looking for a guru, when you have one sitting right here?" I'll never forget that.

Astro is deeply committed to giving back to the community. I've visited less fortunate schools where he has donated clothing made from cancelled orders from buyers. You'll find many people with disabilities working in the factory. Manimurti, for example, is a worker with a disability that affects his hands. After graduating in textiles sciences, he took up a job in quality control and is working his way up to manager. His brother offers his workers free eye surgery.

Astro Apparels was established in 1997 with a team of 300 strong. Astro supplies to brands all over the world, including the North American brands Mark's and Bonnie Togs. They also have embroidery and screen printing machines on the premises. ISO quality standards are strictly followed at all the processing stages (more on that below).

Photo | 1.Top right: Manimurthi in the quality control department. 2. Top left: The only girl is me! The rest is the management team, and Mani is in the center. 3. Center: Kids shelter where Astro donated and made clothing. 4. Bottom left:quality control department 5. Bottom right: Screen printing unit in action.

Mehera Shaw

I met Shari, the founder, in 2015. I found her through a referral and asked if I could stop by for a factory tour. I was instantly drawn to her calm demeanor and positive energy. Shari was born and raised in the U.S. After not being able to find the right manufacturer, she moved to India to open Mehera Shaw, a fair trade factory. What impressed me most was how she communicated with her team. She spoke with the utmost respect, empathy and understanding. She also spoke a little bit of Hindi, which I loved.

Mehera Shaw was founded in 2007. They have created a transparent, vertical supply chain using fair labor standards, sustainable fabrics, and artisan-printed textiles. The small team of 50 specializes in artisanal hand blocking designs using vegetable dyes. In 2012, the Mehera Shaw Foundation Trust was founded as a non-profit organization whose mission is artisan development projects. The Mehera Shaw Foundation uses scrap through an ongoing upcycling project and artisan skills-building program.

Typically, garment workers are paid hourly wages. Mehera Shaw pays all the permanent workers a salary- an uncommon practice. The reason it is so uncommon? Factories cannot rely on buyers who tend to shift factories once a lower price is given to them. The instability makes it difficult for factories to offer permanent jobs with salaries. If the factory has no orders, there is no work. Consistent, reliable orders are what factories depend on to stay in business.

Photo | *Top left:The Mehera Shaw team 2. Top right: hand blocking in action. 3. Bottom left: A garment sewer in action. 4. Bottom right: Tracing the design in paper prior to carving on a wood block.*

2 TIP – Understanding Grows Through A Willingness To Effectively Communicate

When something is not going as planned, we automatically put the blame on others. Ego always gets in the way.

Here's a typical scenario: The factory emails the designer to let them know that the printing is being delayed. Apparently, it's monsoon season. Sounds like an excuse, yet again. Right?

To us, it's a simple rainstorm. Here is what's really going on. To the printing unit, the heavy rainfall is causing high humidity which causes the fabric to stay damp. This, in turn, causes the prints to bleed, and all the prints come out blurry. Worse yet, the monsoon season lasts several months. It's out of their control.

Factories don't have the time to explain the details and struggles they face, especially if you haven't developed that relationship with them. Over time you will have a better understanding of their pain points, which will help you streamline processes, thus calming your fears.

Photo | Top right corner: *a distorted print done during monsoon 2. Top left: table prints with fabric drying 3. Bottom: clear print during regular weather temperatures.*

3 TIP – Source Based On Shared Values

Every potential partner, either personal or professional, brings different strengths and values to the table. It's up to us to decide if they line up with our own.

I genuinely believe that we all need to look beyond the fancy certifications. Even though it's great to see factories that are fair trade or Flo-cert certified, I challenge designers to look beyond the certifications.

Here's why I'm bringing forth the challenge. A few years back, I was thrilled to have come across an online profile of a fair trade certified factory. As I mentioned earlier, the high costs to obtain certifications make it extremely difficult for the smaller players to fork out the dough. The sad truth is most brands are not willing to dish out the money either.

The day I got to the factory, I noticed that most of the workers were women. Nice. The bathrooms were clean. Nice. The showroom was immaculate. Bonus. Everything on the outside looked great! When we were sitting in the showroom, I had asked him if he had any more samples of a product I was interested in. After spending some time with the owner, I noticed that he spoke to his employees in a very loud, disrespectful manner. He asked one of the employees to get more in a very harsh way. When the person returned with the wrong merchandise, he threw it on the floor and told him he brought the wrong stuff. I could sense a lot of fear. Worse yet, he also threw the product around like garbage and expected others to pick it up. True story. I value the hard work that goes into making clothes. I see the skills people have in order to do what they do. Personally, I think it's disrespectful to throw things on the floor. I wouldn't throw a sweater my grandma knitted on the floor, so why would I throw my t-shirt? That's just me.

On the other hand, Mehera Shaw, also a fair trade factory, is very different. Shari took the initiative to learn and speak Hindi. I didn't hear any loud or rude voices. In comparison to the other fair trade factory, who shall remain nameless, the energy was very different. Respect is of the utmost importance to me. I believe respect promotes a healthy environment, thus affecting positive business results. In my opinion, just because a factory is certified doesn't necessarily mean their values are in line with yours. I place respect at the top of my priority list and vet factories accordingly.

4 TIP – Cultivate Patience in a World of Instant Gratification

Just like when your dating, good relationships take to time grow and if you force something it's just going to hurt the relationship. The same holds true for partnering with manufacturers.

I'm a believer that fast fashion exploits workers and negatively impacts the environment. Pressuring the factory to manufacture with short lead times can negatively impact the workers and is often the cause of unethical business practices. And moreover, a trendy product is also one step away from becoming obsolete and headed towards the landfills.

Our lives today are all about instant gratification, and this is even more true in the world of fashion. As a fashion business leader, I understand we need to meet deadlines to succeed, but does it need to be at someone else's expense?

You may not know this, but large corporations have terms and conditions in place for chargebacks. The factory is forced to discount on delays. Working on tight margins can destroy a factory. Many of the "big buyers" know full-well that a factory can't make the delivery date and purposefully add impossible clauses. When the factory breaches the contract, the brand gets the discount. The factory is desperate for orders: no orders means no work. Some buyers go as far as canceling orders and workers end up without pay.

Thus, factories have a massive fear of working with buyers, which therefore affects communication. And, on the flip side, buyers here are afraid of the factories. Empathy and compassion go a long way.

Sew, I'd like to propose the idea of slowing down.

Two quick pointers:

1. *Be better at planning than expecting things on tight deadlines.* Allow enough lead time and plan a few seasons ahead. Allow extra buffer time to account for any delays. Manufacturing and logistics can be unpredictable.

2. *Create classic versus trendy products and move away from season-driven products.* Seasonless, year-round products will reduce the pressure off of needing the product "yesterday" and the time needed to sell your products. You'll feel less pressure meeting delivery dates and deadlines.

If you want something faster, it's also in your control. I challenge you to plan ahead and plan better.

Quality Assurance

Third Party Inspection Services

Throughout this chapter, we've been comparing the factory relationship to dating. However, there is one area of the factory sourcing process that has something that you can't get in the dating world (that is, unless you're willing to hire a private detective, which can be its own can of worms). Namely, third party quality inspection of your prospective factory partners.

Quality is an integral part of creating a successful brand and products that sell. Every brand has different standards which must be upheld. Within the factory, there are numerous steps they take throughout the manufacturing process to ensure standards are met. Beyond that, you can use a third party inspection service, which allows someone outside the factory to come in to do inspections.

Third party inspections can provide many services such as factory audits, product inspections and testing. It is your job to convey what your standards are so they can carry out the inspections effectively. Average prices for the cost of a single visit start from $400 USD. Remember that the costs of doing so will add to the final price of the garment.

Most startups have a random TOP (top of production) sample inspected and request wash and wear testing. As the company grows, third party inspections begin to make sense.

I recommend, Asia Inspect (www.asiainspection.com), a leading global quality assurance and compliance service that can do the inspections for you.

There is also, of course, International Organization For Standardization (ISO) (www.iso.org). The ISO is a global network that develops international standards. If a garment manufacturer is certified right from the purchase of yarn to the packing of the finished garments, the ISO system will help ensure quality. Factories can be accredited for numerous standards. Common ones include: ISO 9002, ISO 9001 and ISO 14001 Certifications. Factories that implement these systems see lower defect rates, lesser rework and only cost savings for large factories.

Based in Geneva, Switzerland, ISO is an independent, non-governmental international organization with a membership of 164 national standards bodies. Each member represents ISO in its country. Individuals or companies cannot become ISO members.

Test Reports

As mentioned earlier, testing in-house is regularly done throughout the manufacturing process. Regardless of whether the factory is working with other subcontractors and suppliers or doing everything in-house, "the fault" always ends up being placed on the factory. For this reason, every supplier or contractor is obligated to provide "unofficial" testing reports to the factory. Factories generally work with contractors and suppliers they trust. For example, at each stage of manufacturing the fabric, the contractor passes on a report. The weaver gives the report to the dyer, who moves another newly created report to the factory, and so forth. For instance, official YKK zippers that are purchased come with an official quality report.

Third party testing labs are contracted to test fabrics, components, and finished products. Tests are conducted to meet both safety and quality requirements. Numerous tests are available, depending on the product. You can request shrinkage tests, colorfastness, fiber identification, and weight. These are some of the standard tests for women's apparel. Flammability and lead testing are vital for childrenswear. Be sure to review the import regulations to check if there are any reports required for the product to be sold in that country (especially with regards to safety).

Testing can be done locally or overseas. If you want a third party lab report from the factory, it comes at an additional cost. This should be discussed before placing the order so they can include the tests in the value of the products. The factory always gets a better price, so it's best to request the reports from the factory.

Two popular global testing labs are Intertek (www.intertek.com) and SGS (sgs.com)

✳ GOLDEN NUGGET

To save money you can ask the factory for the unofficial reports that are supplied to them by the contractors, and for the suppliers to give you a little reassurance.

How far can this relationship go? If you only take away one thing from this chapter, it should be these two words: empathy and communication. Keep mastering those in your relationship with your factory, and the sky's the limit.

"ONLY FROM THE HEART CAN YOU TOUCH THE SKY"
- RUMI

In Part 8, we are going to move forward to something that I feel every business must think about: being responsible. Being responsible is about *ethical production*, a holistic approach to ensuring good health and well-being for everyone in the manufacturing process. Your company's values are everything.

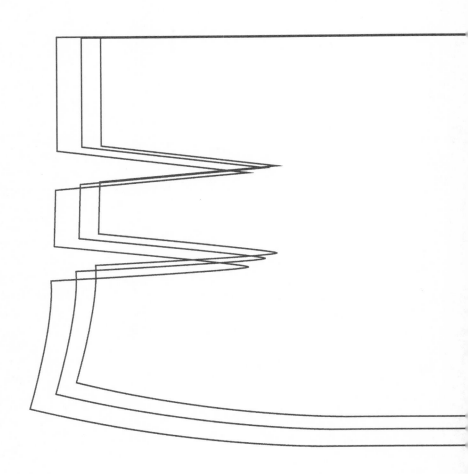

WEAVING YOUR WAY THROUGH RESPONSIBLE MANUFACTURING

OVERVIEW

Fashion is an international experience. Our clothing often travels many miles and touches many hands before making its way into our closets. It is a 3 trillion dollar per year industry. The apparel industry has one of the longest and most complicated supply chains, which makes it difficult to monitor. The negative impacts of the industry are vast and widely felt in two significant ways: there is environmental degradation across the supply chain (from water, waste and chemical use) and perpetual unethical manufacturing practices that negatively impact workers.

Now, let's talk about being responsible. No, I don't mean cleaning your room or doing your taxes (although these are two very responsible things that I would strongly encourage you to do). I'm talking about great responsibility. The kind that superheroes talk about that comes with "great power." Yeah, you know what I mean.

Being responsible in business and manufacturing is more than just doing the right thing; it also means that companies should behave ethically and with sensitivity towards social, cultural, economic and environmental issues. People, planet, profit, a concept known as *the triple bottom line,* embodies the approach to business responsibility. *Sew,* why is that important? Well, for starters, as a business, you are in a position where you can either do a lot of harm, negatively impacting workers and the environment, or do a lot of good. The choice is yours, but we are hoping for the latter. The world needs people like you who can help.

The fashion industry has, for many years, received a lot of bad press. There is very little, if any, transparency, and many consumers are so far removed from how their clothes get made that they do not understand the true value of what it costs to manufacture thoughtfully-made garments, which has consequences for those who make them. For starters, cheap products that are quickly discarded are piling up in landfills, and many of these products take decades to decompose. On top of that, manufacturing clothing is extremely labor intensive, and the workers are generally treated like machines, often borderline enslaved[1]. Unethical factories frequently use child labor and don't pay their workers fair wages.

Now, before we can figure out how to solve this massive problem, we need to re-examine your *why*. Let's figure out how we can incorporate your beliefs and values into an ethical approach. Authenticity speaks volumes to your consumer, and you want to create a brand that speaks directly to the heart. As the author Simon Sinek says, most organizations talk about "what" they do and "how" they do it but seldom talk about "why" they do it. The companies that can articulate and understand their why, or core beliefs, prove to be much more successful. For example, if you value the efforts the factory makes, creating a brand where every garment can be traced from seed to shelf, then visualize it in a way that you would like to see it done.

Responsible businesses come in all shapes, sizes, and colors. While some companies are built as social enterprises - businesses whose core missions solve a problem faced by people or the planet - others may incorporate responsible business practices into their codes of conduct. Can you help save the world with a t-shirt? Or feed a family with a pair of sneakers? Did you know that you have this power right now? You have it in you to make changes you want to see in our world. It all starts with one baby step, and then the climb gets easier from there. All you need to start is what you already have: your business.

We've shown you how to plan your success, helped you understand all the materials, team members, partners and even paperwork that you need to get your designs out of your head and into the world. Now we're going to show you how to use your business to transform the quality of life for thousands of people around the world. I'll walk you through various ways you can create a positive impact through your business. This will be a path with many twists and turns: at times, you might think we're bouncing from one unrelated topic to the next. I ask that you stay the course, as you'll see by the end of this chapter that everything is connected.

Social Enterprise

Social enterprises are businesses that turn a profit, but at the same time serve a social mission. Social enterprises can be operated as non-profit organizations or as for-profit companies. There is no legal structure, certification or other programs that enable a venture to be officially deemed a social enterprise.

A social enterprise has two goals. Beyond earning a profit, it aims to contribute to positive social, cultural, community, economic and/or environmental outcomes. At its core, the mission is to solve a problem and create a better world.

The Triple Bottom Line

Sustainability has become a buzzword over the past decade and is now an often mentioned goal of businesses, non-profits, and governments. Yet, measuring the degree to which an organization is being sustainable or pursuing sustainable growth can be difficult. There is no universal standard method for calculating the Triple Bottom Line (TBL).

The TBL is an accounting framework with three parts: social, environmental (or ecological) and financial. It refers to the three Ps: people, planet, and profit.

The TBL does not have a standard unit of measurement. Profits are measured in dollars, but what about social capital? What about environmental or ecological health? Finding a common unit of measurement is a huge challenge.

The Robin Hood Effect: Do You Have What It Takes?

Robin Hood and social entrepreneurs both have something in common. Robin Hood was portrayed as "robbing the rich to give to the poor." Coincidently, the term "the Robin Hood Effect" refers to an economic occurrence where income is redistributed so that economic inequality is reduced.

Now, obviously, I'm not suggesting that you don a green tunic, take some archery lessons, and hide out in the forest by the highway, waiting for a Bayer (formerly known as Monsanto) truck to pass by. What I am saying is that social entrepreneurs have a mission to help people by using wealth in a positive way. They pursue an innovative idea with the potential to solve a community problem. These entrepreneurs are willing to take on the risk and effort to address social issues and create positive changes in society through their initiatives.

If you are a social entrepreneur, the following words likely speak to you:

You are a **Builder. Maker. Innovator. Game Changer. Disruptor**.

You want to create change. You want to help people. You have a mission.

Shoutouts To Social Enterprises Leading The Way

I love getting inspiration from companies that do good. Here are some of my top picks:

Tonlé (tonle.com) was founded by Rachel Faller after traveling to Cambodia. Her mission is to reduce waste. Rachel's zero waste production process uses around 90% of recycled materials from factories, with 10% coming from sustainable suppliers. Tonlé is closing the loop by making new clothes from existing materials deemed as fabric waste. Additionally, Tonlé pays employees well above the local minimum wage. How cool is that?

Triarchy's mission (triarchy.com) is to change the massive problem apparel faces with water consumption. Did you know it can take up to 3,000 gallons of water to make a pair of jeans? Neither did I! Triarchy is luxury denim made from a Tencel cotton blend, and the Atelier line is all vintage repurposed. Their factory is located in

Mexico where they use 85% recycled water. And you know what's even cooler? It is achieved through a system in which natural bacteria consumes the indigo dye before reintroducing it to the wash process again and again. It was founded in 2011 by three siblings, Ania, Mark and Adam Taubenfligel.

People Tree (peopletree.co.uk), a pioneer in slow fashion, has a mission to produce 100% fair trade and environmentally sustainable clothing. Safia Minney, the founder and CEO, is not only a spokesperson for fair trade fashion but is also the author of *Slave to Fashion*, which raises awareness of modern slavery in the fashion industry.

How do they do it? People Tree partners with artisans and farmers in developing countries to produce ethical, look-good, feel-good clothing. They actively support 34 fair trade groups in 13 developing countries. Not only are the majority of their cotton certified organic and fair trade, but all the clothes are dyed using safe and azo-free dyes. They also do a fantastic job of showcasing manufacturer profiles, including showcasing short videos on their YouTube channel.

These are just a few of the many exemplary activities that social enterprises have accomplished. If they can do it, *sew* can you!

Hands of Fashion

The fashion industry seems to have rediscovered the value of artisanal work. The more a product is visibly handcrafted, and the more consumers are educated on its process, the more the product is perceived as valuable. A handmade product signifies an emotional involvement that industrialized goods do not deliver. This phenomenon has created widespread attention. The artisan sector is the second largest employer in the developing world after agriculture, worth over $32 billion every year, according to the Alliance For Artisans Enterprise[2]. Marketing experts notice there is a clear preference for handmade goods when purchasing a gift for a loved one, with shoppers prepared to pay up to 17% more than they would for a factory-made product.

Artisans are the key to a fashion industry that has culture, ethics and aesthetics. Artisan activity creates jobs and preserves ancient cultural traditions that in many places are at risk of being lost. Hundreds of thousands of people across the globe, particularly women, participate in the artisan sector. Most artisans, especially in developing nations, have been practicing their art for many generations, helping to sustain ancient techniques and preserve culture.

Companies such as Mata Traders and Raven & Lily resist traditional means of overseas factory production by directly hiring fair trade artisans. Many people are forced to relocate from their families to find new jobs, but these two companies provide a stable source of income for families in some of the most impoverished areas. Mata Traders' products are handmade in India and Nepal using artistic traditions like block-printing and embroidery to create flattering designs and colorful patterns. Raven & Lily products are made in eight different countries, and the designs are all thoughtfully made, and consider the impact on people and the planet. In addition, they employ over 1,500 marginalized women on fair trade wages, and their brand was created with a mission to alleviate poverty amongst women.[3]

Laura Siegel, a Canadian womenswear designer, is a pioneer in the emerging world of social enterprise. Inspired by her travels abroad, her mission is to help keep artisanal work alive. Laura's brand employs artisans from rural villages all over the world, sustaining traditional crafts and cultures. Not only does she ensure ethical working conditions and living wages, but she also collaborates with organizations to ensure they receive mentorship to learn how to maintain practicing their craft, business practices, providing for their families and more. Siegel's philosophy also supports ethical, environmental and responsible manufacturing. She's an inspirational example of a person who started small with a mission and managed to profit while contributing to both the planet and people.

Corporate Social Responsibility

Humans are social animals and cannot live in isolation. We are expected to behave in a manner that is socially and morally acceptable to others. The same goes for businesses. Although the primary objective of a business is to earn maximum profits, it's also expected to conduct its operations in a manner that fulfills its social obligations. Let's take employment practices, for example. Although there is no obligation to hire individuals with special needs, it's considered a part of a company's social responsibility to hire people who might be at a disadvantage. Similarly, no binding law states a company *must* engage in activities to clean up the planet. However, taking up projects to help reduce pollution and tend to the planet is considered part of being socially responsible.

Corporate Social Responsibility (CSR) for retailers commonly refers to addressing both social and environmental targets. Reporting mechanisms often differ from one brand to the next. There is no universally agreed-upon definition of CSR, although a commonly understood meaning is outlined by ISO 26000 Working group (2007). It defines CSR this way:

'Social responsibility (is the) responsibility of an organization for the impacts of its decisions and activities on society and environment through transparent and ethical behavior that is consistent with sustainable development and the welfare of society; it takes into account the expectations of stakeholders; is in compliance with applicable law and consistent with international norms of behavior; and is integrated throughout the organization'.[4]

In general, CSR projects aim to reduce the negative social and environmental impacts of a company. From reducing carbon emissions and limiting the environmental impact to strengthening fair labor practices and addressing workers' rights, CSR has a broad mission.

The difference between CSR and a social enterprise is the difference between being reactive and proactive. In practice, CSR often acts as an add-on and is not at the core of what a business does. For example, a company may generate waste throughout the supply chain, and their environmental policy may be to reduce energy use at the factories. It has a positive impact but doesn't change the core of the business. A business with CSR tries to carry out its core business in a responsible way, while a social enterprise focuses its core business on creating social value. A social enterprise exists to solve a more specific problem in society.

Most brands have a page on their website dedicated to CSR that includes information on the company's current CSR activities as well as their future plans. A social enterprise will clearly state the problem they are attempting to solve in the about us and/or mission page of their website, and address how they implement activities to solve the problem. Companies like H&M and Nike (among others) release yearly CSR reports where they report on both social and environmental goals and improvements.

The Benefits of CSR: **The Fruits of Your Labor**

Sew, what's in it for the companies with CSR practices, and *who* cares? It's been proven that CSR improves a firm's competitive advantage, market value, and financial performance. CSR activities are connected to the marketing function of companies and leveraged as a means to enhance reputation. People want to work for companies that care about them and the environment. Consumers have more of an incentive to buy from these companies. Consumers believe it is their right to know how their purchases are made and be able to see the evidence to back it up. Study after study has shown that consumers and employees prefer to purchase from and work for companies that are invested in social and environmental responsibility. Investors and stakeholders care about CSR. It demonstrates how a company operates and what they are doing as part of their business for customers, employees and society at large. CSR is no longer a separate activity from the rest of the organization, but rather has become the heart of how brands operate and is everyone's responsibility within the organization..

Allow me to back up. Here are some stats to support the reasons **WHY** CSR helps improve the bottom line:

Rise in Fair Trade: Consumer demand for sustainable and fair trade products is soaring; global fair trade demand grew from 4.8 billion Euro in 2012, reaching $5.9 billion in sales in 2014. That year also saw a 28% increase in volumes of retail sales of fair trade cotton.[5]

A 2014 Nielsen global online study found that millennials continue to be the demographic most willing to pay extra for sustainable offerings[6].

Demand for Socially Responsible Products: When quality and price are equal, the most critical factor influencing brand choice is a *purpose*. Across the globe, the prominence of products having a purpose as a purchase trigger rose 26% from 2008 to 2012. Forty-seven percent of global consumers buy brands that support a good cause at least monthly, a 47% increase from 2010 to 2012. Seventy-one percent of consumers would help a brand promote their products or services if there is a good cause behind them. Eighty percent of global consumers believe it is vital for companies to make them aware of their efforts to address societal issues.[7]

Photo | *Edelman Goodpurpose 2012 Global Consumer Survey; Social Purpose as Purchase Trigger*

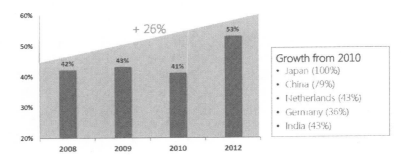

Social Purpose as Purchase Trigger

When quality and price are the same, Social Purpose most important factor

+ 26%

Growth from 2010
- Japan (100%)
- China (79%)
- Netherlands (43%)
- Germany (36%)
- India (43%)

Cause Marketing Increases Sales: The 2007 PR Week/Barkley Cause Survey reveals that philanthropic activities can drive business success. In fact, 72% of consumers say that they have purchased a brand because it supports a cause they believe in. Furthermore, corporate respondents say they see positive PR (65.3%), an increase in sales/retail traffic (26.7%), and an enhanced relationship with their target demographic (52%), as a result of their cause marketing efforts. Fifty-six percent of companies also report heightened staff morale and retention and 14.7% cite improved recruitment of quality candidates.[8]

Green Products = Higher Profits: Leaders of deep green businesses reported greater growth potential, more competitive advantage, higher revenue growth and higher sales prices than their less green peers. According to one article, "deep green businesses were far more likely to report strong revenue growth through the recession from their green products and services than their light green counterparts."[9]

Demand for Good Business Practice: The percentage of consumers who consider transparency and ethical business practices to be essential to a company's product line is growing. According to a report published by the marketing company, Good Must Grow, 60% of American consumers surveyed in 2016 said they felt it was important to purchase goods from companies that demonstrated social consciousness.[10] The number of Americans who prefer to "give back" by purchasing socially responsible products versus donating to charities grew from 18% in 2015 to 22% in 2016. Nearly half (47%) of these respondents believed purchasing socially responsible products was a more effective way to support positive change, while 40% cited convenience. As a result, Fortune 500 corporations and other businesses are opening up and reporting more of their non-financial information.[11]

Rising Demand for Supply-Chain Transparency: "Today's access to information has allowed the social and environmental impacts and challenges of global manufacturing to take center stage," Jorgette Marinez, Associate Director of <u>Business Of Social Responsibility</u>, told TriplePundit. "Manufacturers continue to be challenged by customers, NGOs, rating agencies and investors, retailers, and their own corporate values and colleagues around the sustainability of their products and operations."[12] There is an increasing need, Marinez told us, to make sure that both products and the supply chains that support their manufacture match the ethical values of the consumer. Traceability — the ability to "identify and trace the history, distribution, location, and application of products, parts, and materials" — ensures transparency.

Consumers are making an effort to be responsible citizens of the world, and they expect the same from the businesses they purchase from. They are doing their homework: checking labels before buying, looking at websites for information on manufacturing practices, and much more. Consumers will continue to look for the brands that are proving they are following through with their *green strategy* regardless of whether the brand is big or small.

> "UNLESS SOMEONE LIKE YOU CARES A WHOLE AWFUL LOT, NOTHING IS GOING TO GET BETTER. IT'S NOT."
>
> **– DR. SEUSS, THE LORAX**

Shoutouts To Brands Getting CSR right

A business CSR practices can encompass a wide variety of activities, from donating proceeds to charity and implementing "greener" business operations, to measuring impact and following fair trade practices. If you feel stumped on ideas and activities that you can carry out, seek inspiration from other brands, both small and large.

NIKE (nike.com) went from villain to hero. Back in 1995, there was an outcry from consumers, and news stories were casting Nike in the role of villain amid child labor and sweatshop allegations. Soon afterward, new policies were put into place, and Nike joined forces with the Sustainable Apparel Coalition and is now helping other brands to help create sustainable products. They are committed to sustainable innovation and exploration of advanced innovations. In 2012, Nike partnered with DyeCoo Textile Systems, a Dutch startup, and adopted their new carbon-based dyeing process that dyes garments without using water or chemicals. Way to go, Nike! You truly lived up to your slogan: Just do it!

In 2015, Eileen Fisher (eileenfisher.com), pledged the ambitious VISION 2020 campaign, a bold new plan detailing the steps the brand will take over the course of the next few years toward reaching a goal of 100% sustainability by 2020. The goals focus on eight critical categories: materials, chemistry, water, carbon, conscious business practices, fair wages & benefits, worker voice, and worker & community happiness.

One of the bigger challenges is mapping out every part of its global supply chain, figuring out who they have been investigating, from suppliers and factories to spinners and mills. To assist with supply chain mapping, they use a software called SourceMap, which helps trace products right from the origin of their raw materials. The beauty of SourceMap lies in its use of crowd-sourcing, meaning smaller (sometimes perhaps less known) producers are represented too.

Levi Strauss & Co. (levistrauss.com), the company that invented the blue jean, was also one of the first companies to establish a workplace code of conduct for their manufacturing suppliers. Since then, they have launched Worker Well-Being, a program to improve the lives of apparel workers outside the factory walls, and have made great strides in their commitment in addressing climate change, starting with establishing water quality standards for their suppliers. They also established the Better Cotton Initiative (BCI) (bettercotton.org), an initiative to change the way the largest commodity is grown. BCI focuses on decreasing the environmental impact of cotton, using water efficiently and improving labor standards for farmers. Their commitment to reducing water use in the apparel industry was taken a step further by making their water reduction standards and tools, including Water<Less™ innovations, publicly available to others within and outside our industry.

You don't have to be a big corporation to practice CSR. Even as a small brand, there are many ways to incorporate social responsibility into your supply chain and implement CSR objectives and policies. Even small efforts such as installing energy-efficient lights, toilets, and recycling will not only have a positive impact on the world but will also result in quantifiable cost savings that will be reflected on your bottom line. Every little bit counts. Never discount any effort made.

Walk the Talk

Numerous studies in recent years have shown that consumers prefer to buy from companies that blend social purpose with a corporate mission. It's not always easy for consumers to tell which companies are legit. This is where organizations that help measure and monitor impact come in. It is in a brand's best interest to create consumer trust around their social and environmental standards to improve sales.

Many organizations offer support in this area – here are just a couple to get you started:

Benefit Corporation (bcorporation.net), a/k/a B-Corp, is to business what Fair Trade certification is to coffee. According to their website, "B Corps are for-profit companies certified by the non-profit B Lab to meet rigorous standards of social and environmental performance, accountability, and transparency. Today, there is a growing community of more than 2,100 Certified B Corps from 50 countries and over 130 industries working together toward 1 unifying goal: to redefine success in business."

Your for-profit business could receive this certification if you meet higher standards of social and environmental performance. B Corp status - granted by B Lab, a non-profit -has become a badge of honor for more than 750 businesses since 2007. Some of the bigger names to nab the certification include Ben & Jerry's, Patagonia and Etsy.

Obtaining certifications can be very challenging and costly for startups; however, there is good news! A company can fill out B Lab's free B Impact Assessment Tool (bimpactassessment.net/) anytime to better understand how to measure its impact on employees, the community, and the environment, and get details on more than 150 best practices. The self-assessment tool helps implement processes and provide ideas that will help make the certification process much more manageable. You receive a pending status logo until you are certified.

After you become certified you are required to recertify every two years.If you cannot score the same number of points or more you can lose your certification. It's great because you can benchmark your performance and set goals for continuous improvement. Another awesome perk about B Corp is the sense of community amongst members.

<u>Fair Factories Clearinghouse (FFC)</u> (fairfactories.org). The FFC is a database that helps track and manage social and environmental data. FFC enables members to share the results of audits with other apparel brands doing business in the same factories to improve working conditions. Factories undergo countless and redundant audits, which are counterproductive to their operations, and in turn, can negatively affect working conditions. The FFC reduces the overall number of inspections in factories, thus streamlining processes.

Members have access to software for improving and managing compliance. They will work with each member to configure the FFC software to conform to their business practices and help identify areas for collaboration. Companies with less than 250 million in sales pay $2,500 USD annually.

Mapping Out CSR Objectives

CSR refers to business practices involving initiatives that benefit society. It is the general term often used for the actions that a firm 'voluntarily' undertakes. There are endless ways a company can benefit society; therefore, company leaders need to set clear objectives. Following the establishment of those goals, the CSR activities can support the company's strategic objectives.

Think about your *why* and what areas you want to focus your efforts. Remember back in Chapter 2 we discussed, your why is the purpose, cause, or belief that inspires you to do what you do.

After you have established them, we can organize what and how you want to address your goals. Also consider how your objectives can be addressed into the future.

There are a few broad categories that most companies generally practice. Think about what areas you feel represent your mission, values and brand:

1   **Environmental efforts:** The environment is a primary focus of corporate social responsibility. Regardless of size, every business has a large carbon footprint. Any steps they can take to reduce those footprints are good for both the company and society as a whole.

2   **Philanthropy:** Businesses can address social responsibility by supporting communities and donating to charities, both locally and globally. The many resources that businesses have access to can also benefit charities and local community programs.

3   **Supply Chain Transparency:** This captures the extent to which information about the companies, suppliers and sourcing locations is readily available to end-users and other companies in the supply chain. Ensuring traceability to enable transparency helps consumers to trust.

4   **Ethical labor practices:** By treating employees fairly and ethically, companies can demonstrate their CSR. Businesses that operate in international locations, especially in underdeveloped nations, tend to address these concerns. To improve labor conditions, many companies help better the operating conditions of their suppliers.

5   **Product design:** How will you design and create products? Have you thought about innovation, quality and responsible design and how it may affect society. Think about the life of the product as well as how it will be discarded. Do your products affect animal welfare?

6   **Fair Trade:** Fair trade is a movement that encompasses the above and a bit more, including fair payment of producers and suppliers. The goal is to help producers in developing countries achieve better trading conditions and to promote

sustainability. It's part of an organized social movement, which promotes standards for international labor, environmentalism and social policy in commerce between developed and undeveloped countries.

Mapping Out CSR Activities

Now that you've established the areas where you want to focus your efforts, we can zoom into *what* you want to do to support your objectives. This is the fun part, the possibilities are endless. Let's take a look at examples of CSR objectives that some of the fashion brands across the globe address:

1   Helping people out of poverty and paying living wages.
2   Being transparent with whom you are working (the entire supply chain, everything from trims suppliers to the mills).
3   Ensuring people are treated ethically and fairly.
4   Offering customers "better" eco-friendly alternatives.
5   Providing sustainable employment to artisans in developing countries.
6   Empowering women and underprivileged communities.
7   Ending human trafficking, child labor, and exploitation.
8   Reducing environmental impact and pollution with product, packaging, and logistics.
9   Animal welfare: ensuring that animal rights are voiced and protected, including using faux skins & leathers.
10 Annually self-reporting on operations.
11 Fashion consumption: addressing ways to recycle or close the loop and build quality products that last.
12 Empowering employees to participate in volunteer efforts that support the community.
13 Supporting communities and charitable causes.

Sew, how do some of these awesome companies carry out some activities? Let's look at an example to seek inspiration.

<u>ME to WE</u>, a social enterprise that provides products that make an impact, empowering people to change the world with their everyday consumer choices. *Sew*, what are some of the activities they carry out to support their mission and objective?

> They bring people together and give them tools.
> They provide opportunities for youth, adult, corporate and schools with group trips abroad to volunteer on development projects. They even help with fundraising for the trip.
> They provide resources such as lesson plans and activities to educators.
> They support the ME to WE Charity.
> Also, they created the Me Movement making it easy for anyone to get involved—by offering resources to help create positive social change in local communities and around the world.

CSR Compliance

Sew, you might wonder, who should actually be responsible for your brand's CSR compliance? And the simple answer is: You. CSR compliance is no longer a separate marketing initiative, but rather has become the heart of *how* brands operate and is everyone's responsibility within the organization. Consumers, now more than ever, are insisting that their favorite brands are engaged in CSR initiatives.

How do you ensure that all of your objectives and activities are understood by consumers, employees and stakeholders? Objectives and activities are meaningless if not communicated, articulated and implemented and help you establish your activities.

Depending on a company's size, industry or location, a code of conduct or policy should clearly articulate its beliefs, values, and principles concerning their objectives. It's critical that consumers, employees and stakeholders understand what your company stands for- policies and code of ethics and conduct will help convey your objectives. Strong support and leadership from senior management are essential in conveying these messages to employees and consumers.

A well-written **code of conduct** clarifies an organization's mission, values and principles. It is a set of rules outlining the social norms, religious rules and responsibilities of, or proper practices for, an individual, party or organization. Related concepts include ethical, honor, and moral codes and religious laws.[14]

Monitoring is critical to the success of a code of conduct and gives the code credibility. During the last decade, companies have increasingly created or adopted rules or codes of conduct intended to reduce risks of wrongdoing, such as forced labor. A code of conduct is an effective way to guide the behavior of everyone in CSR: all employees, managers and the CSR Board are governed by it. The code of conduct clearly states the company's firm commitment to behaving honestly and fairly. Some companies actively monitor partners and suppliers through inspections and site visits to ensure they following their policies. Others rely on contractual agreements and certifications. Some do both active monitoring and contracts.

The 2013 Rana Plaza factory collapse in Dhaka, Bangladesh killed more than 1,000 people. It showcases the struggles factory owners often face with retailers pressuring them to lower prices of products, forcing them to ignore ethical labor practices and safety measures. This disaster reignited the conversation around harmful practices in the clothing industry. Consumer question whether the clothes they buy are made in a way that's consistent with their own values on protecting society. Many large factories have signed on to either the Bangladesh Accord or Alliance, a voluntary program. Additionally, corporations have committed to creating stronger safety and inspection measures to work with factories to improve conditions.

Mitigating the risk of wrong doing involves mapping out and disclosing your supply chain. Transparency and traceability of supply chain processes become disproportionately more difficult as brands grow in size and are geographical spread. Large corporations are faced with challenge of knowing who and where the fiber comes from, very trim to each process in manufacturing. Often, order are given to supplier and they little idea who subcontractors are and where materials are sourced.

There are many well established brands in the fashion industry that are doing it right and as a result, reap the benefits. Let's take a look at a few examples:

Gap Inc. has a business code of conduct for everyone in the company, as everyone contributes to protecting the company reputation. Everyone from sales associates to upper-level management and manufacturers can refer to the code of conduct for ethical and legal standards as stated by the corporation.

H&M (sustainability.hm.com) has created a code of conduct specifically to communicate policies and expectations from manufacturers and suppliers. It also helps management make critical decisions with whom they work.

PrAna (prana.com) consciously creates sustainable and ethical travel and yoga wear. They have a social responsibility and traceability manager to implement the goals and commitments of prAna's Social Responsibility program as per the Fair Labor Association (FLA) obligations. Their code of conduct is clearly written on their website. Spot any violations? You can quickly report this directly to an email provided on that page.

How To Create A CSR Plan

I get that as a small brand you may want to make CSR a priority but are faced with difficult issues: limitation of time, energy, resources and money. But even taking a few small steps towards better practices can be instantly rewarding, giving your brand the push to build on what you have.

Undertaking a CSR plan and initiatives is truly a win-win situation. Take some time out to make a plan. Not only will your company appeal to consumers and employees, but you'll also make a real difference in the world. Small businesses have more power than many realize, and using that power to improve the world can bring people of all backgrounds, ages, and interests together. Fashion brands are innovative and need to continuously create new innovative ways of combating sustainability issues.

Remember, no brand is perfect. But given the major social and environmental impacts of the fashion industry and supply chains, it's important to at least have the intention and plans to continue to improve.

Be realistic in the development of a CSR plan and aim for standards that are achievable now, but can be improved as your brand grows and relationships with suppliers develop.

Find examples of codes of conduct from the websites of brands that you look up to for their ethical standards. Do they have goals on their website? Any plans that they share with the media or consumers?

Below are some steps to help you build a CSR Plan

1   *Establish objectives, goals and intentions.* Think about your *why*. What is important to you and your brand? Saving the planet? Motivating the team? What is your vision for the company? What are your future plans for improvement? Write them all down and refine based on what you feel is attainable.

2   *Create a page or add content to your website.* Tie in your objectives to your about us, vision & mission statement and CSR page.

3   *Create a set of rules outlining what your brand stands for.* What is your code of conduct? Do your objectives align with your policies and code of conduct? How are you ensuring any risk of wrongdoing or if a code is broken? Do you have people actively monitoring, certifications or can consumers or employees easily report issues? You can also take your list of objectives and turn them into a policy or code of conduct. For example, let's say you care about animal welfare. You may choose to only use materials free of animals. Or you are

a human rights activist. To ensure there is no forced labor, you regularly have factory audits by a third-party certifier.

4 *Think about what activities support your objectives and policies and how you could carry these out.* You can get suggestions from customers and employees, or even check out other brands. Create a list of ideas.

5 *Establish a budget*: Think about how much you can afford for the year.

6 *Make an actionable yearly plan.* Establish dates and activities, and build a committee to help carry them out. Ensure you're meeting your budget.

The Tug of War

There are many companies out there that have been criticized for having social initiatives that are nothing more than public relations campaigns to boost their brand's reputation. For example, some companies falsely convey to consumers that their products, services or businesses factor environmental responsibility into their offerings and/or operations, when there is, in fact, little to no environmental benefit. This practice is also known as "greenwashing." People want authenticity and can sense it when money is the driving force for doing good, instead of doing good for its own sake.

John Oliver masterly articulates how most fast fashion retailers such as H&M and GAP, are hypocrites for many of their CSR policies. These companies are criticized for offering low prices, which indirectly is a sign of exploiting people offshore. If you haven't watched the John Oliver segment dated April 25, 2015, which has nearly one million views, I highly suggest watching it.[13]

On the one hand, many large corporations want their suppliers to comply with high quality and work standards (such as 8-hour shifts), while on the other hand, they demand suppliers keep prices low and work through 'just in time' management. There is always a tug of war with the moral beliefs and the profits.

Overall, if CSR wants to live up to its mission - to improve the social and economic situation for their workers and their environment, instead of creating a more profitable business model - the demands of workers should be taken into full consideration.

The brands that can authentically tell their story about why they set objectives and follow through with activities are the most respected. Consumers want to be able to trust that when CSR is addressed, it's coming from the heart and employees feel motivated to help grow the company.

Photo | *Cost breakdown of a t-shirt*

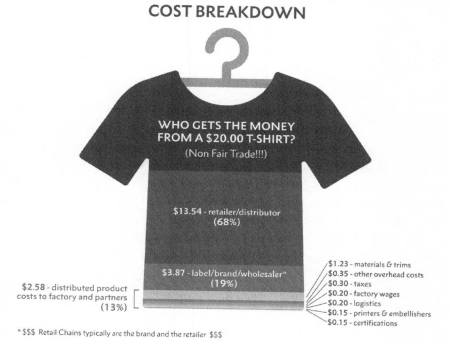

COST BREAKDOWN

WHO GETS THE MONEY
FROM A $20.00 T-SHIRT?
(Non Fair Trade!!!)

$13.54 - retailer/distributor
(68%)

$3.87 - label/brand/wholesaler*
(19%)

$2.58 - distributed product
costs to factory and partners
(13%)

$1.23 - materials & trims
$0.35 - other overhead costs
$0.30 - taxes
$0.20 - factory wages
$0.20 - logistics
$0.15 - printers & embellishers
$0.15 - certifications

* $$$ Retail Chains typically are the brand and the retailer $$$

Fair Trade

"FAIR TRADE IS WHAT WE ASSUME ALL BUSINESSES DO."
- **NELSON MANDELA**

Being fair seems like a no-brainer, right? Still, you'd be surprised how difficult a concept it is for people to grasp. I mean, we pay accountants a retainer before they look at a single receipt, but why is it so difficult for many corporations to pay their suppliers a deposit before they start work? Compared to accountants, not only is their time at stake, but so is procuring essential materials.

Fair trade is about better prices, decent working conditions and reasonable terms of business for farmers and workers. The word "trade" means the buying and selling of goods and services. Good faith, integrity and equitable pay for value should be a given on both sides of any transaction. The significance of "fair" in "fair trade" is a commitment to protect those who do not otherwise have a voice in their industry, or an ability to defend their rights in the workplace.

Sew, how long will people continue to turn a blind eye to the lives of those behind our clothing? Could we be at a turning point on the path to making real change?

Sadly, western-based manufacturers and big fashion brands have historically taken advantage of low wage expectations in developing countries to keep manufacturing costs low and increase profits on finished goods. Also, there are many brands who use fair trade as a public relations asset but with no real commitment to fair trade principles. Although they embrace the policies, they don't have the full understanding needed to put them entirely into action. Most often, it is difficult to be attuned to the cultural, geographic and financial differences that you have to navigate to successfully do business offshore. To be "fair," it's important to understand what is considered "fair" in other parts of the world as well. The best way to navigate this is to first understand what the principles are.

10 PRINCIPLES OF FAIR TRADE

According to their website, *"The World Fair Trade Organization is the global community of Fair Trade Enterprises. Founded in 1989, it has over 400 members across 70 countries. The membership includes over 330 Fair Trade Enterprises, as well as the broader movement of 70 organisations and networks that support them. The WFTO verifies the commitment of its members to Fair Trade through peer reviews and independent audits. "*

To learn more, visit the World Fair Trade Organization.

Other Fair Trade Organizations

To learn even more, check out the Fair Trade Foundation (fairtrade.org.uk) based in the U.K. with branches for Canadians and you can visit *Fair Trade Canada (fairtrade.ca) and Americans can visit Fair Trade USA. (fairtradeusa.org). You can also visit other independent certification and membership organizations such as **Fair***

Trade America *(fairtradeamerica.org),* **and** ***Fair Trade Federation*** *(fairtradefederation.org).*

Sew, how best can we apply these principles as a startup? Simple: become a member of the World Fair Trade Organization. Connecting with the community is the best way to learn and grow. You can find a supplier through WFO, but ensure that you take the time to vet the factory yourself and that both your values align.

In Fair Trade Certified factories, worker satisfaction is high, and turnover is low. Everyone wants to feel supported and empowered and be fairly compensated for the work they do. In Fair Trade factories across the globe, retention rates are higher than average. During the manufacturing process, employees proudly affix the Fair Trade label to each product, and consumers know they are delivering direct financial benefits to the worker's families via Fair Trade premiums.

How can we apply fair trade principles?

1 **Recognize cultural differences.** You cannot expect and impose Western standards on other parts of the world. In eastern countries like India, workers typically don't work regular 9-5 jobs. It's just not their culture, but many companies feel like this isn't fair. Indians generally work later in the day, especially in apparel. Festivals, seasonally severe weather, unreliable power supplies, and religious and state holidays can be important considerations in the manufacturing process. They have way more holidays than we do. As I've mentioned earlier in this book, Holi, a festival in India, can cause a significant production delay, as the company's block printers may travel to their native villages for the festival and then allow their visits to stretch to a week or more. And, if you'll recall, a wedding in the family is not merely a weekend affair. North Americans would never tolerate this as a reason for lateness. India is very different, and their culture must be taken into consideration, as you would with the customs of other non-Western countries.

2 **Be open to adjusting your designs to accommodate different manufacturing processes.** Be ready, willing and eager to learn from the manufacturer and understand their operations. "Trade," after all, means "give and take." What works in the West may be impossible in a developing country, or in a culture influenced by different traditions, business practices or even the weather. The printing and drying process, for example, is affected by the weather, especially monsoons. If you expect a print order at the beginning of summer, the factory has to be sure the fabric can be sourced and printed before the fall monsoons disrupt the production schedule. Pushing a factory to meet unrealistic deadlines is a major cause of unfair treatment of workers. Another reason for delays is that manufacturers can't always get the fabric or in the amount that you may want. Organic cotton is in high demand. Common fabric constructions are easy to source, but special weaves, especially in huge or even small quantities, are not. This can cause delays or require changes in your collection.

3 **Ensure the factory has enough capital to procure materials.** Be prepared to ensure that the factory can purchase fabric and materials to start work. Either pay an advance or open a Letter of Credit with the bank so they can begin to work and pay people for labor. They have to pay their own suppliers and producers up front. Small suppliers can't bear the financial burden of doing business with you if they don't have the capital to pay suppliers.One of the principles of fair trade includes fair payment. Here in Canada, we give retainers to accountants, even graphic designers. What truly boggles my mind is how large corporations can get away with not giving factories deposits, and some go as far as pushing net 30 terms. *Net 30 terms* means a factory may not be paid for over three months from the date of order.

4 **Ensure the factory has enough time to execute orders.** Good things take time. Asking for goods in a short time frame can negatively affect workers. Workers are exploited and the long, laborious hours take a toll on their health and well-being. Chest pain, backache, eye trouble, ulcers, urinary tract infections, headaches and joint pain are some

common occupational ailments.[15] This pressure is often passed onto garment workers, who can suffer as a result from unreachable quotas, insecure employment, and variable income. Allowing longer lead times and ordering earlier is one thing you can do to control the situation.

5 **Communicate frequently and often to truly understand the scope of the manufacturer's work.** As discussed in the previous chapter, in any relationship, open and frequent communication between you and your supplier is absolutely vital. Make a commitment to communicate frequently. Develop a long-term understanding of the nature of the factory's business, as well as your own: this is what makes a true partnership. It's much easier to ensure goods are made by people who are happy where they work and are being treated well. The more you learn about someone else's needs, the easier it becomes to trade fairly. The first step to being "fair" is understanding the other person's situation.

6 **Set the intention that you will try to help the factory grow.** When you contribute to a factory's growth, consider people, processes, and machinery. As a factory improves steadily, both businesses will grow. The underlying principle really is one of fair trading: the "trade" of back-and-forth sharing, developing ideas, making a business work, and growing together. Ask the factory if there are any issues which may be holding them back. The factory's success affects your brand. Certification costs can be challenging, costing factories about $3,000 USD per year to start, which is expensive. Offering to chip in is just one way you can offer some support. Happy workers also affect your success. It is still up to the designer to see what a livable wage might be in the country they work in to ensure the fair trade price is livable for the worker. One of the easiest things you can also do is have a conversation with the factory regarding order quantities ask them what number of units per order will help the factory run efficiently. Minimums just don't cut it.

7 **Consider how culture may affect the way people communicate issues.** Here's one example: it's a norm for Indian business people to be reluctant to say they can't meet a deadline, or otherwise decline a service request that

you make of them. They may respond to a question with a vague or indirect answer that Westerners misinterpret. Be clear about what you want and ensure that they can meet your expectations. It's okay to be open and ask questions in a way that makes them feel that you are a team. How much do *we* pay the workers? What can *we* do to give them incentives? Be patient, be sensitive to nuances, and don't jump to conclusions. Keep rephrasing questions to obtain realistic responses.

Are Chargebacks Fair Practice?

Have you ever ordered your favorite product, only to have the store email you to say it's on backorder? No doubt disappointing, but you likely patiently waited because you get it: sometimes delays happen. For some odd reason, however, when a large corporation doesn't get its order, no matter the reason or the impact, they feel entitled to a discount. In the garment manufacturing world, you see this in the form of chargebacks.

Chargebacks are penalties that corporations enforce on garment factories for delays in shipping orders. Large corporations are extremely strict on meeting delivery dates. Regardless, if there were any unforeseen circumstances behind the delay, big companies give their factories no mercy, enforcing penalties. These penalties are considerable blows to the factory.

Common types of penalties may include:

> Enforcing chargebacks between 2%-5%, which is discounted from the order price.
> Demanding free delivery.
> Or, worst of all, canceling the order. Yes, you heard that right: *canceling*, and without any advance warning given.

Sew, what happens to the factories and people involved in the chargeback? The label maker, weaver, washer, sewer, dyer printer, trim supplier and the managers? Who pays these people if orders are canceled?

We all hear about orders that get shipped that may seem to be defective or not to spec, but what about the monumental losses that factories endure when companies fail to keep their end of the bargain, even if there are no delays? More often than you would believe, these large companies open a letter of credit (LC) with the bank, which states there are funds available in their bank, the factory accepts the LC and ships the order. Without warning, orders get canceled or, worse yet, orders are completed, only to find that the funds are no longer available.

As I mentioned earlier, here in North America, it's standard practice for accountants to work with retainer fees and graphic artists to work on advances, so why are we not doing this for people overseas? This may not apply to your business, but I do want to shed some light on how poorly some factories are treated. There are always two sides to a story. If we're going to be fair, it's vital that we consider the other "party" involved.

The Fashion Police

That's right: the Fashion Police are real, and they're on the case. No, I don't mean those girls in high school who made sure everyone wore pink on Wednesdays. I mean actual, grown-up, third-party accredited inspection houses devoted agents of non-profit organizations who provide the certifications of the world's ethical fashion companies, factories, and suppliers.

For the most part, certifications are costly, and for a startup, it's an added cost for both you and the factory to maintain. As the business owner/entrepreneur, it is critical to work with all employees to establish a company culture and policies that promote human rights. You can start by asking certifiers what questions they ask, then ask the factory similar questions, and do your own due diligence.

If you're able to bear the cost, third party certifiers are helpful. Also, beware of audit fatigue. Many factories have to keep up with so many third party audits that they suffer; straining the factory with daily manufacturing and business operations, which can negatively impact their bottom line.

Check out a few certifiers below:

WRAP (wrapcompliance.org): "Worldwide, Responsible, Accredited Production" is a non-profit dedicated to promoting safe, lawful, humane and ethical manufacturing around the world through certification and education, according to their website.

Their primary activity is the Certification Program, which is the largest independent facility certification program in the world mainly focused on the apparel, footwear, and sewn product sectors. Whereas other similar certifications like Eoko-Tex and Bluesign are material based, WRAP certification is focused on the sewn product portion of the supply chain. Within WRAP certification, there are varying levels of compliance, based on a location's performance. Often times, apparel brands will work with factories that are not currently WRAP certified to help them get to a point where they can be WRAP certified, as long as their desire and willingness to improve is there. Monitoring is an ongoing cost for both the factory and the company involved.

FLOCERT audits producers, traders, and companies to ensure compliance with the internationally agreed fair trade standards: in fact, it is *the* independent certifier for fair trade, often using the trademarked term "fair trade" on its labels. By checking compliance with fair trade standards, the company ensures that the relevant economic, social and environmental criteria are met, and those producers receive the fair trade minimum price and premium. They have become the specialists in custom-made solutions, working with a growing range of partners to offer individualized packages.

FLOCERT auditors are highly qualified, usually based in the countries and regions where they work and familiar with local cultures, languages and legal systems. All auditors are examined on their skills and receive annual training. In 2015, they carried out 2,411 audits around the world and operated in 117 different countries.

Fair Trade International (fairtrade.net) represents the world's largest and most recognized fair trade system. If you become a member, your customers can be confident that the FAIRTRADE Marks (the globally recognized symbols) are only used on products that meet the international Fairtrade standards, and support farmers and workers as they improve their lives and communities. The core of their business remains with Fair Trade, but they are leading the way in finding innovative, customized solutions that help producers, traders, and suppliers to thrive.

Better Work (betterwork.org) brings diverse groups together – governments, global brands, factory owners, and unions and workers – to improve working conditions in the garment industry and make the sector more competitive. The factories that are audited are located in Bangladesh, Haiti, Vietnam, Cambodia, Indonesia, and Ethiopia, to name just a few countries. Brands that are not Better Work partners can purchase reports for factories registered in Better Work programs.

Earning A Living Wage Is A Human Right

Fashion is a $3 trillion global industry. Hourly minimum wages are set by governments, and employers are legally obligated to pay at least that amount. In many parts of the world, people are not being paid what they can actually survive on and struggle to meet their basic needs. Essentially, while the minimum wage sets a bare minimum, the *living* wage aspires to be a socially acceptable minimum. Typically, this is seen as a level that keeps workers out of poverty.

The reality is that the vast majority of the people in developing countries that are making our clothes struggle to survive on wages that are barely enough to cover their daily subsistence needs. When people can't survive, it forces them to work multiple jobs, excessive overtime hours, work through illnesses, and/or force their children to work.

Sew, what can we do, as entrepreneurs, to help these workers?

> Incentivise employers to pay living wages (for example, by increasing orders to those suppliers).
> Build long-term, mutually trusting relationships with suppliers and work together to understand the drivers of prevailing wage levels and how they can be influenced positively.

Clean Clothes Campaign (CCC) is a global alliance dedicated to improving working conditions and empowering workers in the apparel industry. Since 1989, as the garment industry's largest alliance of labor unions and non-governmental organizations, they have been raising public awareness about working conditions in the garment industry. CCC educates and mobilizes consumers, lobbies companies, and governments, and offers direct solidarity support to workers as they fight for their rights and demand better working conditions. Representing the CCC in the UK, Labour Behind the Label campaigns for garment workers' rights worldwide. They both offer really great resources on living wages and supporting workers' rights.

Most of of the world's garments are made in Asia, however the majority of people who make these clothes cannot afford to live off what they are paid. Until recently, it had been difficult to define a living wage. The International Labour Organisation (ILO) has defined a living wage as a fundamental human right under their conventions and recommendations to the Universal Declaration of Human Rights Article.[16] The Asia Floor Wage Alliance, an alliance of Asian trade unions and labor groups have calculated a living wage formula for Asia. The Asia Floor Wage Alliance estimates that a living wage in India is $253 USD a month, which is five times the current minimum wage. Living wage calculations must take into account some common factors, including the number of family members the worker is supporting, the basic nutritional needs of a worker, and other basic needs including housing, healthcare, education and some basic savings.

Traceability & Supply Chain Transparency

Have you ever wondered what the journey of your t-shirt was like and the lives it touched? Many of us have lost the connection between the clothes we wear and the people who make them. The apparel industry has a major challenge in addressing responsible manufacturing practices and supply chain transparency. From seed to shelf, numerous suppliers and hands touch each product and every step should be accounted for to fully understand its impact.

The term *supply chain* refers to the back end of the industry. The *chain* is the link connecting:

> Where the raw materials come from and are processed and manufactured.
> Where factories and suppliers make and finish the garments and materials.
> The distribution network by which the clothes are moved and delivered to consumers.

Consequences of the convoluted manufacturing process include incidents like the devastating five-story building collapse at Rana Plaza in Bangladesh. The clothing, textiles, and footwear industries are incredibly labor intensive, estimated to employ more than *60 million people worldwide.[17] Often, parts of the manufacturing are done elsewhere to meet time constraints. More often, the person placing the order has no clue manufacturing is being subcontracted and has no knowledge of the conditions in those other workplaces.

Traceability and transparency is the ability to identify and trace the history, distribution, location, and application of products, parts, materials, and services. A traceability system records and follows the trail as products, components, materials, and services come from suppliers and are processed and ultimately distributed as final products and services. Transparency means public disclosure of brands' policies, procedures, goals and commitments, performance, progress and real-world impacts on workers, communities and the environment. Transparency requires brands to know precisely who makes their products, from where cotton was farmed, and how the fabric was washed, to where the garments and trims were made.

It is impossible for brands to ensure that environmental practices are sound and human rights are respected if they do not know where and by whom the products are made. Inability to track the origin of products and services may create grounds for violations within a company's supply chain.

The best part about supply chain transparency is the ability to maximize efficiencies in the supply chain, which can reduce a company's supply costs and its environmental footprint. Examples include reducing the energy, water, and natural material use, as well as improving worker health, motivation and productivity. If you're looking for investors, the ability to track your whole supply chain will also help prove there is a lower risk for them to invest.

The concept of transparency is at the forefront of fashion, and many organizations are trying to help move the industry in the right direction.

Like you, many brands are changing the way they approach manufacturing.

The <u>Baptist World Aid Baptist Church</u> (baptistworldaid.org. au) outlines optimistic figures of how brands have shifted their practices. The Ethical Fashion Report graded 407 brands and provides an overall grade on labor rights management systems. For example, Lululemon Athletica got an A-, H&M a B+, Gap a B- and La Senza a D+, and some lesser known brands like Minkpink got an F.

When comparing the findings from 2013 to 2018:

> They have seen a 29% increase in the number of companies working to trace their fabrics (from 49% to 78%).
> They have seen a 25% increase in the percentage of companies working to trace where their raw materials come from (from 17% to 42%).
> Statistics show that the number of final-stage production workers receiving a living wage has almost tripled.

Let's take a closer look at a couple of brands practicing what they preach.

Loomstate's organic cotton apparel (loomstate.org) is made using the Global Organic Textile Standards (GOTS) certified supply chain. GOTS allows companies to develop organic fiber supply chains - from the field to final product - with ease. Loomstate has also created what it calls the 'Loomstate Difference,' an interactive map that follows the journey of the company's newest T-shirt, all 100 percent grown and sewn in America. Their ambition is to create the most traceable tee in the world and to supply the public with full transparency of its supply chain, along with building sustainable business relationships.

Everlane is an American fashion e-retailer and, as of 2018, a brick-and-mortar retailer. It was founded in 2011 and is dedicated to "radical transparency." Everlane's motto is "Know your factories. Know your costs. Always ask why." They claim to openly report the sources and manufacturing processes of their minimalistic designs. For Everlane, environmental friendliness goes beyond using organic farms: they focus on minimizing water and energy consumption. Their pieces are made with quality in mind, which last longer. They do a great job of visually showcasing suppliers with beautiful pictures and personalized profiles. It's a great way to educate consumers and showcase the value of people in the manufacturing process.

Kudos to H&M for being transparent about who their suppliers are. You can explicitly check out their supplier list on the website. The list includes names and addresses, and also lists some of the fabric suppliers. As mentioned earlier, transparency means public disclosure of a brands' policies, procedures, goals and commitments, performance, progress and real-world impacts on workers, communities and the environment. There should be no reason to hold back any information, especially when you've committed to building a relationship with your suppliers.

Embracing Supply Chain Transparency

New organizations are emerging helping with the supply chain transparency, such as the Sustainable Apparel Coalition. They have made great strides to accelerate the implementation of the Higg Index , helping the apparel industry. The World Fair Trade Organization, the Ethical Fashion Forum and Fashion Revolution Day, among others, are all working toward this same goal.

Technology Meets Social Responsibility

The advent of technology in fashion has opened up an avenue of apps and websites to streamline ethical business practices. One such favorite platform is Ulula (ulula.com), which connects businesses, workers, communities, and governments to minimize operational risk and create value across global supply chains. Ulula decided to leverage the ubiquity of mobile phones to gather feedback directly from workers to better understand their working conditions. They can quickly identify the gravest human rights risks: forced labor, child, and human trafficking. Engagement is always voluntary and anonymous so workers can be completely honest, while producers gain feedback on ways to improve conditions to ensure ethical compliance and boost worker satisfaction and productivity.

Vera Belazelkoska, a political economist and Director of Programs at Ulula, has a few tips for us. She comes armed with ten years of experience in international development, with a focus on human rights, economic empowerment, and global supply chains.

Question: How can designers manufacture offshore while safeguarding the people who make our clothing?

Here's what she had to say:
"Governments, companies, workers, and consumers are asking for greater supply chain transparency, as seen with the passing of the Modern Day Slavery Act in France, the UK, and Australia, as well as with growing consumer demand for ethical fashion options. While the complexity of global sourcing can create opaque supply chains that are challenging to navigate, there are growing expectations

that procurement specialists and designers need to show greater traceability of their products - ensuring that there is no forced or child labor in the factories that produce their garments. Apart from social compliance, worker satisfaction and safe working conditions can also have an immensely positive impact on productivity and business outcomes, which benefit everyone involved.

Small and medium-size brands and designers can often feel that their order size and purchasing power are a barrier to requesting greater transparency from their suppliers. Here are a few tips to help brands get on a path to greater transparency:

1 Be extra vigilant if you are sourcing from areas with documented human rights risks. Many sources publish reports on known hotspots of labor rights abuses, which can be specific regions or economic zones where these issues are prevalent. Some good sources for information include the Ethical Trading Initiative, Business and Human Rights Resource Centre, Human Rights Watch, as well as investigative reports by the Guardian and Thomson Reuters. The Responsible Sourcing Tool (responsiblesourcingtool. org) has some great resources as well. Knowing about on-the-ground realities in the production areas where you source is the first step to understanding and mitigating your brand's vulnerability to social risk.

2 If you source from high-risk regions or know that your suppliers sub-contract in these areas, request extra information from them, such as audit results or payroll documentation, or visit their factories more frequently.

3 Find factories that supply socially conscious brands. Follow brands that you know go the extra mile to ensure compliance and look for or request their factory lists.

4 Leverage available innovations that can help you increase transparency. Blockchain - a public ledger - can be leveraged to track and validate the movement of goods in a supply chain. At our company - Ulula - we leverage simple communication technologies (workers' mobile phones) to collect insights directly from workers themselves about their working

conditions. With greater worker insight, we help brands and suppliers identify priorities for improvement.

Case Study

Working with Fair Trade USA, Ulula launched worker voice surveys in two garment factories in Mexico. We asked questions related to workers' wages, overtime, health and safety protocols, among other indicators. Data analytics were shared with buyers and factory management so they could identify areas that need improvement. Workers were also included in the decision-making process on how to spend worker engagement funding (for example, for educational support for children or additional health benefits for workers). Increasing worker inclusivity in the process of workplace improvement can significantly boost worker satisfaction and commitment, and reduce turnover and absenteeism.

Through the efforts tracing your supply chain, a brand can guarantee a sustainable product to their customers and at the same time influence purchase decisions and brand loyalty. Transparency helps people who are concerned about the human and environmental impacts of what they buy to make more informed decisions.

"ULTIMATELY, WE WANT TO SHARE OUR BEST PRACTICES AND BE TRANSPARENT ABOUT THE SUPPLY CHAIN. BEING OPEN ALWAYS BUILDS TRUST; THERE IS VERY LITTLE REASON TO KEEP THINGS PRIVATE."

-VERA BELAZELKOSKA

Shoutouts To Community Organizations Leading The Way

The Ethical Fashion Initiative (ethicalfashioninitiative.org) works in this framework by engaging brands to work with artisans differently. The Ethical Fashion Initiative connects talented but marginalized artisans to an international apparel industry. It is an organization with a goal to build a responsible fashion industry that measures its impact. Beyond their impact assessment, they have cleverly developed their own traceability platform called *Risemap*, which maps the complexity of supply chains and visually showcases the production process with photos and videos.

The Social Innovation Zone (socialinnovation.org) is an excellent community and organization to connect with. They accelerate success and amplify their impact through the power of co-working, community, and collaboration. Beyond shared office space, they are highly community driven and provide numerous support systems to help all sectors across the board create a better world. Offices can be found both in the US and Canada.

Ashoka: Innovators for the Public (www.ashoka.org) was founded by Bill Drayton in 1980 to identify and support leading social entrepreneurs. The foundation operates in more than 60 countries and supports the work of more than 2,000 carefully selected fellows. They cultivate a community of change and accelerate cutting-edge social innovation, whether in social entrepreneurship, education or business.

Echoing Green (www.echoinggreen.org) identifies, funds and supports emerging social entrepreneurs. The non-profit organization provides fellowships, seed-stage funding and strategic support to social entrepreneurs globally. To date, they have invested in more than 700 social entrepreneurs working in more than 75 countries around the world. They have provided a total of $42 million in seed-stage funding and support systems.

The Social Enterprise Alliance (socialenterprise.us) is a membership organization for the rapidly growing social enterprise in sixteen chapters across the United States. They provide resources and support to help develop social enterprises on a national scale and serve as a voice for more sustainable social impact.

Fashion Takes Action (fashiontakesaction.com) began in 2007 and helps advance sustainability in the entire fashion system through education, awareness, and collaboration. They provide support to a membership-based community and host the World Ethical Apparel Roundtable & Design Forward, which brings together like-minded individuals each year. For students, they have an education program called *My Clothes, My World* in Ontario, Canada.

Entrepreneurs are paving the way for positive change on this planet. As we build products and brands, it's essential for everyone, including you, no matter how big or small, to consider what kind of name you want to make for yourself. You have the power to do so much. You can make a difference in people's lives now and for our future.

In Chapter 9, we enter the world of sustainable design. This is where you'll get a better understanding on how to navigate design and your environmental footprint. This chapter addresses a massive topic, but I've condensed it dramatically to give you an overview. This way, you can decide how you want your business to contribute to a better, brighter, greener world.

NOTES

1. McDougall, Dan. "Indian 'slave' children found making low-cost clothes destined for Gap" in The Guardian. Online: https://www.theguardian.com/world/2007/oct/28/ethicalbusiness.retail. Oct 28, 2007
2. Artisan Alliance. Online: http://www.allianceforartisanenterprise.org/. Accessed Jul 8, 2018
3. Fuchs, Christopher, Martin Schreier, & Stijn M.J. van Osselaer (2015), "The Handmade Effect: What's Love Got to Do with It?", Journal of Marketing, 79 (March), 98-110.
4. International Standards Organisation 26000. Online: www.iso2000.info.iso26000. Accessed Jul 8, 2018
5. Fair Trade International Annual Report 2012-2013. (2013). Online: https://www.fairtrade.net/fileadmin/user_upload/content/2009/resources/2012-13_AnnualReport_FairtradeIntl_web.pdf. Accessed Mar 23, 2017
6. Neilsen. The Sustainability Imperative. Online: http://www.nielsen.com/ca/en/insights/reports/2015/the-sustainability-imperative.html. Oct 12, 2015
7. Wren, Erica. "New Study Reveals Cause Marketing an Effective Business Investment" in CSRWire. Online: http://www.csrwire.com/press_releases/15168-New-Study-Reveals-Cause-Marketing-an-Effective-Business-Investment. Oct 23, 2007
8. Ibid.
9. Hembrough, Judi. "Survey finds going green boosts bottom line for small businesses" in Plantronics Soundwave. Online: http://blogs.plantronics.com/small-medium-business/survey-finds-going-green-boosts-bottom-line-for-small-businesses. Jun 12, 2013
10. Small Business Sustainability Report, 2013. (n.d.). Online: http://biggreenopportunity.org/wp-content/uploads/2013/05/Big-Green-Opportunity-Report-FINAL-WEB.pdf. Accessed Mar 23, 2017
11. Ibid
12. Lee, J. (2016, June 21). "Can A Company Be 'Good' Without Transparency?" in Triple Pundit. Online: http://www.triplepundit.com/special/cotton-sustainability-c-and-a-foundation/can-a-company-be-responsible-without-transparency/. Accessed Mar 23, 2017
13. Oliver, John." Fashion: Last Week Tonight." Online: https://www.youtube.com/watch?v=VdLf4fihP78. 26 Apr 2015

14. Wikipedia. Code of Conduct. https://en.wikipedia.org/wiki/Code_of_conduct. Accessed Jul 8, 2018
15. Islam, Tabibul. "Women Suffer Most in Garment Sweatshops" in Inter Press Service. Online: http://www.ipsnews.net/1998/12/labour-bangladesh-women-suffer-most-in-garment-sweatshops/. Dec 29, 1998
16. Anker, R. "Estimating a living wage: A methodological review." Online: ILO. http://www.ilo.org/travail/whatwedo/publications/WCMS_162117/lang—en/index.htm. Aug 31, 2011

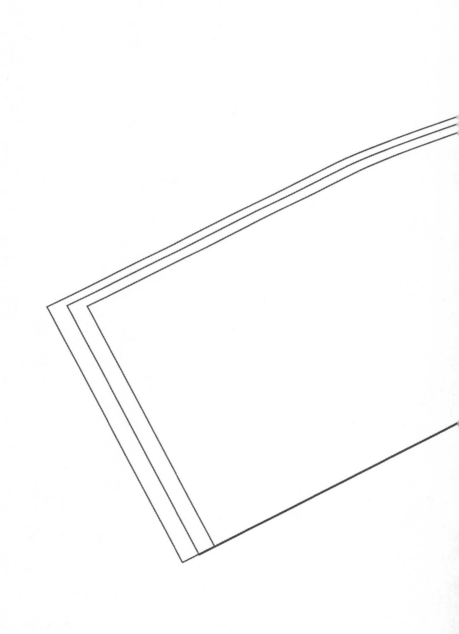

SUSTAINABLE DESIGN

OVERVIEW

Clothing is a basic human need, yet few people realize that the global industry that designs and produces clothing is one of the most environmentally and socially destructive industries in the world. Research on the topic portrays a dismal outlook for our planet, yet we all seem to be turning a blind eye. One of the best opportunities to address this burning issue is at the design stage.

We are all victims of the ruthless practices of global fashion brands that prioritize profits over people and the planet. Brands are in a constant race to get products on the racks. **Fast fashion** refers to cheap alternatives that mimic luxury brands. It offers affordable, basic, and disposable trends produced quickly and in a cost-efficient manner. Many of these fast fashion brands that source offshore have a hidden price tag. In many of these countries, lax regulations give suppliers of international brands a free hand when it comes to using hazardous chemicals to dye and process our clothes. The apparel industry also uses a lot of water. It takes 2,700 liters of water to make one T-Shirt. Approximately 70% of the wastewater from the fashion industry will be dumped and left untreated.[1]

Every morning we make a choice: the clothes we wear. This choice is linked to a massive global environmental, social and economic impact. Low-cost clothing, based on the latest trends, is by nature "a fast response system that encourages disposability."[2] Twenty percent of all freshwater pollution is made by textile treatment and dyeing: that's *a lot* of water. Conventional cotton farming uses approximately 25% of the world's insecticides and more than 10% of the pesticides. Sixty percent of all apparel will end up in a landfill or be incinerated within its first year of life.[3] The list goes on..

Environmental sustainability refers to the ability of something to continue without upsetting the earth's ecological balance. **Sustainable fashion** is a process that respects both people and the planet while remaining economically feasible. Sustainable fashion encompasses the entire supply chain, from agricultural production and fiber processing to design, retail and consumption. Another term for sustainable fashion, called **eco-fashion**, is a part of the growing design philosophy of sustainability. While eco-friendly fashion has never been particularly "glamorous," the best designers of a new generation are stitching sustainability into everything they do. A new generation of designers, of all sizes, such Stella McCartney, and Reformation to Edun, are building brands with a more conscious approach to fashion. A young generation of consumers are demanding it, and brands are finally listening.

The International Standards Organization (ISO) has defined eco-fashion as "identifying the general environmental performance of a product within a product group based on its whole life-cycle to contribute to improvements in key environmental measures and to support sustainable consumption patterns."[4] Unlike fast fashion, **slow fashion** production ensures quality manufacturing to lengthen the life of the garment. It encourages slower production schedules, fair wages, lower carbon footprints and (ideally) zero waste. Think of the same correlation between fast food and slow food: fast food is cheap, but the consequences of eating that food can be deadly. Slow food, on the other hand, from farm to table, is gentler on the planet and the people. The goal is to create a manufactured product that addresses lowering the human impact on the environment, and prioritizes social responsibility. These products often contribute to the slow fashion movement.

Did you know that decisions made in the design phase determine 80% of a product's CO_2 footprint? Integrating sustainability means designing a product and considering all the components, from the use to the end life of a garment. This means taking a closer look at the garment's life-cycle, all the stages from the raw material, through garment manufacture, transportation, how it's worn to how it's disposed of. Not until you have mapped out your product's life-cycle, can you begin to understand and implement strategies to address social and environmental issues. The possibilities are endless and every brand has a unique way of achieving their sustainable goals.We can seek inspiration from other brands and/ or create our own way of being a force for positive change. We can also seek help from other organizations and third- party certifiers.

Navigating the world of sustainable fashion is relatively new, and can feel overwhelming, but help and information is out there. As a designer, it's your vision and you have all the power to create something positive. My goal is to give you the basics so that you feel comfortable but the key is to keep on sharing information and learning from one another. Together we can all make a difference.

Sustainable Design Strategies

All manufactured products have an environmental impact, either during manufacture, use, or disposal. Sustainability goes beyond selecting and disposing of materials – strategy is key. Every point along the product's lifecycle should be considered during design. And there is much to consider: energy use, water, chemicals, and basically everything that might impact the environment. Designing with sustainability has the potential to improve a product's quality, efficiencies, as well as lower environmental impact.

We can evaluate sustainability by looking at the different phases of the product's life cycle and taking action in the stages where it will be most effective to reduce the environmental impact. The insights gained from each phase can assist you in taking the best approach to design and sustainability. It's much easier to create a sustainable product from the start than to do "damage control."

By now you should have a good grip of the product development process. When we talk about garment life-cycle we are looking at all the stages or phases from cradle to grave. The life-cycle begins at fiber (cradle), moving through to garment production, design process, manufacture, distribution, retail, use phase and eventual disposal (grave). Cradle to cradle design aims to bypass the grave to reuse valuable fibers via closed loop manufacturing methods.

For example, fibers in this closed-loop system come from only reused materials - and this is a good place to start. After being used, those recycled fibers are used again, and again, until finally turning into biodegradable waste and being absorbed back into nature. Having a truly closed loop means customers would also need to recycle their garment back to the designer at the end of its life-cycle, providing raw materials for the brand to then break down for reuse. Closed loop systems are very difficult to achieve, especially recycling and reusing different kinds of fabrics. Austrian company Lenzing, for example, has revolutionized the industry with its environmentally-conscious production of Tencel — a natural, man-made fiber also known as Lyocell, made with wood pulp from the Eucalyptus tree. It recovers or decomposes all solvents and emissions through production.

Photo | *The Garment Lifecycle*

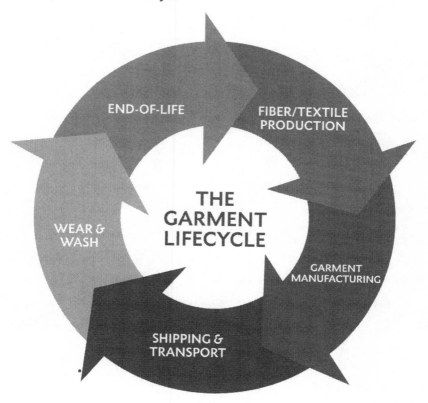

The chart below breaks down the stages of the life-cycle and at which steps in the product development process you can approach sustainability. At every stage you can consider the impacts and approach it with the best strategy.

Photo Credit | *Fig 1. Gwilt, Alison.*[5]

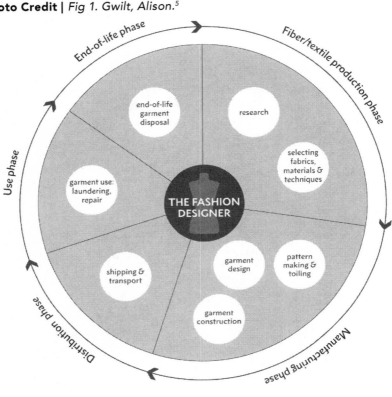

The phases in the life cycle of a garment, detailing the activities in the fashion design process

Below are some things that can be considered at each phase:

1 Fiber Textile Production Phase:

> How much energy and water is used when the fabric is manufactured?
> Can you use fibers that are low impact and can be recycled?
> Are there toxic chemicals used in the yarn, fiber, dyes or textile production that can affect people or the planet?

> Can I select any fabric or trim that has been recycled or can decompose quickly?
> Are there any new sustainable innovations or materials in the apparel industry that can be applied to the product?
> Is the product designed to be multifunctional?
> Is the product designed to be durable?

2 Manufacturing Phase:

> Is the product designed with quality in mind (to maximize the life before it's disposed of)?
> Is the design classic rather than trendy?
> Can the product be designed with lesser maintenance?
> Is your pattern marker laid out with as little waste as possible?
> Is the factory using renewable wind or solar energy etc.?
> Can any of the fabric scraps be used?

3 Distribution Phase:

> When shipping from the factory can you bulk pack items in a single bag that is biodegradable or recyclable? Can these bags also be reused after they're opened?
> What mode can you use that produces the lowest possible amount of carbon emissions?
> Can you reduce the weight of boxes to use less energy?

4 Use Phase

> Is the product designed with value so the consumer is reluctant to replace it?
> Can you provide the consumer with information on how to efficiently use the product?

5 End of life Phase

• Can the product be recycled and did you educate the consumer on how to do this?
• What is the average life of your product and how does it compare to other brands?
• How easy is the product to reuse?
• How easy is the product to recycle?

Get Inspired. Then Make It Your Own.

Many top clothing designers such as Eileen Fisher and Stella McCartney are at the forefront of reforming the fashion industry. Eileen Fisher's company is already using 84% organic cotton and 68% organic linen, and also reducing water use and carbon emissions. It is working to make its supply chain sustainable by 2020.[6]

Establishing your standards and practices from the start is a lot easier than making changes many years down the line. Compared to larger established brands, it is actually easier for new or young companies to enter the sustainably-produced clothing market because they have a chance to introduce themselves to consumers as a sustainable clothing brand right from the get-go, without having to reorganize existing sourcing and manufacturing practices. Large-scale retailers have to spend a lot of money transitioning to more sustainable fabric suppliers, manufacturing processes, etc. When you're small, it's a defining moment to decide how you source and how you manufacture.

Figure out what you can do. Create standards and practices for your organization and implement them early on. Nothing is set in stone: they can evolve over time. For example, a leader like Patagonia moved over to organic cotton after doing an internal audit. Patagonia also began incorporating fair trade certified cotton and started using fair trade factories in 2015.

Brands like Everlane, Edun, People Tree and Alternative Apparel all started with an evident design mission and have since grown their brand names.

Newer Business Models Paving The Way

Upcycling is a concept in which discarded materials and products are reused and given a new life with a higher value. Seek inspiration from brands like Preloved (getpreloved.com) and Nudnik (littlenudniks.com), which provide a new life to garments that would have otherwise gone to the landfill.

Zero-waste designing of apparel is, as the name implies, about minimizing waste. Here, the designing and sourcing processes go hand in hand. According to one article in *Fast Company*, "as much as 15% of fabric ends up trashed in the process of making clothes."[7] This design approach does not conform to the conventional pattern-making style, but instead uses more of a jigsaw puzzle technique to utilize all of the fabric, so there is no wastage. An understanding of textile and design dimensions before beginning the work is essential to zero-waste designing.

With the advent of slow fashion and the rise in demand for sustainable, ethically created clothing, many designers have ventured into the art of creating garments with minimal waste. Brands like Tonle (tonle.com) and Zero Waste Daniel (zerowastedaniel.com) have mastered the art.

If you do generate waste through your manufacturing process and cannot use it, look for other organizations that you could send or sell your scraps to. If you are producing in emerging economies, waste is often burned, sending chemicals from the fabric into the environment. Textile-recycling programs are popping up all over the country. It is up to you to check with your manufacturer to ensure that your waste is handled responsibly.

Deadstock fabrics, a great alternative for many startups, is end-of-roll fabric that would otherwise be discarded. If you can source deadstock fabric, it's a great way to keep things out of the landfill, and the bonus is you won't need to commit yourself to large quantities of fabric.

Capsule collections were initially popularised by Donna Karan in the 1980's when she released an instrumental capsule collection of seven interchangeable work-wear pieces. The idea was to create a capsule wardrobe that features only the most essential or influential pieces from a collection. Capsule dressing - a concept that promises to break the chains of fast fashion - frees up much-needed landfill space while also freeing our minds of the daily pressure involved in getting dressed. These pieces are often interchangeable and color coordinated, providing a wide range of looks from a modest selection. Vetta (vettacapsule.com) is one such brand leading the way.

The lease-return-lease business model comes with a value-added twist for Dutch label Mud Jeans (mudjeans.eu). In 2013, the label launched Lease a Jean to make sustainable fashion affordable. For €7.50 a month, customers can rent a pair of jeans and return them until they are done wearing them, at which point Mud Jeans will recycle them into new items of clothing.

Farm-to-high fashion is very similar to farm-to-table, which became a foodie circle buzzword about a decade ago. Today, the Peggy Sue Collection (peggysuecollection.com) is driven by this concept. Each garment can be traced back to the farmer who grew its fiber, the mill that manufactured the fabric and/or yarn, and the artisan who constructed it. This movement is spreading like wildfire, capturing the imagination of fashion designers and fiber makers across North America.

Repair and reuse is a problematic concept to scale, however, Patagonia (www.patagonia.ca) is leading the way. They are encouraging people to consider the environmental impact of their apparel. They take your old clothes (as long as they're still usable) and give you store credit. Rather than just throwing them out, they fix them up at their repair facility and sell them on their website! They wash used clothes with a waterless technology that helps restore the fabric and then make any needed repairs. Promoting reusing is in line with their core mission of reducing environmental impact. As a designer entrepreneur, you can encourage your consumers to bring back their garments to you for a discount (think "Green Eileen").

The Anti-Fashion Calendar: In the last 50 years, the way we manufacture and purchase clothing has drastically changed. Anyone can afford to wear the short-lived latest trends. Initially, fast fashion was about increasing the speed of production, reducing the time it takes to go from design to getting that product on the shelves. Rather than two collections annually, this made it possible to have a new product in-store with multiple deliveries throughout the year. The ultimate goal was selling more product and having something new that consumers need to get into their wardrobes every few weeks, to be in line with the latest trends. Fast fashion describes the method of imitating trends and styles seen on the runways at Fashion Week and recreating them at a much lower price and quality to sell to the mass market.

The traditional fashion calendar forces brands to release new designs twice a year, surging sales of current products. The seasonal schedule promotes a relentless drive for speed, waste, and over-consumption. Slow Fashion is the movement of designing, creating and buying apparel for their quality and longevity. It encourages slower production schedules, fair wages, lower carbon footprints and (ideally) zero waste. Study NY (study-ny.com) has cleverly crafted the anti-(fashion)-calendar. Tara St James, the founder, and designer, has cleverly challenged the traditional fashion calendar and created a production schedule and a new model based on slow fashion.

Activists Who Inspire

Follow people who want to be a part of the solution. The best and easiest way to learn is through inspiration. Information is always changing, and new studies are constantly being released. Now, I'm not saying that I know *everything* about the topic of sustainability (I have a long way to go), but having people around you who inspire you and are in the thick of the action can provide some great insights. Add them to all your social media. Keep them close. Here are two of my favorites...

The Activist: Dr. Vandana Shiva
Because she is a hero to anti-GMO activists everywhere.

Photo Credit | *Werner, Manfred.*[8]

Before I began my journey into responsible manufacturing, I came across **Dr. Vandana Shiva**, an Indian scholar, environmental activist, eco-feminist and anti-globalization author. There's just something special about her that will make you fall in love. She taught me about genetically modified organisms (GMOs) and GMO seeds. She is opposed by powerful multinational corporations invested in continuing their toxic (though lucrative) agricultural practices. GMO cotton was designed to be resistant to herbicides so that weed killers could be liberally sprayed on crops without worrying about killing the cotton plants.

Here is what I learned from this powerhouse:

Monsanto (now Bayer) invented the genetically modified seed known as Bt cotton, which is resistant to bollworm infestation, the cotton farmer's prime enemy. It "claims" the seeds can reduce the use of pesticides by 25%. GMO cotton was quickly adopted by cotton farmers, and millions of hectares of GMO-modified cotton have been planted worldwide since its introduction in 1996. However, the sad and tragic truth is that the pesticides don't control the bad bugs; many pests have grown immune to many of the toxic pesticides. Unfortunately, the farmers and their families who use the poisonous pesticides suffer from devastating health problems. The toxic chemicals in farming, runoff into nearby water streams and affect the environment and animals, and are directly ingested by people.

These changes come with some potentially problematic environmental challenges. Bees are hugely important in the pollination of many food crops but are unfortunately extremely endangered due to modern agricultural techniques such as GMO crops. As bees fly from crop to crop, they consume the plant nectar that is polluted with pesticides, causing the bees to ingest the toxic chemicals directly. Bees perform a task that is vital to the survival of agriculture: pollination. In fact, one-third of our global food supply is pollinated by bees.[9] Simply put, bees keep plants and crops alive. They are responsible for much of the food on your plate. In addition to bees and butterflies, birds, which also work as biological control agents and pollinators, are also at risk from pesticides, just like bees. Toxins are released into the soil through the plants as well, which jeopardizes the global food supply. Feeding the expanding population without further harming the Earth presents one of the most significant challenges of our time, perhaps of all time.

Furthermore, GMO seeds are expensive. In India, Monsanto's Roundup Ready cotton seed was selling for twice the price of non-GMO seeds. GMO seeds do not regenerate like natural seeds and cannot be used for next season's crop. The high price for the seed led to farmers in India often having to take out loans from moneylenders charging exorbitant interest rates. According to *The New York Times*, 17,107 farmers of all kinds committed suicide in 2003 due to their inability to repay back loans.[10]

The Activist: Safia Minney
Because she's the sustainable style pioneer

Photo Credit | *Odi Caspi.*

I came across Safia Minney on a factory visit back in 2011. I stumbled across some samples being made in the sampling department, just as they were getting the finishing touches. I was instantly drawn to the beautiful garment – it had a radiating energy to it. So I had to ask, "What label is this?" The factory told me it was made for People Tree, and went on to rave about Safia. I was intrigued to learn more, so when I got back home, I Googled her. According to her Wikipedia page, "Safia Minney is a British social entrepreneur and author. She is the founder of People Tree, a pioneering sustainable and Fair Trade fashion label with a mission to provide customers with beautiful clothes." This is how I discovered Safia Minney, and I've followed her ever since.

Here's what I've learned from the Queen of Fair Trade:

People Tree (founded in 1991) is the first apparel brand to achieve the World Fair Trade Organization (WFTO) mark to guarantee fair trade throughout the supply chain, as well as the first to mark their products with the Global Organic Textile Standards (GOTS) certification in the developing world. Safia initiated World Fair Trade Day in 1999, which is endorsed by the WFTO.

Safia is a beautiful storyteller. I was instantly drawn into her world. She has experience and a background in marketing and publishing, which has really helped to convey her messages through everything from social media, keynote talks and films to videos and books. By merely following her on social media, you can gain some insight into past and future events that may be of interest to you. Her books offer a wealth of information and include *Slow Fashion*, *Naked Fashion*, *By Hand*, and *Slave to Fashion*. These books challenge conventional thinking and ways of doing business.

For years, factories have been squeezed from insanely low target prices given by customers. These factories need the business so badly and can get cornered into processing orders just to stay afloat. Not only does Safia pay a fair price, but she also gives *advance payments* to help the factories procure materials and pay their workers in keeping with fair trade principles. She is a catalyst for change in the fashion industry and for change in responsibility in labor practices and environmental protection. She also advocates slow fashion: her designs take six months from idea to customer. Finally, Safia advocates that brands must build a market for ethical fashion in an environment where the prices of retailers do not reflect the true social and environmental cost. To learn more visit her website.

Inspirational Methods To The Madness

To create responsible products and manufacturing, we need to be aware of environmental impacts to be able to incorporate sustainability into the design. Beyond selecting raw materials, transforming a product's sustainability may be achieved through various methods. For example, much of a garment's environmental impact comes from washing and laundering the goods we buy (not just from growing, processing and producing the fabric). As a designer, what you can do is merely add information to the care label to help consumers lower their environmental impact.

Below are some ideas to get you thinking about ways to incorporate sustainability.

Fashion: **A Thirsty Industry**

The fashion industry is highly dependent on water. From growing cotton to manufacturing garments and dying textiles, water is an essential component throughout the entire fashion supply chain.

In the developing world, where the majority of our manufacturing takes place, factories and fabric mills are located directly alongside or close by waterways such as rivers and canals. An estimated 17 to 20% of industrial water pollution comes from textile dyeing and treatment and an estimated 8,000 synthetic chemicals are used throughout the world to turn raw materials into textiles, many of which will be released into freshwater sources.[11]

Why Fresh Water Shortages Will Cause The Next Global Crisis

You might be surprised to learn that, like gold and oil, fresh water is a commodity and it happens to be quite scarce. According to the World Wildlife Fund (WWF), about 70% of the Earth's surface is covered in water, but 97% of it is saltwater, which is useless for human consumption, as it cannot be used for drinking, crop irrigation or most industrial purposes.[12] That leaves us with 3% water, and of that amount, two-thirds is either frozen glaciers or is not consumable by humans. Fresh water simply isn't readily available and free for everyone, especially those who live in poverty-stricken countries. Our ecosystem is becoming stressed by the growing human population. According to the WWF, at the current human growth rate, "[by 2025, two-thirds of the world's population may face water shortages. And ecosystems around the world will suffer even more."[13]

Agriculture consumes most of the water and is incredibly inefficient. You have to look at the cost of water as an inevitable cost of goods. Now, more than ever, it is crucial that we aid and continue to support a transition to a water-conscious garment manufacturing industry. The planet needs our help. It needs *your* help.

The chemicals left in water limit the ability to recycle it, but Levi's has worked with one of its Chinese suppliers to make 100,000 pairs of jeans using 100% recycled water, so it can be done.

The clothing industry is the second largest polluter in the world. It can still take more than 5,000 gallons of water to manufacture a single T-shirt or one pair of jeans. Moreover, wastewater carries a host of different chemicals from the processing of dyes, and the World Bank estimates that textile dyeing and treatment contributes up to 17-20% of total industrial water pollution.[14] It is estimated that 8,000 synthetic chemicals are used throughout the world to turn raw materials into textiles, many of which will be released into freshwater sources. And it's not only the production of raw material that is water intensive; the wet processing of clothing, such as washing and dyeing, also consumes enormous amounts of water.

To learn more, you can check out international river conservationist, Mark Angelo, in the film *RiverBlue,* where he uncovers how the fashion industry plays a part in destroying our world's rivers to get a better understanding of the scope of the issue.

Sew... we are at a crossroads when it comes to sustainability and transparency in the garment manufacturing industry, and how our generation can make a lasting impact. We need to start changing the industry now. Try to find innovative ways of reducing the amounts of water used during manufacture and washing to care.

The Harm Caused by Fabric Dye

Fast fashion brands can be pretty sneaky. While advocating organic cotton, they use conventional dyes that are just as toxic to the environment as conventional cotton. Did someone say greenwashing?

Before chemical dyes existed, people used various sources of natural dyes to add that unique color to their garments. The problem was that most natural dyes faded quickly. The introduction of chemical dyes in the mid-19th Century made this problem a thing of the past; however, the fix brought in a whole new and more dangerous set of challenges to our world today. Water wastage, water pollution, and chemicals that are harmful to the human body and deadly for aquatic life are just a few damaging effects of the process of fabric dyeing.

The process of dyeing requires the fabric to be washed several times to get rid of the excess dye that did not stick to the material in the previous stage. There are several problems with this. First, this process contributes to a massive amount of water wastage. The textile industry wastes about 16-20 liters of water just in the process of dyeing an average t-shirt.[15] This massive water consumption can exhaust water supplies in many regions of the world where water is scarce.

Secondly, chemicals are one of the main components of our clothes. They are used during fiber production, dyeing, bleaching and wet processing of each of our garments. During these washes, much of the dyes used are lost and end up as effluents. Effluent is liquid waste that is discharged into bodies of water, be they lakes, seas or oceans. Given the nature of fabric dyes having to be resistant to fading and washes, they are made to be highly resistant to many factors such as biodegradability, soaps, detergents, light, temperature, weather, etc. This means they end up living in the environment for a very long time and can be extremely harmful to the planet and wildlife.

Chemicals from dyes in the water can affect the transparency of the water, and kill or otherwise harm aquatic life while also decreasing the availability of drinking water, irrigation, and water used for recreation, especially beaches. Moreover, some of these chemicals can be highly toxic to humans. Babies and children are starting to have increased levels of toxic chemicals in their bloodstreams as a result of dyes from their clothing absorbing into their skin. The chemical aniline comes from azo. Azo dyes are most commonly used in our clothing because of their brightness and cheapness.

Also, research has shown that azo dyes can be carcinogenic and prolonged, and/or repeated exposure to it can be cancerous. Additionally, some of these dyes can cause disruptions in DNA and hormones.[16]

Greenpeace leads the Detox Campaign, which challenges top brands to make amends by working with their suppliers to eliminate all hazardous chemicals across the entire lifecycle of their products. They list 11 chemicals that should be avoided, which include azo dyes, amongst others.

This being said, it still doesn't seem like the global demand for chemical dyes is going anywhere. Fortunately, however, many factories are starting to work against the harm of synthetic dyes. Depending on the item being manufactured and the location, factories can dispose of the harmful chemicals safely through treatment plants. The treatment plants will remove the toxic chemicals in dyes and leave the water as pure as it can be. The water will be reused in the manufacturing process.

One way you can ensure that your manufacturer is being responsible with the handling of fabric dyes is by asking for certifications. Look for a factory that is GOTS, Oeko-Tex and/or Bluesign certified. These certifications aim to eliminate unsustainable materials from entering the environment and help to push eco-friendly methods of garment production.

Dyeing...To Give You Some Eco-friendly Tips

Dyeing can be done at almost any stage, from the fiber to the constructed product, and may require whitening pre-treatment. Dyes and printing inks require a pigment and a fixative, or mordant, both of which can utilize toxic chemicals and heavy metals. Azo group chemicals, which release carcinogenic arylamines, are widely used in synthetic dyes and pigments. Dyes are challenging to remove from wastewater and leave it colored, preventing wastewater from supporting plant life by inhibiting aquatic plants' ability to photosynthesize.

1 Ask the dyers if they are connected with a water-effluent treatment plant. Water treatment plants allow factories to recycle and reuse water runoff during the garment manufacturing process, which promotes the three R's: reduce, reuse and recycle. In countries such as India, factories have turned to water treatment plants to reduce the amount of water waste.

Photo | *Water treatment plant in Tirupur, India 2014*

2 The use of low-impact dyes and raw materials are other ways garment factories can reduce their impact on the environment. Low-impact dyes require less water and do not use any heavy metals, resulting in fabric water conservation. They also have a higher absorption rate that sticks to garments with less run-off into the water, ensuring less hazardous waste is dumped into rivers and lakes. Avoid dyes and inks that contain heavy toxic metals. If you're creating your fabric from scratch (which allows more control over the whole process), ask your dyers about the dyes used. Some dyers provide Global Organic Textile Standard (GOTS), and Oeko-Tex® certified low-impact dyes that can be used during the dying process. The <u>Zero Discharge of Hazardous Chemicals</u> (ZDHC) program is working towards zero discharge of hazardous chemicals (more on ZDHC below). You can join the program or check out the list of substances they have banned to ensure you are not using these chemicals.

3   Dye sublimation is the simplest form of imprinting a design on a garment. The outcome of the design is photo quality and very simple to do. All you need is the garment, transfer paper, and dye ink. Sublimation is the chemical process of turning a solid into a gas without it becoming a liquid first. There is no water needed for dyeing. Compared to screen printing, where mass amounts of water are consumed to dye, resulting in polluted water wasted and ground contamination, dye sublimation creates zero water waste. The downside to this process is that the ink can only fuse to polymers, meaning only synthetics. You can't print on garments that are made with natural fibers, such as 100% cotton shirts, but you can use it on a poly/cotton blend.

Do Your Labels Care?

As I mentioned earlier, the care instruction label provides an opportunity to minimize the environmental impact associated with a product's life. Washing in hot water requires energy (via hot water heaters) and so contributes to climate change. Garments that use harsh detergents for washing also pollute our water. Therefore, items that can be washed effectively in cold water and with minimal detergents will have a reduced impact throughout their lives. Where possible, always indicate "cold wash" on the care instruction labels to inform consumers. Finally, encourage people to wash in cold water, hang to dry, and use wet cleaning over dry cleaning.

One statistic, reported by the University of California at Santa Barbara, states that "laundry accounts for 64% of energy consumption and 76% of water consumption in the lifecycle of a poly-cotton t-shirt."[17] What is pulled off or out of your clothing goes back into your water system: chemicals, microfibers, and other particles. Water-based laundry systems just move dirt and particulates from one place to another. Tersus Solutions, a Colorado-based startup, specializes in a technology for cleaning, disinfecting and coating textiles and garments using liquid carbon dioxide in place of water.

Natural Dyes

For the most part, natural dyes have a lesser environmental impact compared to synthetic dyes. Natural dyes are non-toxic, but they are not edible. Natural dyes, a renewable resource, are textile colorants that are derived from plants, insects, and other natural materials. Throughout history, they have been used for generations, with every culture around the world having its own set of prized colors, traditions and meanings. The majority of natural dyes are vegetable dyes from plant sources: roots, berries, bark, leaves, and wood were all used before synthetic dyes came along. The most common natural dyes all come from plants and include madder, cutch, weld and indigo (except cochineal, which comes from an insect).

One thing to keep in mind is that "natural" does not mean "safe." They are not synonyms. Mushrooms can be poisonous. Arsenic is perfectly "natural." Even benign chemicals like potato starch will kill fish and other aquatic life because they encourage the growth of algae that deplete all available oxygen, among other issues (known as BOD or Biological Oxygen Demand). And some so-called "natural" dyes are themselves toxic.

The fiber content determines the type of dye required for a piece of fabric. Combined fibers like those listed below make dyeing complicated:

> Cellulose fibers: cotton, linen, hemp, ramie, bamboo, rayon
> Protein fibers: wool, angora, mohair, cashmere, silk, soy, leather, suede
> Synthetic fibers: nylon, polyester, spandex, acrylic

Natural dyes are less permanent, often requiring the use of mordents to affix the color molecule to the fiber. A dye can sit on top of the fabric and look fine at first, but it easily washes out or fades to a lighter shade very quickly. Another drawback is that the color choices are limited. On the other hand, the fading or slight variations can also add to the beauty and interest of the material. Many people appreciate the look, and the art becomes more important than the actual quality or consistency.

If you're wondering if it's possible to dye large quantities, the answer is yes, it is possible to dye hundreds of pieces at a time. Commercial dye houses like <u>Botanical Colors</u> (botanicalcolors.com) have been at it for the last ten years. The dyes are produced in a concentrated extract form designed for industrial machinery. It is also possible to minimize color variations by careful dyeing and planning.

Do The Right Thing

Both synthetic and natural dyes have drawbacks. Making a choice can be challenging, but the good news is that more dye manufacturers are minimizing the use of harmful chemicals in their products and are more focused on creating dyes with the use of environmentally friendly ingredients. At the same time, the majority of dye producers are treating their dye effluents with organic bacteria to lessen water pollution. The best choice could be perhaps not going for natural or synthetic dyes per se, but going for products that have the least harmful impact on people and nature. When looking for dye products to use for your business, seek help from commercial dyers that offer eco-friendly products. If you're working with a garment manufacturer who is procuring the fabric, ask for certified low-impact dyes. It may add to longer turnaround time, but it is well worth the wait. Also be sure to buy fabric from a supplier that has water treatment in place.

Waste Is A Design Flaw: **Sew, Let's Reduce Waste!**

Waste is only waste if you "waste it." Thirteen million tons of textile waste is created each year in the U.S alone.[18] Recycling is the process of re-using and converting waste materials into new materials and objects. Closing the loop, or a circular economy is a term used in a recycling process. It is basically a production process in which post-consumer "waste," is collected, recycled (broken down) and re-created back into its original form (a bottle gets recycled back into a bottle, for example). Open-loop recycling (downcycling) indicates that it can be recycled into other types of products. This process can be as simple as using recycled plastic to make new bottles (closing the loop), or as complicated as weaving reclaimed plastic bottles into soft polyester for clothing or other products (open-loop).

Stacey Fynn may only be one person taking on this incredibly massive problem, but she is also very irked at the status quo and incredibly trained. She founded the social enterprise Evrnu, which makes fiber from cotton garment waste, thereby closing the loop. This fiber is described as finer than silk but stronger than cotton and uses 98% less water and 90% fewer carbon emissions than cotton and polyester, respectively.

Upcycling

Back in the 1930s and 1940s, when families had little economic and material resources, upcycling was a way of life. Doors became tables, feed sacks became dresses, and curtains became chair covers (or, in the case of *The Sound of Music*, a summer wardrobe for a family of eight). If your grandma can upcycle, *sew* can you.

Upcycling is about refashioning, but still using the same materials as when you started. When you upcycle an item, you aren't breaking down the materials. You are reusing discarded materials in such a way that the upcycled item is of better value or quality.

Taking something old and making it new again can also be done at a scale. Preloved, a made-in-Canada clothing brand, has been at it since 1995. They take vintage clothing, combined with deadstock and overrun fabrics, sort them into similar colors and fibers, completely deconstruct them, then turn them into a material. Creating consistency is an art of the process. To meet the demands of larger retailers that want consistency for each style, they blend that with deadstock materials and overrun materials.

Planet Forward (planetforward.org) is a project of the Center for Innovative Media at the George Washington University School of Media and Public Affairs. It teaches, celebrates and rewards environmental storytelling by college students. According to Planet Forward, in total there are about 21 billion pounds of clothing and textiles in landfills right now, or 70 pounds per person,[19] some 95% of which could be used to make new products. Only about 15% of consumer waste is currently being recycled by consumers.[20]

Encouraging your consumer to recycle *all* of their textile waste can be a powerful tool to reduce waste.

Fabric Scraps

When garments are constructed, there is usually wastage. More than 100 billion garments are produced each year. Fifteen percent of the materials produced in the process go to waste.[21] Recycling textiles aren't always simple, but Fabscrap (fabscrap.org) and FabCycle (fabcycle.ca) want to change that. Both programs are aimed at designers and fashion brands, simplifying the textile recycling process, and by providing pickup services for textile waste.

The fabric that Fabscrap collects is then available to anyone who is interested in using it – from designers to quilters – and can be purchased in both the New York City warehouse, as well as larger pieces, which are available online.

Wearable Collection (wearablecollections.com) is helping to keep textile waste out of landfills and repurpose it instead. This NYC-based company is focused on keeping clothing, textiles, and shoes out of landfills while generating funds for charities. They place collection bins for textiles in apartment buildings. You can request bins or sign up to host a textile collection drive.

You can also do your part to reach out to design schools to see if they can use your scraps, or be sure to donate your scraps to an H&M, or your municipality if they recycle. If you manufacture offshore, check to see what your options are.

Minimize Waste During Patternmaking

Think about ways you can construct the garment differently to reduce waste (e.g. offcuts, end-of-roll). Select textiles that have a repeat pattern (with no beginning or end) so that the entire roll of fabric can be used. Think about whether you can reuse or recycle the waste and offcuts. In a sense, the "waste" is like throwing away money: material has value.

Labeling Garments with Helpful Info

The care label, hang tag and other labels can communicate how the garment can be used and recycled, which helps your customer avoid discarding the garment prematurely.

Packaging Goals

Packaging – much of it single use – has created a rubbish problem that now pollutes every corner of the world. Polybags are critical to ensuring that garments stay clean and protected during transport, but can you opt for bulk packing items in one shipping bag? Can you source recycled polybags? Can you transport products using recycled or reused boxes? Hangtags can use eco-friendly dyes and recycled paper.

Conserve Energy

Energy is not infinitely available. The textile industry retains a record of the lowest efficiency in energy utilization and is one of the major energy-consuming industries.[22] Try to select manufacturers and production processes that are energy efficient, use green, renewable energy, and make efforts to reduce inputs such as water and chemicals. You can ask suppliers to provide you with impact data.

Transportation

The Green Story platform helps brands measure impact and communicate it to their customers. Their goal is to increase conversion rates by turning the positive impacts of a purchase into an interactive experience for customers.

Akhil Sivanandan, the co-founder of Green Story and a sustainability expert, has a few excellent tips to share:

Purely regarding greenhouse gases, three main factors influence transport emissions: Distance, Mode, and Efficiency.

Distance

Distance is pretty straightforward: the less distance you have to transport your goods, the less energy you use, the fewer emissions are generated. So, local is better for emissions.

Mode

When it comes to modes of transport, shipping has the lowest impact for bulk transport, followed by rail, then trucks, with the highest impact being from air transport. There are some exceptions. For example, electric vehicles can have a lower impact than shipping, but only if the electric grid it draws power from is relatively clean. The US grid, for example, has average emissions of over 500 gCO2e/kWh of electricity generated. But the grid in Canada is closer to 150 gCO2e/kWh of electricity generated. So driving an electric vehicle in Canada is cleaner than driving one in the US. An electric grid is how you get electric power. These differ from region to region. For example, Ontario, Canada does not use coal in its power generation; it uses nuclear and hydropower mostly. This is much cleaner than the US, which uses a lot of coal in its power generation.

Efficiency

A factor that many designers often overlook is packing efficiency. In general, the more you can carry in a trip, the more efficient it will be. Think of this concerning carpooling. If it's just you, your travel emissions are close to 240 gCO2e/km, but if there are three more people, your own travel emissions are only 60 gCO2e/km. So, the more tightly packed the goods are, the fewer emissions you have per ton.

Designing A Quality Product Is Directly Related To Sustainability

The sad truth is that most fast fashion companies design products that are deliberately meant to fall apart. When something falls apart, it pushes consumers to go back into the store and buy again.

Longevity of a garment is directly related to sustainability. Beyond the quality of a piece of fabric, poor seams and thread quality result in garments tearing and falling apart, which reduces their lifespan.

These wasteful garments end up in landfills, which present many health and environmental issues. Most of these materials that end up in landfills contain toxins that are eventually released and seep into the soil and groundwater. Greenhouse emissions are produced in landfills and are said to be a significant cause of global warming. Electronics such as computers and batteries contain substances like arsenic, acids, lead and others, which eventually end up in our environment and pose threats to public health. Inhaling even a small amount of mercury vapor can harm our kidneys and cause respiratory failure.

Sourcing Materials

Many experts suggest that sourcing materials closer to home is the key to a sustainable practice. In my opinion, where materials are sourced from and where manufacturing occurs have little bearing on sustainability. It is vital that you understand how fabrics are made.

You can have incredibly unsustainable products made in your backyard, and incredibly sustainable products sourced from across the world. Often, it can be more sustainable to make something overseas with a suitable manufacturing process than in a North American facility with a terribly wasteful process, despite it being right around the corner from where you are.

To help you measure impact, Nike has created a tool called the Nike Making app (on iOS) where you can search fabrics to see their impact. The app provides insightful data and helps to identify materials that have lower environmental impact without compromising the design process. The app ranks materials used in apparel based on four environmental impact areas: water, chemistry, energy, and waste. Making is available to download free of charge from the Apple iTunes store.

Material selection is often the first step that designers will take in reducing the environmental impact of the garment. Environmentally preferred fibers/textiles can significantly reduce the environmental impact and increase the resourcefulness of a product throughout the garment life cycle without changes to the design practice or product development process.

Keep in mind, every process and fiber has its pros and cons. It's a "pick your poison" situation. The question is, which fibers and materials align with your environmental goals?

Fibers

Fibers (natural or manmade) are either cultivated or manufactured (or use a combination of both). Each fiber source and the way it is manufactured comes with its own set of environmental concerns. Textiles are either natural (e.g. cotton, linen, silk, wool), man-made (made from plant based-cellulose, e.g. bamboo, viscose, Tencel, modal versions of rayon), or synthetic (oil used to create polymers, such as polyester, acrylic, and nylon).

All fibers have a negative environmental impact. Natural fibers like cotton, linen, wool, and silk (not plant-based) are created from plant-based cellulose. When they are buried in a landfill, they act like food waste, producing CO_2 and methane emissions. Worse, you can't compost old clothes even if they're made of natural materials. This is a huge problem because they contribute to climate change. Garments are produced in a variety of unnatural and toxic processes, such as bleaching, washing, dyeing, and printing. These chemicals can leach from the textiles and—in improperly-sealed landfills—into groundwater. If you burn these items, you'll release toxins into the air.

Synthetic fibers, like polyester, nylon, and acrylic, have the same environmental drawbacks, and because they are mainly a type of plastic made from petroleum, will take hundreds of years, if not a thousand, to biodegrade. In recent years, polyester has surpassed cotton by far as the material most commonly used for clothing.

Unfortunately, it is cheaper for producers to spin new polyester instead of recycling it.

Conventional Cotton & The Alternatives

Organic cotton is a fiber grown without using any harmful chemical fertilizers or pesticides on it. Its production sustains the health of soils, ecosystems, and people by using natural processes rather than artificial input. Instead of using the harmful chemicals that are used to grow conventional cotton, the cotton farmers use insects, crop rotation, and other methods, including weeding, by using a machine or simply by hand. By doing this, it increases the soil quality and protects the air and water we rely on to survive. Organic cotton uses natural seeds that regenerate. Cotton clothing is only organic if it is certified to an organic cotton standard.

Hurdles to growth include the cost of hand labor for hand weeding, reduced yields in comparison to conventional cotton, and the absence of fiber commitments from brands to farmers before planting the seed. The up-front financial risks and costs are, therefore, shouldered by the farmers, many of whom struggle to compete with economies of scale of corporate farms. Organic cotton is more expensive than conventional cotton because its production takes more time, skill, and hands-on labor.

Conventional cotton, on the other hand, uses genetically modified seeds (GMO), also known as Bt Cotton, yielding higher volumes because the seeds are engineered with toxins to ward off insects and pests. Farmers and farm workers who pick Bt cotton have also complained of skin and respiratory allergic reactions. Many reports have shown that most livestock either fell sick or died after grazing on cotton fields.[23]

Non-organic cotton is one of the most toxic crops on the planet. About 25% of the entire world's use of insecticides comes from growing conventional cotton. To put this into perspective, it takes roughly 1/3 of a pound of chemicals to grow enough conventional cotton to make ONE t-shirt.[24] Keep in mind that most of the world's highly contaminated cotton seeds and cotton gin trash end up in animal feed (especially non-organic dairy) and in low-grade vegetable cooking oils, purchased by consumers or used in fast-food restaurants and school cafeterias.

According to Textile Exchange, "Whether the cotton is grown with chemicals, or organically, each farm and geographic region of the world will have different water usage and impacts. However, the notion that chemical cotton uses less water than organic cotton is false. The bigger issue is that toxic chemicals used in conventional cotton production are poisoning our waters."[25]

Have you ever gone to a mall and walked past some fast fashion retailers and smelled something vile? Most big brands don't use natural fibers, as the cost is much higher. Here's why they smell: "easy care" garments are especially saturated by chemicals, such as formaldehyde and other harsh chemicals, to give clothes features such as anti-microbial, anti-odor or anti-wrinkle characteristics. Formaldehyde - used to eliminate wrinkles, static, odor and bacteria from clothes - is highly toxic and known to cause cancer, skin ulcerations, heart palpitations, eczema, asthma and other health issues. Just *imagine* the condition that garment workers are in!

Some designers have marketed bamboo fiber as an alternative to conventional cotton. Some brands claim that it absorbs greenhouse gases during its life cycle and grows quickly and plentifully without pesticides. The truth is, the conversion of bamboo fiber to fabric is the same as rayon, and is highly toxic. The Federal Trade Commission ruled that labeling of bamboo fiber should read "rayon from bamboo." Bamboo fabric can cause environmental harm in production due to the chemicals used to create a soft viscose from hard bamboo.[26] Just because a plant grows quickly does not mean the fabric that is made from it is sustainable. If harsh chemicals are used in fabric creation and are then pumped into the environment, that resulting material is not sustainable.

Recycled Fabrics

There is something very fishy in our oceans and it's not our fish. It's polyester, a manmade fiber made from petroleum, and one of the world's most common fibers. Despite the fact that it cannot decompose, it has lower energy impacts during the washing and cleaning phase, and is also completely recyclable at the end of its life. But when we wash our polyester clothes, thousands of microplastic fibers are washed into waterways. In fact, it's estimated that a single polyester garment releases 19,000 individual plastic microfibers.[27] Even with every wash at home, we release microfibers. And guess where these microfibers end up? In our oceans, where they threaten ecosystems and end up in our food chain.

It is easiest to find fabrics of recycled materials if you only look for fabrics containing one fiber type. For example, 100% polyester fabric made from recycled polyester waste is quite easy to find. Recycled polyester first made a splash in the market with the launch of "pop-bottle fleece." Since then, textile developers have incorporated recycled poly into a wide variety of knit and woven fabrics.

Blended fibers, e.g. cotton/polyester blends, are sometimes used to increase the strength of yarn and thus increase the lifetime of products, compared to 100% cotton. Once you use 100% recycled polyester yarn to make a fiber blend, the resulting fabric cannot be recycled because there is more than one fiber type in the fabric. Although recycling is one of the best sustainable practices, the costs are incredibly high.

Swerea IVF (swerea.se) is working on a circular technology called *The Regenerator* that uses an earth-friendly chemical to gently separate and regenerate cotton and polyester blends into new, fully useable textile fiber. In short, this innovation will "un-mix" mixes to create tomorrow's fashion. Swerea IVF is also working on a project that will produce guidelines and look at technical solutions on a scientific basis to help the textile industry reduce the emissions of microplastics from their products.

Trims & Embellishments

Trims and embellishments play a big part in a sustainable design. Think about your brand's ethical commitments contributing to a high quality that your customer will appreciate. Every part of your garment has an environmental impact.

Are your printing methods using proper filtration systems and are your inks environmentally friendly? Consider alternatives to materials that cause more harm. Can you select coconut or seashell buttons instead of plastic buttons that will take years to decompose? Most importantly, will you share this information with your customers? They will appreciate all the thought and time that went into designing it.

Manufacturing zippers involves many chemical and carbon-intensive processes. There are environmental effects of extracting petrochemicals for polyester and polyamide (nylon) production as well as smelting metal. YKK has made some visible strides in attempting to address the environmental impact of its products. By 2020, YKK aims to eliminate hazardous chemicals from the manufacturing process following the ZDHC program. The Zero Discharge of Hazardous Chemicals (ZDHC) Program is a collaboration of leading brands, value chain affiliates and associate contributors committed to advancing towards zero discharge of hazardous chemicals in the textile, leather and footwear value chain, thereby reducing harm to the environment and human well-being. As a part of our environmental activities, YKK has developed ECO-DYE® technology that allows the reduction of the amount of water used in the zipper dyeing process to almost zero. They have also created NATULON® zippers, which are made from chemically recycled polyester (post-consumer) and are perpetually recyclable. YKK also has organic cotton zippers and is working on creating plant-based zippers.[28]

One of the most sustainable options for zippers is to reclaim them from old clothes and reuse them in garments. This is definitely the most time intensive, though, as removing zippers involves wrestling with tight stitches to avoid shredding the tape. You can find sellers on Ebay and Etsy that sell bundles of salvaged zippers for the DIYer. Hong Kong-based TYT claims that its Greengear zipper line is made of 100% recycled polymer.[29]

Eco Certifications

Certification takes place when a third party conducts a compliance assessment and determines that a group is properly following a standard. This will help a group ensure they are complying with best practices and also give consumers assurance that a particular product really is made in line with a certifying process. It takes both time and money to become certified, both of which are scarce resources for smaller grassroots organizations. It can be challenging for a new, smaller ethical manufacturer to become certified.

One the easiest things you can do is ask suppliers and manufacturers to provide you with independently verified certifications for environmental management and ethical practices. You can have certifications based on material, product or process. Keep in mind that not all certifications are created equal; in fact, standards that don't require recertification may be particularly suspect.

While there may be some overlap in mission regarding social and environmental responsibility, I've noted a few major players whose mission is to lower environmental impact.

Certifications For Garment & Materials

Global Organic Textile Standards (GOTS): is a crucial certification for products and manufacturers, and is the leading worldwide textile processing standard for organic fibers. According to their website: "The Global Organic Textile Standard (GOTS) was developed through collaboration by leading standard setters with the aim of defining requirements that are recognized worldwide and that ensure the organic status of textiles from harvesting of the raw materials through environmentally and socially responsible manufacturing all the way to labeling in order to provide credible assurance to the consumer."

All organic materials for apparel should be GOTS certified, as it is the most trusted organic certification program for apparel. GOTS was developed with the goal of unifying the various existing standards and draft standards in the field of eco textile processing, and defining worldwide recognized requirements. Processors and manufacturers shall be enabled to supply their organic fabrics, and the standard covers the entire production cycle, from farm to factory, and only textiles that are a minimum of 70% organic fibers can become certified. GOTS also includes critical social criteria based on the key norms of the <u>International Labor Organization</u> (ILO), which includes criteria around forced labor, freedom of association, child labor and living wages. According to the ILO, there is neither a generally accepted definition of what a living wage is, nor is there a generally agreed methodology on how to measure it.[30]

Textile Exchange

According to their website, "Textile Exchange is a global non-profit that works closely with our members to drive industry transformation in preferred fibers, integrity, and standards and responsible supply networks. We identify and share best practices regarding farming, materials, processing, traceability and product end-of-life to reduce the textile industry's impact on the world's water, soil and air, and the human population." Patagonia is one of the founding members. The organization was founded in 2002 and has over 200 members. Each year they also host the Textile Sustainability Conference, bringing together like-minded individuals who want to create a more sustainable and responsible fiber and materials industry."

Cradle to Cradle

Finally, there is a Cradle to Cradle certification. According to their website, "The Cradle to Cradle Products Innovation Institute, a non-profit organization, educates and empowers manufacturers of consumer products to become a positive force for society and the environment, helping to bring about a new industrial revolution. The Institute administers the publicly available Cradle to Cradle Certified™ Product Standard which provides designers and manufacturers with criteria and requirements for continually improving what products are made of and how they are made."

The Institute's *Cradle to Cradle Certified™* Product movement has a growing community, and you can search the database for certified products. What's even cooler is designers can search their database for certified material, certification details, and scorecards, along with the names of suppliers.

Oeko-Tex (oeko-tex.com)
According to their website, "The STANDARD 100 by OEKO-TEX® is a worldwide consistent, independent testing and certification system for raw, semi-finished, and finished textile products at all processing levels, as well as accessory materials used. Examples of articles that can be certified: raw and dyed/finished yarns, woven and knitted fabrics, accessories, such as buttons, zip fasteners, sewing threads or labels, ready-made articles of all types."

Since it was introduced in 1992, their primary focus has been on the development of test criteria. Oeko-Tex Standard 100 certification ensures the fabric has been tested and is certified to be free from harmful levels of more than 100 substances known to be harmful to human health. The certification addresses how the fabric is processed, including things like dyes and finishes.

Blue Sign (bluesign.com)
Typically used by Eileen Fisher and Patagonia along with other larger brands, Blue Sign is challenging to navigate and very costly for a startup. According to the Patagonia website:

"Bluesign® Technologies evaluate and reduce resource consumption in our materials supply chain, and assist us with managing the chemicals, dyes, and finishes used in the process. Bluesign Technologies, based in Switzerland, works at each step in the textile supply chain to approve chemicals, processes, materials, and products that are safe for the environment, safe for workers, and safe for the end customers.

Textile manufacturers that become Bluesign system partners agree at the outset to establish management systems for improving environmental performance in five key areas of the production process: resource productivity, consumer safety, water emissions, air emissions, and occupational health and safety. System partners regularly report their progress in energy, water, and chemical usage and are subject to on-site audits.

The Bluesign system is based on input-stream management. Chemicals are assigned to one of three categories: blue – safe to use; gray – special handling required; and black – forbidden. The Bluesign system helps factories properly manage gray chemicals and replace black chemicals with safer alternatives."[31]

Fashion Positive (fashionpositive.org)
The Fashion Positive initiative leverages Cradle to Cradle Certified™ Product Standard to transform the way fashion products and materials are made. The certification verifies and ensures that material inputs of a product are prepped for people, the planet, and the circular economy.

Fashion Positive members, are leading the fashion industry on a direct path to safe materials. PLUS members, such as Loomstate, Mara Hoffman & H&M are some of the apparel companies driving the circular fashion movement. If you have less than $20M in sales, it will cost $7,500USD to become a member. Certifying a product can get costly; however, they do provide resources and tools for designers that will help you learn about fashion in the circular economy, as well as how to make tangible progress toward certified materials.

Measuring Impact

"Measure impact" has become a mantra for creating environmental and social change. Claims about making a difference are no longer sufficient; evidence of how much difference you're making is now required. We should applaud this trend because results are often unclear and claims often lack evidence. Consumers trust numbers.

Green Story
Green Story is an excellent tool to help startups measure their impact and optimize their marketing initiatives. As mentioned earlier, they help increase conversion rates by helping you understand - and provide your customers with information about - how much energy you've saved, how much water you've saved, and how many emissions you've avoided. How awesome is that?

According to their website:

"Green Story helps increase conversion rates by turning the positive impacts of a purchase into an interactive experience for customers. Your customers want to have an impact, and let's face it, brag about it. Green Story's embeddable graphics transform dry impact data into shareable, interactive assets that let your customers brag about you online. Our calculators, counters, infographics, and social media sharing applications provide an engaging, informative and interactive experience to your customers at each and every point of their interaction with you."

> Unagalli (ungalli.com), with the help of Green Story, purposefully measures impact. Unigalli wants to raise awareness of the negative impact the mainstream clothing industry has on people, wildlife, and the planet. Customers can buy with confidence. Every Unigalli jogger purchased by a consumer diverts eight plastic bottles from the landfill, eliminates two kilometers' worth of driving emissions, conserves 110 days of drinking water, and saves one light bulb! How cool is that?

SUSTAINABLE APPAREL COALITION (apparelcoalition.org)
The Sustainable Apparel Coalition is an incredible resource for any brand looking to build sustainability, even small startups. Launched in 2009 by the odd couple, Walmart and Patagonia, it has brought together 175 members whose companies account for more than 40% of the global apparel industry. They have been building what they expect to be the principal driver of change in the industry: a set of three online tools, known as the Higg Index that measures the social and environmental impact of brands, manufacturing facilities, and products. It helps inform designers about sustainability opportunities from prototype to finished product, guiding them to make better choices at every stage of a product's development.

Brands are asked practice-based, qualitative questions to gauge environmental sustainability performance and drive behavior for improvement. Information is then collected from their own operations and their suppliers, all of it going into a database that coalition members can use to evaluate suppliers. About 6,000 factories have provided information about their social and environmental impact.

It is a learning tool for both small and large companies to identify challenges and capture ongoing improvement. Merely reviewing the HIGG Index modules will give you a visible picture of what sustainability should be, because it encompasses *all* aspects of production. This online module program can be downloaded for *free* and is user-friendly: merely enter data about your business practices, and the Higg Index examines the different areas within your company, from design and manufacturing policy, to logistics and end-of-life practices, and rates them regarding their sustainability. It then highlights areas that can be improved. Also, check out the Materials Sustainability Index (MSI) to rate materials you are thinking of using in your designs to understand their impacts on the environment and compare them to other materials.

Zero Discharge of Hazardous Chemicals (ZDHC) (roadmaptozero.com) Established in 2011, the ZDHC is a group of apparel and footwear brands and retailers working together to lead the industry towards zero discharge of hazardous chemicals. It was founded by six leading brands and today consists of 98 contributors. They have a ZDHC MRSL list of chemical substances that should be banned from intentional use by the industry in the production of textile, apparel, leather, and footwear.

According to their website:

"Our mission is to advance towards zero discharge of hazardous chemicals in the textile, leather and footwear value chain to improve the environment and people's well-being.

Our vision is widespread implementation of sustainable chemistry and best practices in the textile, leather and footwear industries to protect consumers, workers, and the environment.

Our goal is to eliminate the use of priority chemicals by focusing on the following areas: Manufacturing Restricted Substances List

(MRSL) & Conformity Guidance, Wastewater Quality, Audit Protocol, Research, Data and Disclosure, and Training."

The ZDHC Roadmap to Zero Program takes a holistic approach to tackle the issue of hazardous chemicals in the global textile, leather and footwear value chain.

Inditex Group (inditex.com), the parent company of Zara stores, has a strategic environmental policy. Under their Global Water Management Strategy, they are committed to zero discharge of hazardous materials by 2020. They also intend to promote eco-friendly alternatives in the development of new products and reduce energy consumption across all retail locations.

How To Get Started In The World Of Sustainability

1 Understand

Do your homework. Research and analysis should always be done as the first step to any sustainable strategy. Get inspired by other brands. Find and attend raw material, wholesale and retail trade shows and events to gain insight into new developments in the field of sustainable design. Subscribe to newsletters of organizations, certifying bodies or any type of expert so you and stay on top of what is happening in the industry. Attend sustainability events and become members of associations. Connecting with people opens doors.

Ask your supplier questions and develop a relationship with them. Sustainability is always evolving. Suppliers are in the "thick of what is going on" and can offer insights to problems and solutions. They can also be an invaluable source in finding sustainable materials.

What hits home for you? With all that information that you've gathered, here are some things to consider:

> Do you want sustainability to be a cornerstone of your brand story or an addition to it?
> Can you help solve a sustainability issue?

- > What resources have you found that you can incorporate into your design or brand strategy?
- > While doing your research, have you come across sustainable textiles and trims that can be used for your products?
- > Have you found creative ways to minimize waste in design or post-production?
- > If you are using a single fiber in your garments, like 100% cotton or 100% polyester, you can encourage post-consumer recycling of your garments. This can be done by sharing information on how to do that on your website.
- > Can you encourage upcycling of your products by offering a discount on a new product to your customers when they give you your well-loved garments back?
- > Have you found a supplier that is GOTS certified? Are your printers and dyers using a water treatment plant?

2 Plan

Take a look at the product life-cycle and phases. Go back to the beginning of the chapter. At each phase you can consider the best strategy.

Jane Goodall said it best: "What you do makes a difference and you have to decide what kind of a difference you want to make." Your research will guide, not determine, your strategy.

The list of possibilities to build a social brand is infinite.

3 Create

Now that you have a plan, you can start designing your product and working through product development armed with knowledge. With all that information under your belt, you're on your way to being thoughtful in design and running your business. You can confidently consider reducing impact during each step of the product development life-cycle, from construction, materials and finishing, to producing a high-quality product that will have a long life.

Don't forget to utilize the HIGG MSI scores to compare different materials, identifying which have the highest/lowest impact. The

Sustainable Apparel Coalition's Higg Index product tools will help provide you with information to make better choices at every stage of a product's development.

4 Implement

Tell your brand story. What was your journey like? How did you get to where you are? You've done a lot of work to get there, and sharing your story will only help build your relationship with your customers.

Talk about your past, present and future. The story of your company and brand starts with the founder and why you started the business. Share your process in developing products, your values, and your goals in helping save the planet.

Educate your customers. How are your customers washing your garments? Why is it important to do what you do? Can you provide tips on how they can keep their garments fresh without over-washing? Make sure your marketing initiatives incorporate your sustainable journey and goals.

5 Measure

Have you made a positive impact in the world? Can you quantify the progress your company has made? Look to the experts, join organizations, and get help to measure the difference you have made. Not only does it give your customers confidence, but it will also really show you what achievements you have made.

The fashion industry is fast-paced and demanding. If sustainability is important to you, give yourself time to understand your options to produce the best product possible. Learning and improving is an ongoing process. Your ability to design sustainable products will become better and stronger with each year that passes. Give yourself permission to start where you are, and your brand will become more sustainable over time.

Endings & Beginnings

I'm finding it a bit bittersweet that the book is coming to an end. Yes, the end is nearing, but for many of you, this is where your journey will begin. I've been there: nothing entirely describes that feeling when you envision that dream and then see it materialize.

I still remember, the first time I visited the first factory I did business with. Believe it or not, my mom was there with me. Yes, my Mom! She wasn't there to chaperone me, we were on vacation and she was doing me a favor by spending some of her vacation time visiting a factory with me. Thanks mom! I had never set foot in a factory before, and when I entered, boy was I amazed. It was like the North Pole during the final few days before Christmas! Elves frantically creating something magical.

It was a bit overwhelming and I tried not to let my lack of experience show. I was eager to learn and understand how it all worked from the factory's side. I may have been very young, 22, but I also had really good questions to ask. I think both my mom and the owner were impressed. Sure, I was nervous, but I was also super excited. I was eager to learn, and I still am today!

After I got back home, I received a package from the factory with my counter samples. I remember sitting there on the floor like it was my birthday, tearing open all the boxes and bags (I know, so not environmentally friendly!). Sure, the samples were not perfect, but they were mine! I made these! My drawings come to life! Unfortunately, I no longer work with that factory, they had well over 1000 sewing operators. Although it wasn't a good business fit, I still have a relationship with them. And whenever I have a problem, or yes - yet another question, I'm lucky enough to have someone I can reach out to! The owner's industry expertise has always been a great help.

As you forge ahead on this exciting yet challenging journey, keep in mind those qualities and skills demonstrated by successful designer-entrepreneurs in the industry.

*Always maintain a thirst to learn – never stop gathering inspiration for innovative design or researching the ever-changing in-and-outs of this dynamic industry.

*Be true to your creative vision and always stay driven in bringing it to fruition through all the obstacles you encounter along the way. At the same time, be smart, be practical, and know when to compromise to ensure the success of your brand.

*Never underestimate the good that you can do for the world and for all those in it. Be a part of driving this industry in the right direction. Learn from the pioneers and be one too!

*Be fearless. Don't let anyone or anything intimidate you. Believe in yourself and in what you have to offer all those potential customers out there. Always strive for more – more growth, more progress, and more change for the better.

*Above all, your team and the factory, (your ride or die), is key to unlocking the door to success. Pick your tribe wisely and learn to always improve your communication and grow your relationships.

I hope that this book has given you a clearer picture of the entire process that is involved in getting from idea to product. With the roadmap that I've provided, you are better equipped to transform that dream into reality. Create your own unique brand and process, and a plan that works for you. I genuinely hope you use all the information I have given you to move forward with confidence!

You can do this. You've got this. This is your year.

NOTES

1. "Cotton's Water Footprint: How One T-Shirt Makes a Huge Impact on the Environment (VIDEO)" in The Huffington Post. Online: https://www.huffingtonpost.com/2013/01/27/cottons-water-footprint-world-wildlife-fund_n_2506076.html. Jan 27 2013
2. Annamma Joy et al. "Fast Fashion, Sustainability, and the Ethical Appeal of Luxury Brands" in Fashion Theory. Vol 16, Issue 3. Victoria: UBC Press, P. 275.
3. Drennan, Kelly. "How Fashion is Ripe for Disruption." Fashion Takes Action. Online: https://fashiontakesaction.com/fashion-is-ripe-for-disruption/. Oct 30, 2017
4. Petz, Bob. "Waste Couture: Environmental Impact of the Clothing Industry" in Ecology Today. Online: http://www.ecology.com/2010/11/02/environmental-impact-clothing-industry/. November 2, 2010
5. The Fashion Design for Sustainability model template. In "Integrating sustainable strategies in the fashion design process: A conceptual model of the fashion designer in haute couture". Melbourne: RMT University, School of Architecture and Design, 2012. p.95.
6. Lockwood, Lisa, and Arthur Friedman. "Eileen Fisher Aims for Total Sustainability" in WWD. Online: https://wwd.com/fashion-news/designer-luxury/eileen-fisher-total-sustainability-10099173/. Mar 19, 2015
7. Peters, Adele. "5 New Solutions for the Fashion Industry's Sustainability Problem" in Fast Company. Online: https://www.fastcompany.com/3055925/5-new-solutions-for-the-fashion-industrys-sustainability-problem. Feb 1, 2016
8. Vandana Shiva on the "green carpet" for the Save the World Awards 2009. 24 July 2009. Online: https://it.m.wikipedia.org/wiki/File:Save_The_World_Awards_2009_show03_-_Vandana_Shiva.jpg
9. Yang, Sarah "Pollinators help one-third of world's crop production, says new study" in UC Berkeley News. https://www.berkeley.edu/news/media/releases/2006/10/25_pollinator.shtml. Oct 25, 2006
10. Sengupta, Somini. "On India's Farms, a Plague of Suicide" in The New York Times. Online: http://www.nytimes.com/2006/09/19/world/asia/19india.html?pagewanted=1&_r=1&ei=5094&en=ce312104d42deb70&hp&ex= 1158724800&partner=homepage. Sep 19, 2016

11. Ravasio, Pamela. "How can we stop water from becoming a fashion victim?" in The Guardian. Online: https://www.theguardian.com/sustainable-business/water-scarcity-fashion-industry. Mar 7 2012

12. World Wildlife Fund. "Water Scarcity." Online: https://www.worldwildlife.org/threats/water-scarcity. Accessed Jul 8, 2018

13. Ibid

14. "Dye Industry." Worst Polluted. Online: http://www.worstpolluted.org/projects_reports/display/105. Accessed Jul 8, 2018

15. Wang, Irina. "Environmental Chemistry - Fashion" in Prezi. Online: https://prezi.com/o5liaqprixy_/environmental-chemistry-fashion-and-environment/. Apr 15, 2013

16. European Commission Health and Food Safety Scientific Committee. "Opinion on Risk of Cancer Caused by Textiles and Leather Goods colored with Azo-Dyes." Online: http://ec.europa.eu/health/scientific_committees/environmental_risks/opinions/sctee/sct_out27_en.htm. Jan 18, 1999

17. Tersus Solutions "Why Your Dirty Laundry Matters." Online: http://www.tersussolutions.com/tersusblog/2017/3/21/why-your-dirty-laundry-matters. Mar 21, 2017

18. Frazee, Gretchen. "How To Stop 13 million tons of clothing from getting trashed every year" in PBS. Online: https://www.pbs.org/newshour/nation/how-to-stop-13-million-tons-of-clothing-from-getting-trashed-every-year. Jun 7, 2016

19. Russell, Aspen. "Closing the loop in clothing manufacturing." Planet Forward at GW. Online: https://www.planetforward.org/idea/closing-the-loop-in-clothing-manufacturing. May 31, 2016

20. Runnel, Ann. "How much does garment industry actually waste?" Reverse Resources. Online: http://reverseresources.net/news/how-much-does-garment-industry-actually-waste. Aug 31, 2016

21. Ibid

22. Prince, Aravin. "Energy conservation in textile industries & savings" in Fire2fashion. Online: http://www.fibre2fashion.com/industry-article/3377/energy-conservation-in-textile-industries-savings. Accessed Jul 8, 2018

23. Branford, Sue. "Indian farmers shun GM for organic solutions" in The Guardian. https://www.theguardian.com/environment/2008/jul/30/gmcrops.india. Jul 30, 2008

24. Franzen, Harold. "Here's Why Your Next T-Shirt Should Be Made of Organic Cotton." Organic Consumers Association: https://www.organicconsumers.org/news/heres-why-your-next-t-shirt-should-be-made-organic-cotton. Jun 1, 2017

25. Textile Exchange. "Quick Guide to Organic Cotton." Online: http://textileexchange.org/quick-guide-to-organic-cotton/. Accessed Jul 8, 2018

26. Biome. "Bamboozled...Are Bamboo Sheets & Socks Eco-Friendly?" Online: https://www.biome.com.au/blog/bamboo-sheets-bamboo-socks-eco-friendly/. Apr 4, 2017

27. O'Connor, Mary Catherine. "Inside the lonely fight against the biggest environmental problem you've never heard of" in The Guardian. Online: https://www.theguardian.com/sustainable-business/2014/oct/27/toxic-plastic-synthetic-microscopic-oceans-microbeads-microfibers-food-chain. Oct 27 2014

28. YKK Fastening. "Sustainability." Online: https://www.ykkfastening.com/sustainability/. Accessed Jul 8, 2018

29. Striepe, Becky. "Fab Fabrics: Zippers" in Crafting a Green World. Online: https://craftingagreenworld.com/articles/fab-fabrics-zippers/. Accessed Jul 8, 2018

30. Reynaud, Emmanuel. The International Labour Organization and the Living Wage: A Historical Perspective. Geneva: ILO. 2017

31. Patagonia. Bluesign System. Online: https://www.patagonia.com/bluesign.html. Accessed Jul 8, 2018

GLOSSARY OF TERMS TO KNOW & UNDERSTAND

ACCELERATOR – a business that connects startups with mentors, guidance, resources, and funding *(50, 51)*

ARTISAN – a highly-skilled craftsperson who makes small quantities of high-quality or unique products, usually by hand or using traditional methods *(224, 241, 250, 251, 259, 274, 275, 277, 286)*

ASTM / AMERICAN SOCIETY FOR TESTING AND MATERIALS – an international standards organization that dictates the specifications and test methods for the physical, mechanical, and chemical properties of textiles and fabrics *(97, 115)*

AZO DYES – organic compounds used to dye textiles, often used for clothing due to its brightness and low cost, but believed to have negative effects on people's health *(250, 293, 294)*

BASIC BLOCK – a pattern silhouette that is re-used season after season with only minor changes *(20, 120)*

BOM / BILL OF MATERIALS – a list of raw materials and other components, and the quantities of each, needed to manufacture an end product *(142, 147)*

BRAND IDENTITY – the components of the brand that identify and distinguish the brand in the customer's mind, the way a business presents itself and is perceived by consumers *(57, 122)*

BRAND LABELS – also referred to main label, that is affixed to a product. the brand label communicates the company name to the consumer. it contains the brand name or brand logo of the buyers such as h&m, gap etc.*(111, 113, 115)*

BUYING AGENT / BUYING HOUSE – a person or firm that locates supplies at the best prices *(222)*

CA NUMBER – the ca identification number is obtained by applying to the canadian competition bureau. commonly referred to as "ca number", is registered for exclusive use of a canadian dealer on the label of a consumer textile article in place of a name and postal code. *(115)*

CAD / COMPUTER-AIDED DESIGN – precise, technical illustrations created using computer software, which clearly illustrate design requirements *(5, 79, 80, 119, 128, 135, 140, 143, 147, 150, 174, 175, 230)*

CAPSULE COLLECTION – a collection released by a designer featuring a limited number of essential pieces aimed at being functional, interchangeable, and timelessness *(286)*

CARBON FOOTPRINT – the total emissions of carbon dioxide and carbon compounds from the actions performed by a particular person, group, or business *(258, 280, 287)*

CARE LABEL – the label on a piece of clothing that communicates the item's washing or dry-cleaning instructions *(5, 45, 111, 113, 114, 115, 150, 170, 172, 205, 291, 299)*

CAUSE MARKETING – a promotional strategy where a business's sales are connected to a charitable cause to which a portion of the profits is donated *(254)*

CAD – cad, or computer aided design is the use of computer systems to aid in the creation or modification of a design. *(84)*

CB - *cb or center back. is the vertical line taken from the center back neck point to the waistline leven (88)*

CENTER-SELVAGE VARIATION – centre to selvedge variation is a critical problem in open width fabric processing. for solid fabrics shade of the fabric varies between center and selvage. *(195)*

CHARGEBACKS – penalties that corporations enforce on garment factories for delays in shipping orders *(244, 268)*

CLOSURES – mechanical devices that close, fasten, or secure garments while wearing them *(39, 87, 88, 103 – 105, 108, 109, 118)*

CMT (CUT, MAKE, TRIM) FACTORY – a factory that will cut and sew the fabric, and attach the trimmings, but where you provide the materials, patterns, and cutting marker *(223)*

CODE OF CONDUCT – guidelines a business provides for its members to ensure they understand and comply with its ethics and objectives *(256, 260 - 262)*

COMBING – a mechanical process used align the fibers in yarn to make it smoother *(180)*

COMPACTING – a mechanical process of finishing a textile using heated rollers that can improve it in a number of ways, including lowering shrinkage and increasing smoothness *(172, 182, 205)*

COMPETITIVE RESEARCH – seeking and evaluating information on companies selling to the consumers in your target market *(34, 36)*

COMPOSITION – composition, also referred to fiber content, is what the fabric is made of. fabrics can be made of either natural or manufactured fibers or a combination. *(33, 62, 63, 70, 132, 163)*

CONVERTER – a person or firm that purchases unprocessed goods directly from a fabric mill, and then dyes, finishes, prints and/or washes them to create finished fabrics *(124, 125)*

CORPORATE CULTURE – a corporation's values, policies, practices, and behaviors that collectively create its unique workplace environment *(71)*

COST SHEETS – a document outlining the cost of items and services needed for a particular project within a business *(80)*

COUNTER SAMPLE – a sample developed by the factory based on the prototypes, reference samples, and tech packs provided by the designer, that the factory uses to achieve sewing efficiencies, establish machinery requirements, and source all other materials needed, and that the designer comments on or approves *(7, 13 - 16, 18, 19, 21, 23, 24, 96, 118, 123, 126, 128, 132, 136, 141, 142, 147 – 154, 156, 158, 159, 175 - 177, 203, 204, 227 - 230, 314)*

CPL / CUT PANEL LAUNDRY – cut panel laundry (cpl) is a process used in knits garment manufacturing to control shrinkage. to improve dimensional stability of the fabric panels of fabric are cut at specific points, then washed and tumble dried before cutting the pattern pieces and stitching. *(173)*

CRADLE TO CRADLE DESIGN – a method of designing via closed loop manufacturing, for example, creating products that are made from reused materials and that can themselves be reused or recycled *(281, 307, 308)*

CROWDFUNDING – a method of raising money for a project or an organization from a large number of individual donors or investors *(217)*

CSR / CORPORATE SOCIAL RESPONSIBILITY – the responsibility of an organization for the impacts of its policies and practices on the welfare of society and the environment *(251 - 253, 255 - 263)*

CUSTOMS BROKER – a licensed individual, with customs and import/export knowledge, who acts as an agent on behalf of an importer or exporter by handling fees, documentation, and the clearing of goods through customs *(12, 17, 25, 86, 112, 113, 199, 202, 203)*

CUT-AND-SEW FACTORIES – also refered to as a cmt (cut, make, trim) factory will produce a product from start-to-finish. they cut the fabric, sew the fabric pieces together and attach the trimming such a s hangtags, labels and buttons etc. the buyer sources the material and components. generally. most domestic factories are cmt factories. *(10, 33, 205)*

CUTTING MARKER – a cutting marker, also known as a marker, is a guide or template made typically made by computer and printed out and used in the cutting process. all the pattern pieces for any given style(s), including sizes - are laid out in a formation intended to reduce fabric waste. after the marker is made, the fabric is laid out in layers and it is laid on top of the fabric to trace and cut by machine.*(223)*

DEAD INVENTORY – products that sit in a warehouse and are not selling. *(210)*

DEADSTOCK FABRICS – the end-of-roll fabric that would otherwise be discarded *(286, 298)*

DENIER – a unit of weight used to measure the fineness of fabrics like nylon yarn, rayon, or silk *(69, 181)*

DESIGN SKETCH – a hand drawn sketch of a design made with paper and pen or pencil. *(78 - 80, 83, 85, 135)*

DYE SUBLIMATION – a method of imprinting a design onto a garment without using water *(295)*

ECONOMIES OF SCALE – a reduction of costs arising from a business increasing in size *(178, 190 – 192, 196, 303)*

EMBELLISHMENT – a decorative detail or feature added to a product to make it more attractive or enhance its appearance without having any functional purpose *(14, 19, 23, 45, 87, 103, 104, 128, 131, 135, 141, 150, 154, 163, 168, 170, 178, 185, 189, 194, 238, 305)*

FABRIC EASE – the measurable difference between the measurement of the body and the measurement of the garment which allows for movement and comfort for the wearer *(102)*

FABRIC STANDARD – the material /textile provided as a level of quality to try to attain. *15, 63, 69, 126, 127, 147, 148, 217, 226 - 228)*

FABRIC STRUCTURE – the way a fabric is formed, either a knit, woven or non-woven. *(10, 11, 17, 64, 66, 68, 82, 132, 189, 217, 225, 229)*

FABRIC SWATCH – a small sample piece of a textile that looked at before purchasing in bulk. *(14, 23, 72, 126, 127, 138, 139, 160, 162)*

FABRIC WHOLESALER – a business that sells textiles in bulk quantities for commercial use. *(11)*

FAIRTRADE – an independent non-profit foundation advocating for improved social and environmental standards, particularly in relation to products and commodities exported from developing countries *(112, 196, 237, 240, 243, 250, 251, 253, 255, 256, 258, 264 - 268, 270, 275, 276, 285, 290, 291)*

FARM-TO-HIGH FASHION – the concept of creating a garment that can be traced back to the farmer who grew its fiber, the mill that manufactured the fabric and/or yarn, and the artisan who constructed it *(286)*

FASHION ILLUSTRATION – an artistic visualization of a model wearing a garment, used by a designer to brainstorm their ideas and vision for a garment in an fantastical and inspirational way *(79)*

FAST FASHION – cheaply made garments, often created to mimic luxury brands, which are affordable, basic, and take the form of disposable trends *(19, 43, 183, 196, 244, 263, 279, 280, 286, 287, 292, 301, 303)*

FIT MODEL – a fit model used by a designer or manufacturer to check the fit, drape, and appearance of a garment on a person's body *(14, 77, 87, 101, 119 – 123, 137, 153, 154, 157, 203)*

FIT SESSION – a meeting with the fit model, pattern maker and possibly the sample sewer, where samples are tried on by the fit model for evaluation *(19, 120, 122, 124, 130, 137, 156, 157)*

FLA / FAIR LABOR ASSOCIATION – a non-profit group that promotes labor laws and audits factories to evaluate their compliance with fair labor practices *(261)*

FOB / FREE ON BOARD – a value of goods stated on a commercial invoice - includes all the costs related to materials, production, and transportation to the closest loading point to the factory. *(24, 202)*

FOCUS GROUPS – a tool for market research where a small group of people is introduced to a product which they discuss, aimed at gathering data which represents preferences and beliefs of the general population *(38, 39, 41 - 43, 152)*

FPP FACTORY / FULL PACKAGE PRODUCTION FACTORY – a factory that takes care of the entire production process, everything from fabric purchase, cutting, and sewing, to trimming and packaging, the designer supplies only the designs and specifications *(223)*

GLOBAL SUPPLY CHAIN – the worldwide network of all of the entities, such as producers, warehouses, producers, distributors, and retailers, that all serve in getting the product from creation to sale to the customer *(256, 275)*

GRADING – the process of scaling the sample size to the range of sizes for retail *(87, 89, 106, 152, 158, 159, 211, 223)*

GREENWASHING – a company falsely conveying to customers that they benefit a social or environmental initiative when they don't, simply to boost their brand's reputation *(263, 292)*

GREIGE – an unfinished knitted or woven fabric that has not been dyed or bleached *(71, 182, 211)*

GSM / GRAMS PER SQUARE METRE – the most common method of measurement of fabric weight used in the industry *(67 - 69, 126, 180)*

HAUTE COUTURE – exclusive, custom-fitted, high fashion garments designed by high-end designers or fashion houses, and constructed by hand with expensive materials and extreme attention to detail *(4)*

HIGG INDEX – a tool for measuring the social and environmental impact of brands, manufacturing facilities, and products *(275, 310, 312)*

INCUBATOR – a firm that helps entrepreneurs through their development stage into profitability, by teaching them how to run a successful startup, and assisting them in locating financial resources *(50, 51)*

ISO / INTERNATIONAL STANDARDS ORGANIZATION – a global body made up of representatives from various national standards organizations that promotes industrial, proprietary, and commercial standards *(237, 240, 245, 246, 252, 280)*

JOBBER – a person or firm that buys overruns, leftover goods from manufacturers, and seconds, which they then sell with lower minimums *(125)*

L/C / LOC / LETTER OF CREDIT – a letter issued by a bank to another bank to serve as a guarantee for payments made to a specified person under specified conditions *(24, 129, 198 - 200, 267, 269)*

LAB DIP – swatches of fabric test dyed to hit or match a color standard a designer provides *(15, 71, 126, 127, 141, 148, 150, 154, 160 - 162, 174, 205)*

LEAD-TIME – aka turnaround time, the total amount of time needed to complete a product from receiving an order to the shipment of goods to the distributor *(10, 12, 28)*

LIGHTBOX – a fabric color matching cabinet machine that allows one to evaluate color samples under different light sources *(160)*

LINE SHEET – a single "snapshot" of your purchase order containing colorized front and back technical drawings of all styles on order, and detailing all necessary information *(23, 75, 80, 82, 127, 130, 137 - 139, 147)*

LOOKBOOK – A PRODUCT CATALOGUE OF PHOTOS SHOWCASING A DESIGNER'S STYLES FOR MARKETING PURPOSES *(71, 213)*

MAIN LABELS – refer to brand labels *(5, 115)*

MARGIN – a margin is simply a measure of profitability, it quantifies the earnings or profit that is left after you subtract out the costs of what it took to produce the products. *(13, 183, 184, 186, 188,189,193, 198,208,204,225,244,252, 280)*

MARKER – a marker, also known as a cutting marker, is a guide or template made typically made by computer and printed out and used in the cutting process. all the pattern pieces for any given style(s), including sizes - are laid out in a formation intended to reduce fabric waste. after the marker is made, the fabric is laid out in layers and it is laid on top of the fabric to trace and cut by machine.**(192,193,210,223,286)**

MARKET RESEARCH – identifying a specific market, measuring its size and characteristics, and collecting data regarding its customers' preferences and behaviors *(34 - 36, 38, 40, 47, 48, 52)*

MEDIA KITS – an information packet containing promotional material about a product or a business *(51)*

MERCHANDISER – merchandisers or factory merchandiser is responsible for coordinating production orders and is the main point of contact for the buyer. *(27,90,97,109, 145-147,152,153,176,202,214,216, 229,231)*

MOCK PO / MOCK PURCHASE ORDER – an order put together, outlining the styles, targets costs, colors, and the quantities for each size, as well as delivery dates and testing requirements . the order is provided to help the factory gauge a buyers requirements . *(23, 75, 127, 128, 130, 134, 138, 139, 142, 147, 194, 197,)*

MOCK-UP – samples or materials sourced by the factory and provided to a buyer for an approval to proceed with production. *(15)*

MOOD BOARD – An arrangement of images, materials, pieces of text, etc. placed on a canvas intended to evoke or project a particular style or concept. *(19, 32, 34, 45, 71, 72, 74, 78, 79, 81, 118, 130, 133)*

MOQ / MINIMUM ORDER QUANTITY – the lowest number of items that the manufacturer needs to accept an order *(27, 28, 134, 190, 192 - 194, 196, 207, 208, 215, 224 - 228)*

MORDANT – a substance that is combined with dye or stain to affix the color molecule to the fibers of a textile or material *(294, 297)*

NET 30 TERMS – A specific type of trade credit where the payment is due in full 30 days after the item is purchased, (can also be net 15, 45 etc). *(267)*

NICHE MARKET – a tightly focused target group comprised of a specific segment of a much larger market based on particular interests and demographics *(40, 56, 57)*

OPENING ORDERS – the first purchase order placed with a factory. *(178, 197)*

OVERHEADS / OVERHEAD EXPENSES – ongoing expenses involved in a business's operations, such as rent and utilities *(183, 208)*

OVERRUNS - excess finished fabrics from mills and converters *(125, 298)*

PANTONE NUMBER – a universal color system for matching ink or dye colors *(103, 110, 126, 127, 132, 135, 160, 162, 170, 174, 209)*

PI / PROFORMA INVOICE – a document that shows a commitment on the part of the seller to sell the goods according to the pre-decided terms, prices, and conditions *(24, 199)*

POLYBAGS – bags made of plastic and used to ship items and typically used to protect garments. *(299, 300)*

POM / POINT OF MEASURE – a specific point on a garment that is used to help determine a garments measurement. *(85, 86, 89, 90, 100, 101, 156, 158, 159, 175)*

POP-UPS / POP-UP SHOPS *(38, 217)*

PRE-PRODUCTION PACKAGE – a set of documents that the designer submits to the factory, that the factory reviews in order to source fabric options and eventually produce an estimate *(14, 15, 23, 127, 138, 147, 175, 207)*

PRODUCTION-READY SAMPLE – a counter sample created by a factory that has is approved for production. *(118, 203)*

PSYCHOGRAPHICS – information on a particular group's social attitudes and values, in other words, how they think *(43, 49)*

QR CODE / QUICK RESPONSE CODE – a machine-readable barcode that contains information about an item *(274)*

RN NUMBER – RN stands for Registered Identification Number. It is a number issued by the FTC to U.S. businesses that manufacture, import, distribute, or sell products covered by the Textile, Wool, and Fur Acts. *(115)*

SALES CHANNEL – the way in which one brings products to the market to be purchased by customers *(217)*

SALES SAMPLES – samples made in the exact approved fabric and colors, using all trims and labels approved for production *(25, 129, 141, 148, 150 - 152, 204, 234)*

SAMPLE SIZE / BASE SIZE – typically, the most medium size of a designer's chosen size range to assist with establishing the right fit and pattern measurements. *(83, 85, 89, 92, 93, 119 - 121, 158)*

SECONDARY RESEARCH - data that's already compiled and organized for you, and which is provided by third party market research firms *(38, 47, 48)*

SELVAGE EDGE - the edge generally on top or bottom, produced on a woven fabric during manufacture that prevents it from unravelling. *(112)*

SHOPPING THE MARKET – purchasing physical samples of garments from a variety of retail stores to gain practical information and design inspiration *(5, 18, 32, 44, 72, 78, 128, 130, 131, 203)*

SHOWROOM – a room or area used for the purpose of displaying a company's products *(46, 217, 230, 239, 243)*

SKU / STOCK KEEPING UNIT – an identification code, usually alphanumeric, of a particular product that allows it to be tracked for inventory purposes *(82, 159, 164, 207)*

SLOW FASHION – a method of manufacturing that ensures quality and lengthens the life of the garment, and encourages slower production schedules, fair wages, lower carbon footprints and (ideally) zero waste *(250, 280, 285, 287, 290, 291)*

SOCIAL ENTERPRISE – a for-profit business whose core missions solve a problem faced by people or the planet, alongside the earning of revenue *(248 - 252, 259, 278, 298)*

SPEC SHEET / SPECIFICATION SHEET - a technical document that contains a technical diagram/sketch of the garment, and all the measurements including grading presented in an easy-to-read chart along with illustrations *(89)*

STAPLE PIECES – basic styles that are carried season after season. *(20)*

STRIKE-OFFS – during sampling swatches of the print, embroidery, or color created for approval to be able to proceed with an order. *(141, 148, 163, 169, 170, 174, 175)*

STYLE NUMBER – a number assigned to each design to help identify it *(23, 24, 82, 127, 128, 137 – 140, 155, 157)*

SWEATSHOP – a business that subjects its workers to extremely harsh and often dangerous conditions, and pays them unfairly low wages *(255)*

TBL / TRIPLE BOTTOM LINE - an accounting framework that focuses a business's goals in three areas: the social, the environmental (or ecological) and the financial, rather than being solely profit driven *(247 - 249)*

TECH PACK / TECHNICAL PACK - an information sheet that designers create to communicate with the manufacturer all of the necessary components needed to construct a product *(5, 11, 19, 45, 70, 78, 80, 84 - 87, 89, 91, 96, 99 - 103, 106, 110, 114 -123, 127, 130, 135 - 139, 147, 150, 155 - 159, 175, 203, 208 and others)*

TECHNICAL DESIGNER – is a liaison between design and production helping to digitally create designs (provided by a designer) and create tech packs. *(5, 77, 80, 81, 83, 84, 87 – 89, 101, 118, 122, 131, 133, 135)*

TECHNICAL DRAWING – a vector (cad) flat illustration of a garment. it is used as a guide to the pattern maker and manufacturer create a garment. *(5, 82, 90)*

TECHNICAL FLAT – a black and white computerized line drawing that shows a garment as if it were laid flat, detailing all seams, topstitching, hardware, and any other design details, in order to form a basis for further product development *(79, 80, 82, 86, 89, 137)*

TEX – a unit of weight used to measure the density of yarns *(69, 181)*

THREAD COUNT / THREADS-PER-INCH – a measure of the coarseness or fineness of finished woven fabric, the number of warp ends and filling picks per inch *(69, 181)*

TNA CALENDAR / TIME AND ACTION CALENDAR – a calendar that helps to establish the time an order takes to complete, from the moment the factory receives the order to the final shipment to the buyer, listing all key processes and planned dates of action *(9, 24, 26 - 28, 152, 234)*

TOP SAMPLE / TOP OF PRODUCTION SAMPLE – a random garment pulled after the bulk production. this is the final sample stage where the buyer gets to see one of the pieces prior to delivery. *(25, 234, 245)*

TRADE ASSOCIATIONS / TRADE ORGANIZATIONS – a membership association or organization that has a group of people or companies in a particular business or trade organized to promote their common interests. *(38, 50)*

TRADE SHOW – a large trade event aimed at facilitating direct contact amongst members of a certain industry, such as between the manufacturers and the distributors or sellers *(38, 46, 47, 52, 60, 62, 217, 221, 230, 234, 311)*

TREND FORECASTING SERVICES – companies helping fashion designers and brands with upcoming trends - forecast and predict fabrics, colors, styles, materials, graphics prints and more which will be predicted at runway shows and popular with consumers. *(52)*

TRIMS – additions that enhance the aesthetic and/or functionality of a garment, and are required for the proper construction or fit of the garment *(23, 86, 103, 104, 109, 119, 127, 128, 131 - 136, 139 - 142, 147 – 151, 154, 175, 177, 185, 194, 203 – 205, 223, 283, 305, 312 and others)*

UPCYCLING - reusing discarded materials in such a way that the upcycled item is of better value or quality *(241, 285, 298, 312)*

VECTOR OR VECTOR FILE – a computer generated graphics file that uses paths and not pixels. no matter how big or small you make a vector, it will always look sharp as the original.*(80, 89,163, 164)*

WEARING EASE the basic rule that the wearer must be able to move, bend, breathe, sit, raise their arms, and walk without the garment pulling, pinching, stretching, or straining beyond a natural relaxed position *(102)*

WORK BACK SCHEDULE – a guide to plan what needs to be done when to stay on track with deadlines, by starting from the date you want to receive your goods and working backwards *(10, 13, 16, 17)*

Made in the USA
San Bernardino, CA
18 December 2019